TWO-STORY HOMES

D1373552

478 Designs
for 1½ and 2 Stories

1,200 to 7,200 square feet

HOME PLANNERS, INC.

Contents

Note: Many of the homes featured in this book have a matching or corresponding Landscape or Deck plan available from Home Planners, Inc. Some have both. These plans have an ■L or a ■D following their design number and square-footage notations. For information on how to order plans for landscapes and decks, see pages 398-405.

Published by Home Planners, Inc.

Editorial and Corporate Office:
  3275 West Ina Road, Suite 110
  Tucson, Arizona 85741
Distribution Center:
  29333 Lorie Lane
  Wixom, MI 48393

President and Publisher: Rickard D. Bailey
Publications Manager: Cindy J. Coatsworth
Editor: Paulette Mulvin
Front Cover Graphic Design: Paul Fitzgerald

10   9   8   7   6   5   4

Library of Congress Number: 90-084445
ISBN: 0-918894-86-7

ON THE COVER: Plans for this impressive Two-Story Georgian, Design V22683 can be found on page 148.
House by Kellett & Saylor Builders, Bloomington, Michigan.
Photographer: Laszlo Regos

How To Read
Floor Plans and Blueprints

Selecting the most suitable house plan for your family is a matter of matching your needs, tastes, and lifestyle against the many designs we offer. When you study the floor plans in this book, and the blueprints that you may subsequently order, remember that they are a two-dimensional representation of what will be a three-dimensional reality.

Floor plans are easy to read. Rooms are clearly labeled, with dimensions given in feet and inches. Most symbols are logical and self-explanatory: The location of bathroom fixtures, fireplaces, planters, tile floors, cabinets and counters, sinks, appliances, closets, and sloped or beamed ceilings will be obvious.

A blueprint, although much more detailed, is also easy to read; all it demands is concentration. The blueprints that we offer come in many large sheets, each one of which contains a different kind of information. One sheet contains foundation and excavation drawings, another has a precise plot plan. An elevations sheet deals with the exterior walls of the house; section drawings show precise dimensions, fittings, doors, windows, and roof structures. This provides all the construction information needed by your contractor. Also available is a helpful materials list with size and quantities of all necessary components. Using this list, your contractor and suppliers can make a start at calculating costs for you.

When you first study a floor plan or blueprint, imagine that you are walking through the house. By mentally visualizing each room in three dimensions, you can transform the technical data and symbols into something more real. Interior space should be organized in a logical way, based on the intended use of such space. Usually the space is divided into rooms which fall into one of three categories. The sleeping area includes bedrooms and bathrooms; the work area includes the kitchen, laundry, utility room, garage and other functional rooms; the living area includes the living and dining rooms, family room, and other gathering areas as well as entrance ways.

To begin a mental tour of the home, start at the front door. It's preferable to have a foyer or entrance hall in which to receive guests. A closet here is desirable; a powder room is a plus.

Look for good traffic circulation as you study the floor plan. You should not have to pass all the way through one main room to reach another. From the entrance area you should have direct access to the three principal areas of a house—the living, work, and sleeping zones. For example, a foyer might provide separate entrances to the living room, kitchen, patio, and a hallway or staircase leading to the bedrooms.

Study the layout of each zone. Most people expect the living room to be protected from cross traffic. The kitchen, on the other hand, should connect with the dining room—and perhaps also the utility room, basement, garage, patio or deck, or a secondary entrance. A homemaker whose workday centers in the kitchen may have special requirements: a window that faces the backyard; a clear view of the family room where children play; a garage or driveway entrance that allows for a short trip with groceries; laundry facilities close at hand. Check for efficient placement of kitchen cabinets, counter, and appliances. Is there enough room in the kitchen for additional appliances, for eating in? Is there a dining nook?

Perhaps this part of the house contains a family room or a den/bedroom/office. It's advantageous to have a bathroom or powder room in this section.

As you study the plan, you may encounter a staircase, indicated by a group of parallel lines, the number of lines equaling the number of steps. Arrows labeled "up" mean that the staircase leads to a higher level, and those pointing down mean it leads to a lower one. Staircases in a split-level will have both up and down arrows on one staircase because two levels are depicted in one drawing and an extra level in another.

Notice the location of the stairways. Is too much floor space lost to them? Will you find yourself making too many trips?

Study the sleeping quarters. Are the bedrooms situated as you like? You may want the master bedroom near the kids, or you may want it as far away as possible. Is there at least one closet per person in each bedroom or a double one for a couple? Bathrooms should be convenient to each bedroom—if not adjoining, then with hallway access and on the same floor.

Once you are familiar with the relative positions of the rooms, look for such structural details as:
- Sufficient uninterrupted wall space for furniture arrangement.
- Adequate room dimensions.
- Potential heating or cooling problems—i.e., a room over a garage or next to the laundry.
- Window and door placement for good ventilation and natural light.
- Location of doorways—avoid having a basement staircase or a bathroom in view of the dining room.
- Adequate auxiliary space—closets, storage, bathrooms, countertops.
- Separation of activity areas (will noise from the recreation room disturb sleeping children or a parent at work?).

As you complete your mental walk through the house, bear in mind your family's long-range needs. A good house plan will allow for some adjustments now and additions in the future.

Take time to notice special amenities: fireplaces and raised hearths, work islands in the kitchen, pass-through countertops between kitchen and breakfast nook, whirlpool baths. Note the placement of decks and balconies. Your family may find the listing of favorite features a most helpful exercise. Why not try it?

How To Shop For Mortgage Money

Most people who are in the market for a new home spend months searching for the right house plan and building site. Ironically, these same people often invest very little time shopping for the money to finance their new home, though the majority will have to live with the terms of their mortgage for as long as they live in the home.

The fact is that not all lending institutions are alike, nor are the loans that they offer.

- Lending practices vary from one city and state to another. If you are a first-time builder or are new to an area, it is wise to hire a real estate (not divorce or general practice) attorney to help you unravel the maze of your area's laws and customs.
- Before talking with a lender, write down all your questions and take notes so you can make accurate comparisons.
- Do not be intimidated by financial officers. Do not hesitate to reveal what other institutions are offering; they may be challenged to meet or better the terms.

A GUIDE TO LENDERS

Where can you turn for home financing? Here is a list of sources for you to contact:

Savings and Loan Associations
Savings Banks/Mutual Savings Banks
Commercial Banks
Mortgage Banking Companies
Some Credit Unions

Each of the above institutions generally offers a variety of loan types, interest rates, and fees. It is recommended that you survey each type of institution in your area to determine exactly what type of financing is available so that you can make an intelligent and informed decision.

A GUIDE TO LOAN TYPES

Conventional Loans

These types of loans usually require a minimum down payment of 10% of the lower of the purchase price or appraised value of the property. However, in many cases, this down payment requirement has been increased to 15% to 20% depending on the type of loan and the requirements of the lending institution. Often, the minimum down payment requirement is applied to owner-occupied residences and is usually increased if the property is purchased as a vacation home or investment.

The most common type of conventional loan is the **fixed-rate loan** which has a fixed interest rate and fixed monthly payments. The term of the loan may vary, but such loans generally are available in fifteen- and thirty-year terms. The obvious advantage of a fifteen-year term is an earlier loan payoff as well as reduced interest charges.

Other types of conventional loans are called **adjustable rate mortgages (ARM's)**. This type of loan usually has a lower initial interest rate than the fixed-rate loan, but the interest rate of payment may change depending on the loan terms and economic conditions. The frequency of these interest/payment adjustments depends on the individual loan, but they usually occur every twelve months.

Some key terms to understanding ARM loans are listed below:

Adjustment Period - The period between one rate change and the next. Therefore, a loan with an adjustment period of one year is known as a One Year ARM.

Index - The interest rate change is tied to an index rate. These indexes usually go up and down with the general movement of interest rates. If the index rate moves up, so does your monthly payment. If the index rate goes down, your monthly payment may also go down. There are a variety of indexes. Among the most common is the weekly average yield on U.S. Treasury securities adjusted to a constant maturity of one, three, or five years.

Margin - To determine the interest rate on an ARM, lenders add a few percentage points to the index rate. These percentage points are called the margin. The amount of the margin can differ from one lender to the next, but is usually constant through the life of the loan.

Caps - Most ARM loans limit the amount that the interest rate can increase. There are periodic caps which limit the increase from one adjustment period to the next and overall caps which limit the interest rate increase over the life of the loan.

Negative Amortization - Several ARM loans contain negative amortization which means that your mortgage balance can increase even though you are making regular monthly payments. This happens when the interest rate of the loan increases while your monthly payment remains the same.

Convertibility or Conversion Option - This is a clause in your agreement that allows you to convert the ARM to a fixed-rate mortgage at designated times. Not all ARM loans contain this option.

There are other types of less-common conventional loans which are offered by many institutions: Graduated Payment Mortgages, Reverse Annuity Mortgages, and Bi-Weekly Mortgages. Consult with a financial officer of a lending institution for details on these other loan types.

Government Loans

FHA loans are government insured and have substantially lower down payments than conventional loans; however, there are maximum allowable loan amounts for these loans depending on the location of the property.

Another type of government loan is through the Veteran's Administration (VA). Like the FHA, the VA guarantees loans for eligible veterans and the spouses of those veterans who died while in the service. Down payment requirements are also extremely low on these types of loans.

There are a variety of loan types available under these government programs including fixed rate, ARM's and graduated payment mortgages. The financial officer of the lending institution will be able to explain these various loan types and the qualification standards.

The Cost of a Mortgage

Monthly principal and interest per $1,000 of mortgage

Mortgage rate	15-year loan	20-year loan	25-year loan	30-year loan
5.000%	7.91	6.60	5.85	5.37
5.125%	7.97	6.67	5.92	5.44
5.250%	8.04	6.74	5.99	5.52
5.375%	8.10	6.81	6.07	5.60
5.500%	8.17	6.88	6.14	5.68
5.625%	8.24	6.95	6.22	5.76
5.750%	8.30	7.02	6.29	5.84
5.875%	8.37	7.09	6.37	5.92
6.000%	8.44	7.16	6.44	6.00
6.125%	8.51	7.24	6.52	6.08
6.250%	8.57	7.31	6.60	6.16
6.375%	8.64	7.38	6.67	6.24
6.500%	8.71	7.46	6.75	6.32
6.625%	8.78	7.53	6.83	6.40
6.750%	8.85	7.60	6.91	6.49
6.875%	8.92	7.68	6.99	6.57
7.000%	8.99	7.76	7.07	6.66
7.125%	9.06	7.83	7.15	6.74
7.250%	9.13	7.91	7.23	6.83
7.375%	9.20	7.98	7.31	6.91
7.500%	9.28	8.06	7.39	7.00
7.625%	9.35	8.14	7.48	7.08
7.750%	9.42	8.21	7.56	7.17
7.875%	9.49	8.29	7.64	7.26
8.000%	9.56	8.37	7.72	7.34
8.125%	9.63	8.45	7.81	7.43
8.250%	9.71	8.53	7.89	7.52
8.375%	9.78	8.60	7.97	7.61
8.500%	9.85	8.68	8.06	7.69
8.625%	9.93	8.76	8.14	7.78
8.750%	10.00	8.84	8.23	7.87
8.875%	10.07	8.92	8.31	7.96
9.000%	10.15	9.00	8.40	8.05
9.125%	10.22	9.08	8.48	8.14
9.250%	10.30	9.16	8.57	8.23
9.375%	10.37	9.24	8.66	8.32
9.500%	10.45	9.33	8.74	8.41
9.625%	10.52	9.41	8.83	8.50
9.750%	10.60	9.49	8.92	8.60
9.875%	10.67	9.57	9.00	8.69
10.000%	10.75	9.66	9.09	8.78
10.125%	10.83	9.74	9.18	8.87
10.250%	10.90	9.82	9.27	8.97
10.375%	10.98	9.90	9.36	9.06
10.500%	11.06	9.99	9.45	9.15
10.625%	11.14	10.07	9.54	9.25
10.750%	11.21	10.16	9.63	9.34
10.875%	11.29	10.24	9.72	9.43
11.000%	11.37	10.33	9.81	9.53
11.125%	11.45	10.41	9.90	9.62
11.250%	11.53	10.50	9.99	9.72
11.375%	11.61	10.58	10.08	9.81
11.500%	11.69	10.67	10.17	9.91
11.625%	11.77	10.76	10.26	10.00
11.750%	11.85	10.84	10.35	10.10
11.875%	11.93	10.93	10.44	10.20
12.000%	12.01	11.02	10.54	10.29
12.125%	12.09	11.10	10.63	10.39
12.250%	12.17	11.19	10.72	10.48
12.375%	12.25	11.28	10.82	10.58
12.500%	12.33	11.37	10.91	10.68
12.625%	12.41	11.45	11.00	10.77
12.750%	12.49	11.54	11.10	10.87
12.875%	12.58	11.63	11.19	10.97
13.000%	12.66	11.72	11.28	11.07

Note: Multiply the cost per $1,000 by the size of the mortgage (in thousands). The result is the monthly payment, including principal and interest. For example, for an $80,000 mortgage for 30 years at 10 percent, multiply 80 x 8.78 = $702.40.

How To Choose A Contractor

Contractors are part craftsmen, part businessmen, and part magicians. Transforming your dreams and drawings into a finished house, they are responsible for the final cost of the structure, for the quality of the workmanship, and for the solving of all problems that occur quite naturally in the course of construction.

There are two types of residential contractors: the construction company and the carpenter-builder, often called a general contractor. Each of these has its advantages and disadvantages.

Carpenter-builders work directly on the job as field foremen. Because their background is that of a craftsman, their workmanship is probably good—but their paperwork may be slow or sloppy. Their overhead—which you pay for—is less than that of a large construction company. However, if the job drags on for any reason, their interest may flag because your project is overlapping their next job and eroding profits.

Construction companies that handle several projects concurrently have an office staff to keep the paperwork moving and an army of reliable subcontractors. Though you can be confident that they will meet deadlines, they may sacrifice workmanship in order to do so. Emphasizing efficiency, they are less personal to work with than a general contractor and many will not work with an individual unless there is representation by an architect.

To find a reliable contractor, start by asking friends who have built homes for recommendations. Check with local lumberyards and building supply outlets for names of possible candidates and call departments of consumer affairs. Keep in mind that these watchdog organizations can give only the number of complaints filed; they cannot tell you what percent of those claims were valid. Remember, too, that a large-volume operation is logically going to have more registered complaints against it than will an independent contractor.

Interview each of the potential candidates. Find out about specialties—custom houses, development houses, remodeling, or office buildings. Ask each to take you into—not just to the site of—current projects. Ask to see projects that are complete as well as work in progress, emphasizing that you are interested in projects comparable to yours. A $300,000 dentist's office will give you little insight into a contractor's craftsmanship.

Ask each contractor for bank references from both a commercial bank and any other appropriate lender. If in good financial standing, the contractor should have no qualms about giving you this information. Also ask about warranties. Most will give you a one-year warranty on the structure; some offer as much as a ten-year warranty.

Ask for references, even though no contractor will give you the name of a dissatisfied customer. Ask about follow-through. Was the building site cleaned up or did the owner have to dispose of the refuse? Ask about the organization of business. Did the paperwork go smoothly, or was there a delay in hooking up the sewer because of a failure to apply for a permit?

Talk to each of the candidates about fees. Most work on a "cost plus" basis; that is, the basic cost of the project— materials, subcontractors' services, wages of those working directly on the project, but not office help—plus a fee. Some have a fixed fee; others work on a percentage of the basic cost. A fixed fee is usually better for you if you can get one. If a contractor works on a percentage, ask for a cost breakdown of the best estimate and keep very careful track as the work progresses. A crafty contractor can always use a cost overrun to good advantage when working on a percentage.

Do not be overly suspicious of a contractor who won't work on a fixed fee. One who is very good and in great demand may not be willing to do so and may also be reluctant to submit a competitive bid.

Give the top two or three candidates each copies of the plans and your specifications for materials. If they are not each working from the same guidelines, the competitive bids will be of little value. Give each the same deadline for turning in a bid; two or three weeks is a reasonable period of time. Make an appointment with each of them and open the envelopes at this time.

If one bid is remarkably low, the contractor may have made an honest error in the estimate. Don't insist that the contractor hold to a bid if it is in error. Forcing a building price that is too low could be disastrous for both of you. You may want to review the bids with your architect, if you have one, or with your lender to discuss which to accept. They may not recommend the lowest. A low bid does not necessarily mean that you will get the best quality with economy.

If the bids are relatively close, the most important consideration may not be money at all. A bid from a contractor who is easy to talk to and inspires confidence may be the best choice. Any sign of a personality conflict between you and a contractor should be weighed when making a decision.

Once you have financing, you can sign a contract with the builder. Most have their own contract forms, but it is advisable to have a lawyer draw one up or, at the very least, review the standard contract. This usually costs a small flat fee.

A good contract should include:
- Plans and sketches of the work to be done, subject to your approval.
- A list of materials, including quantity, brand names, style or serial numbers. (Do not permit any "or equal" clause that will allow the contractor to make substitutions.)
- The terms—who (you or the lender) pays whom and when.
- A production schedule.
- The contractor's certification of insurance for workmen's compensation, damage, and liability.
- A rider stating that all changes, whether or not they increase the cost, must be submitted and approved in writing.

Of course, this list represents the least a contract should include. Once you have signed it, your plans are on the way to becoming a home.

A Checklist For Plan Selection

Developing an architectural plan from the various wants and needs of an individual or family that fits into lifestyle demands and design elegance is the most efficient way to assure a livable plan. It is not only possible but highly desirable to design a plan around such requirements as separate bedrooms for each member of the family, guest suites, a quiet study area, an oversized entertainment area, a two-car garage, a completely private master suite, and a living room fireplace. Incorporated into this can be such wants as Tudor styling, 1½-stories, a large entry hall, decks and balconies, and a basement.

While it is obviously best to begin with wants and needs and then design a home to fit these criteria, this is not always practical or even possible. A very effective way around this problem is to select a professionally prepared home plan which meets all needs and incorporates as many wants as possible. With careful selection, it will be possible to modify sizes and make other design adjustments to make the home as close to custom as can be. It is important to remember that some wants may have to be compromised in the interest of meeting budgetary limitations. The trick is to build the best possible home for the available money while satisfying all absolute needs.

Following are some cost-controlling ideas that can make a big difference in the overall price of a home:

1. Square or rectangular homes are less expensive to build than irregularly shaped homes.
2. It is less expensive to build on a flat lot than on a sloping or hillside lot.
3. The use of locally manufactured or produced materials cuts costs greatly.
4. Using stock materials and stock sizes of components takes advantage of mass production cost reductions.
5. The use of materials that can be quickly installed cuts labor costs. Prefabricating large sections or panels eliminates much time on the site.
6. The use of prefinished materials saves significantly on labor costs.
7. Investigating existing building codes before beginning construction eliminates unnecessary changes as construction proceeds.
8. Refraining from changing the design or any aspect of the plan after construction begins will help to hold down cost escalation.
9. Minimizing special jobs or custom-built items keeps costs from increasing.
10. Designing the house for short plumbing lines saves on piping and other materials.
11. Proper insulation saves heating and cooling costs.
12. Utilizing passive solar features, such as correct orientation, reduces future maintenance costs.

To help you consider all the important factors in evaluating a plan, the following checklist should be reviewed carefully. By comparing its various points to any plan and a wants-and-needs list, it will be possible to easily recognize the deficiencies of a plan or determine its appropriateness. Be sure to include family members in the decision-making process. Their ideas and desires will help in finding exactly the right plan.

CHECKLIST

The Neighborhood

1. _____ Reasonable weather conditions
2. No excess
   _____ *a.* wind
   _____ *b.* smog or fog
   _____ *c.* odors
   _____ *d.* soot or dust
3. _____ The area is residential
4. There are no
   _____ *a.* factories
   _____ *b.* dumps
   _____ *c.* highways
   _____ *d.* railroads
   _____ *e.* airports
   _____ *f.* apartments
   _____ *g.* commercial buildings
5. _____ City-maintained streets
6. No hazards in the area
   _____ *a.* quarries
   _____ *b.* storage tanks
   _____ *c.* power stations
   _____ *d.* unprotected swimming pools

7. Reasonably close to
   _____ *a.* work
   _____ *b.* schools
   _____ *c.* churches
   _____ *d.* hospital
   _____ *e.* shopping
   _____ *f.* recreation
   _____ *g.* public transportation
   _____ *h.* library
   _____ *i.* police protection
   _____ *j.* fire protection
   _____ *k.* parks
   _____ *l.* cultural activities
8. _____ Streets are curved
9. _____ Traffic is slow
10. _____ Intersections are at right angles
11. _____ Street lighting
12. _____ Light traffic
13. _____ Visitor parking
14. _____ Good design in street
15. _____ Paved streets and curbs
16. _____ Area is not deteriorating
17. _____ Desirable expansion
18. _____ Has some open spaces

19. _____ Numerous and healthy trees
20. _____ Pleasant-looking homes
21. _____ Space between homes
22. _____ Water drains off
23. _____ Near sewerage line
24. _____ Storm sewers nearby
25. _____ Mail delivery
26. _____ Garbage pickup
27. _____ Trash pickup
28. _____ No city assessments

The Lot

1. _____ Title is clear
2. _____ No judgments against the seller
3. _____ No restrictions as to the use of the land or the deed
4. _____ No unpaid taxes or assessments
5. _____ Minimum of 70 feet of frontage
6. _____ House does not crowd the lot
7. _____ Possible to build on
8. _____ Few future assessments (sewers, lights, and so forth)
9. _____ Good top soil and soil percolation
10. _____ Good view
11. _____ No low spots to hold water
12. _____ Water drains off land away from the house
13. _____ No fill
14. _____ No water runoff from high ground
15. _____ If cut or graded there is substantial retaining wall
16. _____ Permanent boundary markers
17. _____ Utilities available at property line
18. _____ Utility hookup is reasonable
19. _____ Utility rates are reasonable
20. _____ Taxes are reasonable
21. _____ Water supply is adequate
22. _____ Regular, simply shaped lot
23. _____ Trees
24. _____ Do not have to cut trees
25. _____ Privacy for outside activities
26. _____ Attractive front yard
27. _____ Front and rear yards are adequate
28. _____ Front yard is not divided up by walks and driveway
29. _____ Outdoor walks have stairs grouped

The Floor Plan

1. _____ Designed by licensed architect
2. _____ Purchased from a reputable stock plan company
3. _____ Supervised by skilled contractor
4. Orientation
   _____ a. sun
   _____ b. view
   _____ c. noise
   _____ d. breeze
   _____ e. contour of land
5. _____ Entry
6. _____ Planned for exterior expansion
7. Planned for interior expansion
   _____ a. attic
   _____ b. garage
   _____ c. basement
8. _____ Simple but functional plan
9. _____ Indoor recreation area
10. _____ Wall space for furniture in each room
11. Well-designed hall
   _____ a. leads to all areas
   _____ b. no congestions

_____ c. no wasted space
_____ d. 3' minimum widths
12. _____ Easy to clean
13. _____ Easy to keep orderly
14. _____ Plan meets family's needs
15. _____ All rooms have direct emergency escape
16. Doorways functional
   _____ a. no unnecessary doors
   _____ b. wide enough for moving furniture through
   _____ c. can see visitors through locked front door
   _____ d. do not swing out into halls
   _____ e. swing open against a blank wall
   _____ f. do not bump other subjects
   _____ g. exterior doors are solid
17. Windows are functional
   _____ a. not too small
   _____ b. enough but not too many
   _____ c. glare-free
   _____ d. roof overhang protection where needed
   _____ e. large ones have the best view
   _____ f. easy to clean
   _____ g. no interference with furniture placement
   _____ h. over kitchen sink
   _____ i. open easily
18. _____ No fancy gadgets
19. _____ Room sizes are adequate
20. _____ Well-designed stairs
   _____ a. treads are 9" minimum
   _____ b. risers are 8" maximum
   _____ c. 36" minimum width
   _____ d. 3' minimum landings
   _____ e. attractive
   _____ f. easily reached
21. _____ Overall plan "fits" family requirements
22. _____ Good traffic patterns
23. _____ Noisy areas separated from quiet areas
24. _____ Rooms have adequate wall space for furniture
25. _____ Halls are 3'6" minimum

The Living Area

1. _____ Minimum space 12' x 16'
2. _____ Front door traffic does not enter
3. _____ Not in a traffic pattern
4. _____ Windows on two sides
5. _____ Has a view
6. _____ Storage for books and music materials
7. _____ Decorative lighting
8. _____ Whole family plus guests can be seated
9. _____ Desk area
10. _____ Fireplace
11. _____ Wood storage
12. _____ No street noises
13. _____ Privacy from street
14. _____ Acoustical ceiling
15. _____ Cannot see or hear bathroom
16. _____ Powder room
17. _____ Comfortable for conversation
18. Dining room
   _____ a. used enough to justify
   _____ b. minimum of 3' clearance around table
   _____ c. can be opened or closed to kitchen and patio
   _____ d. can be opened or closed to living room
   _____ e. electrical outlets for table appliances

19. Family room
    _____ a. minimum space 10' x 12'
    _____ b. room for family activities
    _____ c. room for noisy activities
    _____ d. room for messy activities
    _____ e. activities will not disturb sleeping area
    _____ f. finish materials are easy to clean and durable
    _____ g. room for expansion
    _____ h. separate from living room
    _____ i. near kitchen
    _____ j. fireplace
    _____ k. adequate storage
20. _____ Dead-end circulation
21. _____ Adequate furniture arrangements

The Entry

1. _____ The entry is a focal point
2. _____ The outside is inviting
3. _____ The landing has a minimum depth of 5'
4. _____ Protected from the weather
5. _____ Has an approach walk
6. _____ Well planted
7. _____ Coat closet
8. _____ Leads to living, sleeping, and service areas
9. _____ Floor material attractive and easy to clean
10. _____ Decorative lighting
11. _____ Space for table
12. _____ Space to hang mirror
13. _____ Does not have direct view into any room

The Bedrooms

1. _____ Adequate number of bedrooms
2. _____ Adequate size—10' x 12' minimum
3. _____ Open into a hall
4. _____ Living space
5. _____ Children's bedroom has study and play area
6. _____ Oriented to north side
7. In quiet area
    _____ a. soundproofing
    _____ b. acoustical ceiling
    _____ c. insulation in walls
    _____ d. thermal glass
    _____ e. double doors
    _____ f. closet walls
8. _____ Privacy
9. _____ 4' minimum wardrobe rod space per person
10. Master bedroom
    _____ a. bath
    _____ b. dressing area
    _____ c. full-length mirror
    _____ d. 12' x 12' minimum
11. Adequate windows
    _____ a. natural light
    _____ b. cross-ventilation
    _____ c. windows on two walls
12. _____ Room for overnight guests
13. _____ Bathroom nearby
14. _____ Wall space for bed, nightstands, and dresser
15. _____ Quiet reading area

The Bathroom

1. _____ Well designed
2. _____ Plumbing lines are grouped
3. _____ Fixtures have space around them for proper use
4. _____ Doors do not interfere with fixtures
5. _____ Noises are insulated from other rooms
6. _____ Convenient to bedrooms
7. _____ Convenient to guests
8. _____ Ventilation
9. _____ Heating
10. _____ Attractive fixtures
11. _____ No windows over tub or shower
12. _____ Wall area around tub and shower
13. _____ Light fixtures are water tight
14. _____ Large medicine cabinet
15. _____ Children cannot open medicine cabinet
16. _____ No bathroom tie-ups
17. _____ Good lighting
18. _____ Accessible electrical outlets
19. _____ No electric appliance or switch near water supply
20. _____ Towel and linen storage
21. _____ Dirty clothes hamper
22. _____ Steamproof mirrors
23. _____ Wall and floor materials are waterproof
24. _____ All finishes are easy to maintain
25. _____ Curtain and towel rods securely fastened
26. _____ Grab bar by tub
27. _____ Mixing faucets
28. _____ Bath in service area
29. _____ No public view into open bathroom door
30. _____ Clean-up area for outdoor jobs and children's play

The Kitchen

1. _____ Centrally located
2. _____ The family can eat informally in the kitchen
3. _____ At least 20' of cabinet space
    _____ a. counter space on each side of major appliances
    _____ b. minimum of 8' counter work area
    _____ c. round storage in corners
    _____ d. no shelf is higher than 72"
    _____ e. floor cabinets 24" deep and 36" high
    _____ f. wall cabinets 15" deep
    _____ g. 15" clearance between wall and floor cabinets
4. _____ Work triangle is formed between appliances
    _____ a. between 12' and 20'
    _____ b. no traffic through the work triangle
    _____ c. refrigerator opens into the work triangle
    _____ d. at least six electric outlets in work triangle
    _____ e. no door between appliances
5. _____ No space between appliances and counters
6. _____ Window over sink
7. _____ No wasted space in kitchen
8. _____ Can close off kitchen from dining area
9. _____ Snack bar in kitchen
10. _____ Kitchen drawers are divided
11. _____ Built-in chopping block
12. _____ Writing and telephone desk
13. _____ Indoor play area visible from kitchen
14. _____ Outdoor play area visible from kitchen
15. _____ Exhaust fan
16. _____ Natural light
17. _____ Good lighting for each work area
18. _____ Convenient access to service area and garage
19. _____ Durable surfaces
20. _____ Dishwasher
21. _____ Disposal
22. _____ Built-in appliances
23. _____ Bathroom nearby

24. _____ Room for freezer
25. _____ Pantry storage

The Utility Room

1. _____ Adequate laundry area
2. _____ Well-lighted work areas
3. _____ 240-volt outlet
4. _____ Gas outlet
5. _____ Sorting area
6. _____ Ironing area
7. _____ Drip-drying area
8. _____ Sewing and mending area
9. _____ On least desirable side of lot
10. _____ Exit to outdoor service area
11. _____ Exit near garage
12. _____ Sufficient cabinet space
13. _____ Bathroom in area
14. _____ Accessible from kitchen
15. _____ Adequate space for washer and dryer
16. _____ Laundry tray
17. _____ Outdoor exit is protected from the weather
18. _____ Window

Working Areas

1. _____ Home repair area
2. _____ Work area for hobbies
3. _____ Storage for paints and tools
4. _____ Garage storage
5. _____ Incinerator area
6. _____ Refuse area
7. _____ Delivery area
8. _____ Near parking
9. _____ 240-volt outlet for power tools

Storage

1. _____ General storage space for each person
2. _____ 4' of rod space for each person
3. _____ Closet doors are sealed to keep out dust
4. _____ Minimum wardrobe closet size is 40" x 22"
5. _____ Cedar closet storage for seasonal clothing
6. _____ Bulk storage area for seasonal paraphernalia
7. _____ Closets are lighted
8. _____ Walk-in closets have adequate turnaround area
9. Storage for:
   _____ a. linen and towels
   _____ b. cleaning materials
   _____ c. foods
   _____ d. bedding
   _____ e. outdoor furniture
   _____ f. sports equipment
   _____ g. toys—indoor
   _____ h. toys—outdoor
   _____ i. bicycles
   _____ j. luggage
   _____ k. out-of-season clothes
   _____ l. storm windows and doors
   _____ m. garden tools
   _____ n. tools and paints
   _____ o. hats
   _____ p. shoes
   _____ q. belts
   _____ r. ties
   _____ s. bridge tables and chairs
   _____ t. camping equipment
   _____ u. china
   _____ v. silver
   _____ w. minor appliances
   _____ x. books

10. _____ Closets are ventilated
11. _____ Closets do not project into room
12. _____ Toothbrush holders in bathrooms
13. _____ Soap holders in bathrooms
14. _____ Adequate built-in storage
15. _____ Drawers cannot pull out of cabinet
16. _____ Drawers slide easily
17. _____ Drawers have divided partitions
18. _____ Adult storage areas easy to reach
19. _____ Children storage areas easy to reach
20. _____ Guest storage near entry
21. _____ Heavy storage areas have reinforced floors
22. _____ Sides of closets easy to reach
23. _____ Tops of closets easy to reach
24. _____ No wasted spaces around stored articles
25. _____ Sloping roof or stairs do not render closet useless
26. _____ Entry closet

The Exterior

1. _____ The design looks "right" for the lot
2. _____ Design varies from other homes nearby
3. _____ Design fits with unity on its site
4. _____ Definite style architecture—not mixed
5. _____ Simple, honest design
6. _____ Garage design goes with the house
7. _____ Attractive on all four sides
8. _____ Colors in good taste
9. _____ Finish materials in good taste
10. _____ Has charm and warmth
11. _____ Materials are consistent on all sides
12. _____ No false building effects
13. _____ Well-designed roof lines—not chopped up
14. _____ Window tops line up
15. _____ Bathroom windows are not obvious
16. _____ Does not look like a box
17. _____ Easy maintenance of finish materials
18. _____ Windows are protected from pedestrian view
19. _____ Attractive roof covering
20. _____ Gutters on roof
21. _____ Downspouts that drain into storm sewer
22. _____ Glass area protected with overhang or trees
23. _____ Dry around the house
24. _____ Several waterproof electric outlets
25. _____ Hose bib on each side
26. _____ Style will look good in the future

Outdoor Service Area

1. _____ Clothes hanging area
2. _____ Garbage storage
3. _____ Can storage
4. _____ On least desirable side of site
5. _____ Next to indoor service area
6. _____ Near garage
7. _____ Delivery area for trucks
8. _____ Fenced off from rest of site

Outdoor Living Area

1. _____ Area for dining
2. _____ Area for games
3. _____ Area for lounging
4. _____ Area for gardening
5. _____ Fenced for privacy
6. _____ Partly shaded
7. _____ Concrete deck at convenient places
8. _____ Garden walks

9. _____ Easy access to house
10. _____ Paved area for bikes and wagons
11. _____ Easy maintenance

Landscaping

1. _____ Planting at foundation ties
2. _____ Garden area
3. _____ Well-located trees
4. _____ Healthy trees
5. _____ Plants of slow-growing variety
6. _____ Landscaping professionally advised
7. _____ Garden walks
8. _____ Easy maintenance
9. _____ Extras as trellis or gazebo

Construction

1. _____ Sound construction
2. _____ All work complies to code
3. _____ Efficient contractor and supervision
4. _____ Honest builders
5. _____ Skilled builders
6. _____ Constructed to plans
7. Floors are well constructed
    _____ a. resilient
    _____ b. subfloor diagonal to joints
    _____ c. flat and even
    _____ d. slab is not cold
    _____ e. floor joists rest on 2" of sill—minimum
    _____ f. girder lengths are joined under points of support
8. Foundation is well constructed
    _____ a. level
    _____ b. sill protected from termites
    _____ c. vapor barrier
    _____ d. no cracks
    _____ e. no water seepage
    _____ f. no dryrot in sills
    _____ g. garage slab drains
    _____ h. waterproofed
    _____ i. walls are 8" thick
    _____ j. basement height 7'6" minimum
    _____ k. sills bolted to foundation
    _____ l. adequate vents
9. Walls are well constructed
    _____ a. plumb
    _____ b. no waves
    _____ c. insulation
    _____ d. flashing at all exterior joints
    _____ e. solid sheathing
    _____ f. siding is neat and tight
    _____ g. drywall joints are invisible
10. Windows are properly installed
    _____ a. move freely
    _____ b. weatherstripped
    _____ c. caulked and sealed
    _____ d. good-quality glass
11. Doors properly hung
    _____ a. move freely
    _____ b. exterior doors weatherstripped
    _____ c. exterior doors are solid-core
    _____ d. interior doors are hollow-core
12. Roof is well constructed
    _____ a. rafters are straight
    _____ b. all corners are flashed
    _____ c. adequate vents in attic
    _____ d. no leaks
    _____ e. building paper under shingles
13. _____ Tile work is tight

14. _____ Hot water lines are insulated
15. _____ Mortar joints are neat
16. _____ Mortar joints do not form shelf to hold water
17. _____ Ceiling is 8'0" minimum
18. _____ No exposed pipes
19. _____ No exposed wires
20. _____ Tight joints at cabinets and appliances
21. _____ Stairs have railings
22. _____ Neat trim application
23. _____ Builder responsible for new home flaws

The Fireplace

1. _____ There is a fireplace
2. _____ Wood storage near the fireplace
3. _____ Draws smoke
4. _____ Hearth in front (minimum 10" on sides; 20" in front)
5. _____ Does not project out into the room
6. _____ Has a clean-out
7. _____ Chimney top 2' higher than roof ridge
8. _____ No leaks around chimney in roof
9. _____ No wood touches the chimney
10. _____ 2" minimum air space between framing members and masonry
11. _____ No loose mortar
12. _____ Has a damper
13. _____ Space for furniture opposite fireplace
14. _____ Doors minimum of 6' from fireplace
15. _____ Windows minimum of 3' from fireplace
16. _____ On a long wall
17. _____ Install "heatilator"
18. _____ Install glass doors to minimize heat loss

Equipment

1. _____ All equipment listed in specifications and plans
2. _____ All new equipment has warranty
3. _____ All equipment is up to code standards
4. _____ All equipment is functional and not a fad
5. _____ Owner's choice of equipment meets builder's allowance
6. _____ Public system for utilities
7. _____ Private well is deep; adequate and healthy water
8. Electrical equipment is adequate
    _____ a. inspected and guaranteed
    _____ b. 240 voltage
    _____ c. 120 voltage
    _____ d. sufficient electric outlets
    _____ e. sufficient electric circuits—minimum of six
    _____ f. circuit breakers
    _____ g. television aerial outlet
    _____ h. telephone outlets
    _____ i. outlets in convenient places
9. Adequate lighting
    _____ a. all rooms have general lighting
    _____ b. all rooms have specific lighting for specific tasks
    _____ c. silent switches
    _____ d. some decorative lighting
    _____ e. light at front door
    _____ f. outdoor lighting
10. _____ Plumbing equipment is adequate
    _____ a. inspected and guaranteed
    _____ b. adequate water pressure
    _____ c. hot water heater—50-gallon minimum
    _____ d. shut-off valves at fixtures

_____ e. satisfactory city sewer or septic tank
_____ f. septic tank disposal field is adequate
_____ g. septic tank is large enough for house (1000 gallons for three-bedroom house, plus 250 gallons for each additional bedroom)
_____ h. water softener for hard water
_____ i. siphon vertex or siphon reverse-trap water closet
_____ j. clean-out plugs at all corners of waste lines
_____ k. water lines will not rust
_____ l. water pipes do not hammer
_____ m. waste lines drain freely
_____ n. cast iron with vitreous enamel bathtub

11. _____ Good ventilation through house and attic
12. Heating and cooling systems are adequate
_____ a. insulation in roof, ceiling, walls
_____ b. air conditioning system
_____ c. heating and cooling outlets under windows
_____ d. air purifier
_____ e. thermostatic control
_____ f. walls are clean over heat outlets
_____ g. comfortable in hot or cold weather
_____ h. automatic humidifier
_____ i. furnace blower is belt-driven
_____ j. quiet-heating plant
_____ k. ducts are tight

13. _____ Windows are of good quality
_____ a. storm windows
_____ b. secure locks
_____ c. screened
_____ d. double glazed in extreme weather (thermal)
_____ e. glass is ripple-free
_____ f. safety or safe thickness of glass
_____ g. moisture-free
_____ h. frost-free

14. Doors are of good quality
_____ a. secure locks on exterior doors
_____ b. attractive hardware
_____ c. hardware is solid brass or bronze

15. All meters easily accessible to meter readers
16. _____ Fire extinguisher in house and garage
17. _____ Acoustical ceiling
18. _____ Facilities to lock mail box
19. _____ Facilities to receive large packages
20. _____ Gas or electric incinerator
21. Adequate small hardware
_____ a. soap dishes
_____ b. toilet-paper holders
_____ c. toothbrush holders
_____ d. towel holders
_____ e. bathtub grab bars
_____ f. door and drawer pulls

The Garage

1. _____ Same style as the house
2. _____ Fits with house
3. _____ Single garage 12' x 22' minimum
4. _____ Double garage 22' x 22' minimum
5. _____ Larger than minimum size if used for storage or workshop
6. _____ Protected passage to house
7. _____ Doors are safe
8. _____ Access to overhead storage

Financial Checklist

1. _____ Do you understand conveyancing fees (closing costs)?
2. _____ Is the house a good investment?
3. _____ Is the total cost approximately three times your annual income?
4. _____ Have you shopped for the best loan?
5. _____ Do you have a constant payment plan (sliding principal and interest)?
6. _____ Is there a prepayment penalty?
7. _____ Will a week's salary cover the total housing expense for one month?
8. _____ Are all the costs itemized in the contract?
9. Do you understand the following closing costs?
_____ a. title search
_____ b. lawyer
_____ c. plot survey
_____ d. insurance, fire, and public liability
_____ e. mortgage tax
_____ f. recording mortgage
_____ g. recording deed
_____ h. bank's commitment fee
_____ i. state and county taxes
_____ j. state and government revenue stamps
_____ k. title insurance (protects lender)
_____ l. homeowner's policy (protects owner)
_____ m. transferring ownership
_____ n. mortgage service charge
_____ o. appraisal
_____ p. notarizing documents
_____ q. attendant fee (paying off previous mortgage)
_____ r. personal credit check

10. _____ Do you have extra cash to cover unforeseen expenses?
11. Can you afford to pay the following?
_____ a. closing costs
_____ b. old assessments or bonds
_____ c. new assessments or bonds
_____ d. downpayment
_____ e. immediate repairs
_____ f. immediate purchases (furniture, appliances, landscape, tools, fences, carpets, drapes, patio)
_____ g. adequate insurance
_____ h. mortgage payments
_____ i. general maintenance
_____ j. utilities (water, heat, electricity, phone, gas, trash pickup)
_____ k. special design features wanted
_____ l. extras not covered in plans and contract
_____ m. prepayment of interest and taxes for first month of transition
_____ n. moving
_____ o. gardener
_____ p. travel to work
_____ q. interest on construction loan
_____ r. advances to contractors

12. _____ Who will pay for the following?
_____ a. supervision costs of architect or contractor
_____ b. inspection fees
_____ c. increased costs during building
_____ d. building permits
_____ e. difficulties in excavation
_____ f. dry wells
_____ g. extra features the building inspector insists upon

The above Checklist is used with permission. It is taken from Home Planners' Guide to Residential Design _by Charles Talcott, Don Hepler, and Paul Wallach; 1986;_ McGraw-Hill, Inc.

EARLY COLONIAL DESIGNS . . .

as found in this section feature a wide variety of sizes and shapes with a myriad of charming exterior design details which recall our architectural heritage. The saltbox and gambrel roofed structure has been an enduring and highly identifiable form. These houses, together with full two-story, are depicted here with a wide range of living potential for varying budgets and family sizes. Worthy of note are the fine traffic patterns that emanate from the numerous center entry houses shown here. With the excellent sleeping, living and work area potential these are truly homes for family living.

Design V22666

First Floor: 988 square feet
Second Floor: 1,147 square feet
Total: 2,135 square feet

● Charming Colonial detailing in multi-paned windows and twin coach lamps grace the exterior of this two-story. A spacious country kitchen highlights the interior. Its features include an island workcenter, fireplace, beamed ceiling, and sliding glass doors leading to the rear terrace. A washroom and a side door are only steps away. A second fireplace is in the large living room which also has sliding glass doors to the rear.

13

Design V22998

First Floor: 2,243 square feet
Second Floor: 1,532 square feet
Total: 3,775 square feet

● Symmetrical and simply lovely, this gambrel-roofed two-story is a fine example of historical homes. Its details will enchant the most particular enthusiast of early architecture. The floor plan is a classic as well. Note the formal dining and living rooms flanking the entry hall. The living room has a fireplace and the dining room a bay window. A media room/study also sports a fireplace and has access to a rear terrace. The family room connects to the kitchen via a through snack bar. There's also another fireplace here. On the second floor are three bedrooms and two full baths. The third floor contains unfinished space which acts as superb storage and can be developed later into more bedrooms if needed.

Design V22990

First Floor: 2,615 square feet
Second Floor: 1,726 square feet
Guest Bedroom: 437 square feet
Total: 4,878 square feet

● Designed to resemble the St. George Tucker house in Williamsburg, this stately home offers a floor plan for today's family. First-floor rooms include a family room with informal dining space at one end of the plan and a formal living room at the other end. In between are the media room, guest powder room, dining room and kitchen. Three second-floor bedrooms include a luxurious master suite with sitting room. There is also a guest room with private bath over the garage.

Design V22994

First Floor: 1,736 square feet
Second Floor: 1,472 square feet
Total: 3,208 square feet

BEDROOM
14⁰ X 13⁴ 17⁴

BATH

MASTER BATH

HER WALK-IN CLOSET

HIS WALK-IN CLOSET

WHR POOL

SEAT

LINEN

DN

OPEN BELOW

RAILING

LINEN

BEDROOM
15⁰ X 13⁴

SEAT

MASTER BEDROOM
18⁴ X 13⁴

60'-0"

GARAGE
21⁶ X 21⁰

LAUNDRY

GREENHOUSE

DRIP DRY

SERVICE ENTRANCE

53'-6"

REF'G

BRKFST RM
11⁰ X 11⁰

FAMILY RM
18⁴ X 14⁰

KITCHEN
15⁴ X 13⁰

CHINA

COOK TOP

OVEN

PDR RM

RAISED HEARTH

WOOD BOX

SHELVES

SHLVS

BUTLER'S PANTRY

DINING RM
16⁰ X 13⁶

FOYER

LIVING RM
18⁴ X 13⁶

PORCH

● Modeled after the homes of successful merchants in Amherst, New Hampshire, this lovely two-story plan presents an historical facade. Two chimney stacks, fluted pilasters and a bracketed pediment add their distinctive details. The floor plan is equally as classic with center hall separating living and dining rooms and leading back to the family room. All three living spaces have fireplaces. The second floor holds three bedrooms including a gracious master suite with two walk-in closets and whirlpool tub. Secondary bedrooms share a full bath with dual lavatories.

Design V22989

First Floor: 1,972 square feet
Second Floor: 1,533 square feet
Total: 3,505 square feet

● This dramatic residence, patterned after one built in 1759 by Major John Vassall in Cambridge, offers a floor plan that is intriguing in its wealth of amenities. On the first floor are the formal living and dining rooms, each with fireplace. A front study connects to the family room with built-ins and another fireplace. Opening to the rear terrace is a most-welcome sun room with pass-through snack bar to the kitchen. Upstairs are three bedrooms. The master has a sitting room, double vanity, whirlpool tub, His and Hers closets, and built-in vanity. Two family bedrooms share a full bath.

Design V22687
First Floor: 1,819 square feet
Second Floor: 1,472 square feet; Total: 3,291 square feet

L D

● Exterior styling of this home is reminiscent of the past but its floor plan is as up-to-date as it can get. Its many unique features include: a greenhouse, 78 square feet, off the country kitchen, a media room for all the modern electronic equipment, a hobby/laundry room with a washroom and a deluxe master bath.

BEDROOM
12⁴x12⁸

BEDROOM
12⁰x9⁰

VANITY

WHIRLPOOL

DRESSING RM.

BATH

WALK-IN CLOSET

DN

LINEN

DRESSER SPACE

BATH

BEDROOM
14⁰x15⁴

MASTER BEDROOM
17⁸x15⁴

69'-8"

GARAGE
23⁴x23⁸

TERRACE

GREENHOUSE

CURB

HOBBIES/LAUNDRY
17¹⁰x13⁰

WASH RM.

WORK CENTER

COUNTRY KITCHEN
30¹⁰x13⁰

COOK TOP

REF'R

DINING RM.
14⁰x12⁸+BAY

56'-0"

DN

BROOM CL.

OVENS

PANTRY

CHINA

STUDY/MEDIA RM.
14⁰x15⁴

FOYER

UP

LIVING RM.
20⁰x15⁴

PORCH

Design V22399

First Floor: 1,301 square feet
Second Floor: 839 square feet
Total: 2,140 square feet

● From Early Colonial America comes this Salt Box. Narrow, horizontal siding, muntined windows, a massive centered chimney, carriage lamps and a classic front entrance set the exterior character. Inside, three bedrooms, three baths and two living areas. And much more.

Design V22691 First Floor: 1,550 square feet
Second Floor: 1,142 square feet; Total: 2,692 square feet

● This stately Georgian adaptation can trace its styling heritage to the 18th Century. Notice the typical Georgian symmetry of design. This home offers comfort plus elegance with dormer windows looking out from three bedrooms, all on the second floor. Downstairs, there's a parlor in addition to a gathering room. There's a breakfast room in addition to a dining room. Note the mud room off the washroom and three-car garage. A porch overlooks a rear terrace.

74'-0"

34'-0"

TERRACE

PORCH

DINING RM.
13⁰x13⁰+BAY

KITCHEN
12⁰x13⁰

BREAKFAST RM.
14⁸x13⁰

MUD RM.

WASH RM.

PARLOR
18⁰x15⁰

FOYER

GATHERING RM.
17⁰x15⁰

3 CAR GARAGE
23⁴x30⁸

MASTER BEDROOM
16⁰x13⁴

BEDROOM
14⁰x9⁸

BEDROOM
11⁴x13⁴

BATH

WALK-IN CLOSET

BATH

WALK-IN CLOSET

ROOF

Design V23379 First Floor: 1,086 square feet
Second Floor: 902 square feet; Total: 1,988 square feet

● Colonial styling is perfect in this two-story, narrow-lot plan. With the garage facing toward the front, the home is protected from street noise and works well on a lot that allows very little clearance on the sides. Living areas are concentrated in the formal living and dining rooms and the media room with nearby powder room. The kitchen holds a large snack bar counter through to the breakfast room. Sliding glass doors here allow easy access to the rear terrace. The bedrooms are on the second floor and include a master with fireplace and garden whirlpool and two family bedrooms. One of the secondary bedrooms includes a large walk-in closet.

Design V22253 First Floor: 1,503 square feet; Second Floor: 1,291 square feet; Total: 2,794 square feet

● The overhanging second floor sets the character of this Early American design. Study the features, both inside and out.

Design V21179 First Floor: 1,378 square feet; Second Floor: 1,040 square feet; Total: 2,418 square feet

● Loads of livability. This home could be called upon to serve as a five bedroom design. It will function admirably however you choose.

Design V21700 First Floor: 1,836 square feet; Second Floor: 1,232 square feet; Total: 3,068 square feet

● Good zoning, fine traffic circulation, efficient work center, first floor laundry are among convenient living features.

Design V21900

First Floor: 1,672 square feet
Second Floor: 1,287 square feet
Total: 2,959 square feet

● The history of the Colonial Salt Box goes back some 200 years. This unusually authentic adaptation captures all the warmth and charm of the early days both inside as well as outside. To reflect today's living patterns, an up-dating of the floor plan was inevitable. The result is a room arrangement which will serve the active family wonderfully. Formal living and dining take place at one end of the house which is free of cross-room traffic. Informal living activities will center around the family room and expand through sliding glass doors to the terrace. The mud room area is strategically located and includes the laundry and a full bath. An extra study/bedroom supplements four bedrooms upstairs. Count the closets and the other storage areas.

Design V22654

First Floor: 1,152 square feet
Second Floor: 844 square feet
Total: 1,996 square feet

● This is certainly an authentic traditional salt-box. It features a symmetrical design with a center fireplace, a wide, paneled doorway and multi-paned, double-hung windows. Tucked behind the one-car garage is a garden shed which provides work and storage space. The breakfast room features French doors which open onto a flagstone terrace. The U-shaped kitchen has built-in counters which make efficient use of space. The upstairs plan houses three bedrooms.

Design V22978 First Floor: 1,451 square feet
Second Floor: 1,268 square feet; Third Floor: 746 square feet
Total: 3,465 square feet

● The Nathaniel Hawthorne house in Salem, Mass. was the inspiration for this New England gambrel-roofed design. It was orignally constructed around 1730. This 20th Century version offers a heap of living potential. The family's favorite spot will be in front of the fireplace in the spacious country kitchen. However, there are other places to retire to such as the formal living room, the adjacent library, the bedrooms, or the areas on the third floor. The full basement offers the potential for the development of additional recreational space. Don't overlook the mud room strategically located with access from the garage and both yards.

Design V22659
First Floor: 1,023 square feet
Second Floor: 1,008 square feet; Third Floor: 476 square feet
Total: 2,507 square feet

L **D**

● The facade of this three-storied, pitch-roofed house has a symmetrical placement of windows and a restrained but elegant central entrance. The central hall, or foyer, expands midway through the house to a family kitchen. Off the foyer are two rooms, a living room with fireplace and a study. The windowed third floor attic can be used as a study and studio. Three bedrooms are housed on the second floor.

First floor plan (49'-8" x 32'-0"): TERRACE, DINING RM. 12⁰ x 9⁶ + BAY, BREAKFAST RM. 11⁶ x 11⁶, KITCHEN 11⁶ x 11⁶, GARAGE 13⁴ x 21⁴, DESK, OVEN, RANGE, REF'G., MUD ROOM, WASH RM., LIVING RM. 14⁰ x 17⁶, FOYER, STUDY 10⁸ x 9⁸, PORCH, CURB

Second floor plan: DRESSING ROOM, BATH, BATH, BEDROOM 13⁰ x 12⁴, SHELVES, LINEN, MASTER BEDROOM 14⁰ x 17⁶, BEDROOM 13⁰ x 12⁴

Third floor plan: ROOF, CEILING CLIP, RAILING, STUDIO/SEWING 14⁰ x 14⁰, STUDENT STUDY 13⁰ x 14⁰, ROOF

Design V22799 First Floor: 1,196 square feet
Second Floor: 780 square feet; Total: 1,976 square feet

● This two-story traditional design's facade with its narrow clapboards, punctuated by tall multi-paned windows, appears deceptively expansive. Yet the entire length of the house, including the garage, is 66 feet.

BEDROOM 12⁰x11⁰   BEDROOM 10⁸x10⁰
CL.
CL.
LIN.
CL.   CL.   HALL
DN
STOR.   BATH
LEDGE
BATH
S
VANITY
MASTER BEDROOM 12⁰x15⁸   DRESSING ROOM   WALK-IN CLOSET

66'-0"

TERRACE

STORAGE
CURB

POWDER RM.
CL.
MUD RM.
REF'G.
S   S   DW
BRKFST RM. 9⁰x11⁶
RANGE
KITCHEN 10⁰x11⁶
FAMILY RM. 17⁰x11⁶
RAILING

D. W. LT.
PANTRY
OVEN
DESK   BRM. CL.
DN

26'-0"

GARAGE 19⁸x25⁴
DINING RM. 12⁰x13⁶
UP
FOYER
CL.
CL.
LIVING RM. 19⁸x12⁶

PORCH

56'-0"

TERRACE

STOR.
STOR.
CL.
CL.

CURB

GARAGE
23⁸ x 23⁴

FAMILY RM.
11⁰ x 18⁸

PASS THRU
S. D.W.
KITCHEN
10⁰ x 9⁰
REF'G.

DINING RM.
10⁰ x 13⁶

31'-0"

PANTRY
COOK TOP
OVENS
CHINA
DN

P
PDR. RM.
CL.
FOYER
UP

LIVING RM.
16⁸ x 12⁶

PORCH

L D

BEDROOM
11⁰ x 10⁰
CL.
BATH
VANITY
BEDROOM
10⁰ x 11⁴
CL.
LINEN

WALK-IN CLOSET
LINEN
DN
CL.
CL.
CL.

WALK-IN CLOSET

BEDROOM
11⁰ x 13⁸
S.
BATH

MASTER BEDROOM
13⁴ x 13⁴

● What an appealing low-cost Colonial adaptation. Most of the livability features generally found in the largest of homes are present to cater to family needs.

54'-0"

TERRACE

DINING RM.
11⁰ x 10⁰

BRKFST.
8⁸ x 8⁰
S. D.W.
SNACK BAR

KITCHEN
11⁴ x 10⁰
RANGE

30'-0"

PANTRY
BRM. CL.
REF'G.
CL.
PDR. RM.
DN

CURB

STORAGE
STORAGE
UP

LIVING RM.
13⁶ x 17⁰

FOYER

STUDY
10⁰ x 9²

GARAGE
21⁸ x 23⁴

PORCH

Design V22870 First Floor: 900 square feet
Second Floor Left Suite: 467 square feet
Second Floor Right Suite: 493 square feet
Total: 1,860 square feet

BEDROOM
13² x 10⁴
CL.
CL.
BEDROOM
13² x 10⁴

CABINET
BOOKS
CABINET
LINEN
LINEN

BATH
SUITE ENT. HALL
DN
STOR.
STOR.
BATH
CL.
CL.

MASTER BEDROOM
11² x 13⁴
WALK-IN CLOSET
SHELVES
CL.
MASTER BEDROOM
11² x 13⁴

● This colonial home was designed to provide comfortable living space for two families. The first floor is the common living area, with all of the necessary living areas; the second floor has two two-bedroom-one-bath suites. Built-ins are featured in the smaller bedroom.

Design V22653

First Floor: 2,016 square feet
Second Floor: 1,656 square feet
Total: 3,672 square feet

● Livability and special features are absolutely
outstanding in this Colonial design. Imagine a
living room with beamed ceiling and fireplace
that measures more than 20 x 27 feet. And the
second fireplace in the luxurious master suite.
Make a special note about all the built-ins
featured in the dining room.

First Floor

71'-8"

STORAGE

TERRACE

LAUNDRY

FAMILY RM
19⁰ x 13⁸

KITCHEN
14⁶ x 13⁸

SERVICE
ENTRANCE

GARAGE
23⁴ x 23⁴

SEAT   BRM. CL.

PANTRY   OVEN

DINING RM.
14⁰ x 13⁰

DN

UP

50'-0"

LIVING RM.
20⁸ x 27⁴

FOYER

LIBRARY
16⁰ x 14⁰

PORCH

Second Floor

ROOF

BED RM./
STUDY
15⁰ x 11⁸

BATH

ROOF

LINEN

ATTIC

ATTIC

WALK-IN
CLOSET

BED RM.
13⁸ x 13⁰

BATH

DRESSING
ROOM

SHELVES

SHELVES

WALK-IN
CLOSET

DN

LINEN

MASTER
BED RM
20⁸ x 16⁰

HALL

BED RM.
13⁸ x 14⁰

Floor plan labels:

- 62'-0"
- 42'-0"
- TERRACE
- GARAGE 11⁴x22⁴
- PORCH
- DINING RM 12⁴x11⁰+BAY
- KITCHEN 12⁰x11⁴
- FAMILY DINING 16⁴x11⁴
- MUD ROOM
- CURB
- RAISED HEARTH
- WASH RM
- RAISED HEARTH
- FAMILY LIVING 19⁸x13⁴
- PARLOR 14⁴x17⁰
- FOYER
- COVERED PORCH
- PORCH

- BATH
- BATH
- STOR
- BEDROOM 18²x8⁰-11⁴
- DRESSING RM
- STOR
- MASTER BEDROOM 21⁰x9⁴-14⁸
- BEDROOM 17⁴x10⁸-13⁴

Design V22681

First Floor: 1,350 square feet
Second Floor: 1,224 square feet
Total: 2,574 square feet

● The charm of Early America is exemplified in this delightful design. Note the three areas which are highlighted by a fireplace. The three-bedroom second floor is nicely planned. Make special note of the master bedroom's many fine features. Study the rest of this design's many fine qualities.

Design V22625

First Floor: 1,640 square feet
Second Floor: 1,072 square feet
Total: 2,712 square feet

● A 19th-Century Farmhouse! So it might seem. But one with contemporary features . . . like the U-shaped kitchen with a built-in desk and appliances as well as a separate dining nook. Or the 20' by 13' family room. There, a beamed ceiling and raised-hearth fireplace add traditional warmth to a modern convention.

Design V21763
First Floor: 1,246 square feet; Apartment: 624 square feet
Second Floor: 1,054 square feet; Total: 2,924 square feet

● A charming New England saltbox designed to satisfy the needs of the large family, plus provide facilities for a live-in relative! Many houses can be a problem in adapting to the living requirements of an in-residence relative. But, not this one. Your family will have all the space it needs, while your relative will enjoy all his or her privacy and independence. This apartment area may also function as a doctor's suite.

Design V22623 First Floor: 1,368 square feet
Second Floor: 1,046 square feet; Total: 2,414 square feet

L D

● Take note of this four bedroom saltbox design. Enter through the large entrance hall to enjoy this home. Imagine a living room 13 x 27 feet. Plus a family room. Both having a fireplace. Also, sliding glass doors in both the family room and nook leading to the rear terrace.

Design V21814
First Floor: 1,471 square feet
Second Floor: 1,052 square feet
Total: 2,523 square feet

● A saltbox design that has all of the usual traditional exterior features. The interior shows what up-to-date floor planning can do inside the charm of yesteryear's exterior. A central entrance hall routes traffic directly to all major areas. The work area can be made to capture that cozy country kitchen atmosphere.

Design V22641

First Floor: 1,672 square feet
Second Floor: 1,248 square feet
Total: 2,920 square feet

● This Georgian adaptation is from the early 18th-Century and has plenty of historical background. The classical details are sedately stated. The plan promises up-to-date livability. The size of your site need not be large, either.

STORAGE

CL.
VANITY
BATH
DRESSING RM.
CL.
WALK-IN CLOSET
BED RM. 15⁸ x 12⁶

LINEN
BATH
MASTER BED RM. 18⁰ x 13⁶
BED RM. 15⁸ x 12⁶

48'-0"

TERRACE
GARAGE 23⁴ x 22⁰
FAMILY RM. 16⁰ x 19⁸
STOR.
CL.
52'-0"
OVENS RANGE PANTRY
HALL
LAUNDRY
STUDY-BED RM. 13⁰ x 11⁶
NOOK 8⁰ x 12⁶
KIT. 10⁰ x 12⁶
PDR. RM.
CL.
DINING RM. 18⁰ x 12⁶
ENTRANCE HALL
LIVING RM. 18⁰ x 13⁶
PORCH

Design V22102

First Floor: 1,682 square feet
Second Floor: 1,344 square feet
Total: 3,026 square feet

● This Early Colonial adaptation has its roots deep in the past. While it is long on history, it is equally long on 20th-Century livability features. The narrow horizontal siding, the appealing window treatment, the exquisite door detailing, the hip-roof, the massive chimneys and the cupola are exterior architectural features which set the character. It would certainly be difficult by today's living standards to ask for more than what this floor plan offers. From the first floor laundry with its adjacent washroom to the study with its adjacent powder room, the interior is replete with convenient living appointments. There is a wealth of "little" features such as the built-ins, the raised hearths, the pantry, the pass-through to breakfast room and the beamed ceiling.

● Small house with big house features and livability. Some of the features include two full baths and extra storage upstairs; laundry, washroom and two fireplaces, each with a wood box on the first floor. Two sets of sliding glass doors lead to the terrace.

Design V21856
First Floor: 1,023 square feet
Second Floor: 784 square feet
Total: 1,807 square feet

D

● The appeal of this Colonial home will be virtually everlasting. It will improve with age and service the growing family well. Imagine your family living here. There are four bedrooms, 2½ baths, plus plenty of first floor living space.

Design V22211 First Floor: 1,214 square feet
Second Floor: 1,146 square feet; Total: 2,360 square feet

L **D**

● A Garrison type adaptation that projects all the romance of yesteryear. The narrow horizontal siding, the wide corner boards, the window detailing, the overhanging second floor and the massive, centered chimney help set this home apart.

Design V21849

First Floor: 1,008 square feet
Second Floor: 1,080 square feet
Total: 2,088 square feet

Design V22640 First Floor: 1,386 square feet
Second Floor: 1,232 square feet; Total: 2,618 square fe

D

● Here is a gracious exterior which adopts many features common to New England-style Federal homes. The symmetry and proportions are outstanding. Inside, a fine functioning plan. Note stairs to attic for additional storage and livability.

Design V22649

First Floor: 1,501 square feet
Second Floor: 1,280 square feet
Total: 2,781 square feet

● This design's front exterior is highlighted by four pedimented nine-over-nine windows, five second-story eyebrow windows and a massive central chimney. Note the spacious kitchen of the interior. It is large in size and features an island range, pantry and broom closets, breakfast room with sliding glass doors to the rear porch and an adjacent laundry room which has access to the garage.

Design V21202
First Floor: 1,246 square feet
Second Floor: 1,052 square feet
Total: 2,298 square feet

First floor:
TERRACE
DINING RM. 13⁴ x 13⁰
KIT. 10⁰ x 11⁰
FAMILY RM. 12⁴ x 13⁰
GARAGE 23⁸ x 23⁴
LAUND.
BATH
BOOKS
LIVING RM. 13⁴ x 20⁰
ENTRY
STUDY 12⁸ x 13⁴
60'-8"
36'-8"
38'-0"
34'-0"

Second floor:
BED RM. 13⁰ x 10⁰
BED RM. 13⁰ x 10⁰
LINEN
BATH
VANITY
MASTER BED RM. 13⁴ x 18⁰
BATH
BED RM. 12⁸ x 12⁴

Design V21266
First Floor: 1,374 square feet
Second Floor: 1,094 square feet
Total: 2,468 square feet

Second floor:
BED RM. 12⁸ x 10⁰
BED RM. 12⁸ x 10⁰
LINEN
BATH
VANITY
MASTER BED RM. 13⁴ x 18⁸
BED RM. 12⁸ x 13⁴

First floor:
TERRACE
DINING RM. 13⁴ x 13⁰
KIT. 10⁰ x 13⁰
SNACKS
FAMILY RM. 20⁸ x 13⁰
GARAGE 23⁴ x 23⁴
RANGE O. PANTRY
BOOKS
BATH
BOOKS
LIVING RM. 13⁴ x 20⁰
ENTRY HALL
UP
STUDY BED RM. 12⁸ x 13⁴
68'-8"
44'-8"
24'-0"
34'-0"

Design V21142 First Floor: 1,525 square feet; Second Floor: 952 square feet
Total: 2,477 square feet (2,578 square feet Optional Four Bedroom)

Upper floor plan (three bedroom):

BED RM. 13⁸ x 10⁰ — CL. — CL. — LIN. — BATH — DN. — CL. — CL. — WALK IN CL. — VANITY — BATH — S. — MASTER BED RM. 13⁸ x 20⁰ — BED RM. 12⁸ x 14⁶

Lower floor plan (four bedroom):

BED RM. 12⁸ x 10⁰ — CL. — CL. — BED RM. 12⁸ x 10⁰ — CL. — CL. — CL. — LINEN — BATH — STORAGE — DN. — LIN. — S. — VANITY — CL. — MASTER BED RM. 13⁴ x 18⁰ — BATH — VANITY — BED RM. 12⁸ x 12⁴

First floor plan:

78'-8" — 52'-8" — 26'-0" — 34'-0" — 38'-0"

QUIET TERRACE — PLAY TERRACE — CHINA — DINING RM. 13⁸ x 13⁰ — KIT. 12⁰ x 13⁰ — S. — D.W. — RANGE — CL. — SNACK BAR — FAMILY RM. 24⁰ x 13⁰ — WOOD BOX — RAISED HEARTH — GARAGE 25⁴ x 23⁴ — REF.G. — BRM. — CHINA — PDR. RM. — BATH — W. D. — SEAT — CL. — STORAGE — CL. — DN. — LIN. — BOOKS — CL. — UP — LIVING RM. 13⁸ x 20⁰ — ENTRANCE HALL — STUDY-B.R. 12⁸ x 12⁰ — PORCH

● This design comes with details for both three and four bedroom construction. The first floor remains the same for both versions. Study this plan carefully, it has a great deal to offer the active, growing family.

Design V22999

First Floor: 2,547 square feet
Second Floor: 2,128 square feet
Guest Apartment: 1,186 square feet
Total: 5,861 square feet

WIDTH 80'-10"
DEPTH 52'-2"

● Recalling the grandeur of its Maryland ancestors, this manor house is replete with exterior details that make it special: keystoned lintels, fluted pilasters, a dormered attic and pedimented doorway. The centerhall floor plan allows formal living and dining areas to the front of the plan. Complementing these are the cozy library and large family room/breakfast room area. A service entrance off the garage holds a laundry room and wash room. Upstairs bedrooms allow more than adequate space. Over the garage is a complete guest apartment with living area, office, bedroom, bath and kitchen.

Design V22992

First Floor: 1,541 square feet
Second Floor: 1,541 square feet
Third Floor: 1,016 square feet
Total: 4,098 square feet

L **D**

TERRACE

BREAKFAST RM
13⁰ × 11⁰

FAMILY RM
22⁶ × 13⁴

LAUNDRY

PORCH

SNACK BAR

KITCHEN
14⁴ × 13⁴

ISLAND

CHINA

PDR RM

LIVING RM
17⁰ × 13⁴

FOYER

DINING RM
17⁰ × 13⁴

PORCH

44'-0"

32'-0"

ROOF

WALK-IN CLOSET

LINEN

SEAT

BATH

GUEST BEDROOM
12⁴ × 19⁰

STUDIO
17⁰ × 19⁰

DN

DESK

TWL-S

ROOF

MASTER BEDROOM
21⁴ × 13⁴

BEDROOM
13⁰ × 13⁴

BATH

WALK-IN CLOSET

LINEN

LINEN

OPEN TO BELOW

WALK-IN CLOSET

VANITY

WHIRLPOOL

MASTER BATH

SEAT

SEAT

BEDROOM
17⁰ × 13⁴

● The Dalton house, built between 1750 and 1760 in Newburyport, Massachusetts, inspired our plan shown here. Its lovely proportion and graceful exterior give way to a floor plan designed for the times. Left of the entry foyer is the formal living room; to the right formal dining. Both rooms have warming hearths. A family room to the rear of the plan connects with a unique glass-enclosed breakfast room. Nearby is the kitchen with pass-through snack bar. The second floor holds three bedrooms — the master suite and two family bedrooms. On the third floor is a guest bedroom with private bath and studio.

Design V22733 First Floor: 1,177 square feet; Second Floor: 1,003 square feet; Total: 2,180 square feet

L D

● This is definitely a four bedroom Colonial with charm galore. The kitchen features an island range and other built-ins. All will enjoy the sunken family room with fireplace, which has sliding glass doors leading to the terrace. Also a basement for recreational activities with laundry remaining on first floor for extra convenience.

CUSTOMIZABLE

Custom Alterations? See page 413 for customizing this plan to your specifications.

Design V22598

First Floor: 1,016 square feet
Second Floor: 890 square feet
Total: 1,906 square feet

● An impressive, Early Colonial adaptation with a projecting two-car garage and front drive court. It will not demand a large, expensive piece of property. In days of high-cost building, this relatively modest-sized two-story will be a great investment. Note the huge living room. The basement lends itself to recreational facilities.

Design V22622

First Floor: 624 square feet
Second Floor: 624 square feet
Total: 1,248 square feet

L D

● Appealing design can envelope little packages, too. Here is a charming, Early Colonial adaptation with an attached two-car garage to serve the young family with a modest building budget.

Design V22308

First Floor: 1,807 square feet
Second Floor: 1,195 square feet
Total: 3,002 square feet

● If yours is a corner lot you might want to give this attractive Colonial adaptation your consideration. Or, perhaps more significantly, if you have a large family this may be the design to solve your housing problem. Certainly you won't have to invest in a huge piece of property to enjoy the livability this home has to offer. In addition to the formal living room and informal family room, there is the separate dining room and kitchen eating space. Further, in addition to the three upstairs bedrooms, there is a fourth downstairs. The library could function as the fifth, if desired.

Design V22103

First Floor: 1,374 square feet
Second Floor: 1,056 square feet
Total: 2,430 square feet

D

Design V23552

First Floor: 1,784 square feet
Second Floor: 1,192 square feet
Total: 2,976 square feet

● Smart exterior features mark this home as a classic: second-story pop-outs with half-round windows above multi-paned windows, charming lintels, and a combination of horizontal wood siding and brick. Its interior floor plan contains both formal and informal areas, two fireplaces, a cozy solarium and three bedrooms with a sitting room. A three-car garage provides all the space necessary for the family vehicles and plenty of additional paraphernalia.

Design V22610

First Floor: 1,505 square feet
Second Floor: 1,344 square feet
Total: 2,849 square feet

● This full two-story traditional will be worthy of note wherever built. It strongly recalls images of a New England of yesteryear. And well it might; for the window treatment is delightful. The front entrance detail is inviting. The narrow horizontal siding and the corner boards are appealing as are the two massive chimneys. The center entrance hall is large with a handy powder room nearby. The study has built-in bookshelves and offers a full measure of privacy. The interior kitchen has a pass-thru to the family room and enjoys all that natural light from the bay window of the nook. A beamed ceiling, fireplace and sliding glass doors are features of the family room. The mud room highlights a closet, laundry equipment and an extra wash room. Study the upstairs with those four bedrooms, two baths and plenty of closets. An excellent arrangement for all.

Design V22188

First Floor: 1,440 square feet
Second Floor: 1,280 square feet
Total: 2,720 square feet

● This design is characteristic of early America and its presence will create an atmosphere of that time in our heritage. However, it will be right at home wherever located. Along with exterior charm, this design has outstanding livability to offer its occupants. Begin- ning with the first floor, there are formal and informal areas plus the work centers. Note the center bath which has direct access from three adjacent areas. Built-in book shelves are the feature of both the family room and the study/bedroom. Built-ins are also featured in the garage. Ascending up to the second floor, one will be in the private sleeping area. This area consists of the master suite, three bedrooms and full bath. Folding stairs are in the upstairs hall for easy access to the attic.

● This inviting Early American design will be outstanding in any area. Note the uniqueness of the front, covered porch entry to the family room. Interior features are many. Note the snack bar, study, vestibule, mud room and oversized garage.

70'-0"

TERRACE
P
GARAGE
21'⁴x27'⁴
STOR.
FAMILY RM.
12'⁰x19'⁴
STEP
KITCHEN
11'⁴x15'⁰
OPEN
THREE
SHELVES
MUD RM.
WASH RM.
STUDY
13'⁴x9'⁰
CL.
W.
DN.
CL.
P'TRY.
SNACK BAR
COVERED PORCH
DINING RM.
13'⁴x14'⁰
ENTRY HALL
VESTIBULE
CL.
LIVING RM.
13'⁴x20'⁰
PORCH

32'-0"

BEDROOM
13'⁴x12'⁴
BATH
MASTER BEDROOM
13'⁴x15'⁴
CL.
CL.
CL.
CL.
LINEN
DN.
OPEN
CL.
CL.
BEDROOM
13'⁴x12'⁴
BATH
CHEST
BEDROOM
13'⁴x11'⁴

Design V21278
First Floor: 1,336 square feet
Second Floor: 1,080 square feet
Total: 2,416 square feet

Design V22138

First Floor: 1,464 square feet
Second Floor: 1,144 square feet
Total: 2,608 square feet

First Floor Plan labels:
66'-0"
24'-0" · 16'-0" · 26'-0"
44'-0"

TERRACE

LAUND.

COUNTRY KITCHEN 19⁴ x 13⁶

REF'G.

FAMILY RM. 16⁰ x 19⁴

ISLAND CABINET

GARAGE 21⁰ x 23⁴

OVEN · RANGE

CL.

PDR. RM.

DINING RM. 12⁶ x 12¹⁰

WOOD BOX

STOR.

COVERED PORCH

FOYER

UP

STOR.

CAB.

LIVING RM. 25⁴ x 13⁶

Second Floor Plan labels:
ROOF

BED RM. 12⁶ x 10⁰

MASTER BED RM. 12⁶ x 18⁰

WALK-IN CL.

DN.

BATH

CL.

DRESS. RM.

WALK-IN CL.

BATH

SLIDING DOOR

PDR. RM.

ROOF

CL.

BED RM. 12⁶ x 10⁰

BED RM. 12⁶ x 13⁶

First Floor Plan labels:
54'-0"
30'-0"

TERRACE

DINING RM. 12⁸ x 11⁶

KITCHEN 11⁰ x 11⁶

NOOK 9⁴ x 9⁶

REF'S.

RANGE

B-O. OVEN

PANTRY

CL.

CURB

PDR. RM.

LAUNDRY

WASH. DRY.

GARAGE 19⁸ x 21⁴

CL.

DN.

UP

LIVING RM. 12⁸ x 17⁶

ENTRANCE

STUDY 10⁰-12⁴ x 11⁰

PORCH

Design V22731
First Floor: 1,039 square feet
Second Floor: 973 square feet; Total: 2,012 square feet

L **D**

● The multi-paned windows with shutters of this two-story highlight the exterior delightfully. Inside the livability is ideal. Formal and informal areas are sure to serve your family with ease. Note efficient U-shaped kitchen with handy first-floor laundry. Sleeping facilities on second floor.

Second Floor Plan labels:
ROOF

CL.

BATH

WALK-IN CLOSET

BED RM. 17⁰ x 11⁶

ROOF

LINEN

BATH

DN.

RAILING

MASTER BED RM. 12⁸ x 17⁶

BED RM. 12⁴ x 12²

Design V22295

First Floor: 1,947 square feet
Second Floor: 1,092 square feet
Total: 3,039 square feet

● This L-shaped two-story will make efficient use of your building site. The floor plan and how it functions is extremely interesting and practical. Study it carefully.

● Angular in its configuration, this inviting home offers loads of livability. There are five bedrooms, study, family room and a 27 foot long living room.

Design V22322

First Floor: 1,480 square feet
Second Floor: 1,172 square feet
Total: 2,652 square feet

D

Design V22346

First Floor: 1,510 square feet
Second Floor: 1,009 square feet
Total: 2,519 square feet

● A fine mixture of exterior materials, window treatment, and roof planes help set the character here. Envision your family enjoying all that this design has to offer.

Design V22539

First Floor: 1,450 square feet
Second Floor: 1,167 square feet
Total: 2,617 square feet

● This appealingly proportioned gambrel exudes an aura of coziness. The beauty of the main part of the house is delightfully symmetrical and is enhanced by the attached garage and laundry room. The center entrance routes traffic directly to all major zones of the house.

Design V21141
First Floor: 1,360 square feet
Second Floor: 939 square feet; Total: 2,299 square feet

● A 27-foot end living room, a fireplace in the breakfast room and master bedroom and a generous area over the garage for possible future development are highlights of this design. Don't overlook the many other features which include the family room, extra washroom, dining room, etc.

Design V22538

First Floor: 1,503 square feet
Second Floor: 1,095 square feet
Total: 2,598 square feet

L **D**

● This saltbox is charming, indeed. The livability it has to offer to the large and growing family is great. The entry is spacious and is open to the second floor balcony. For living areas, there is the study in addition to the living and family rooms.

Expandable Cape Ann Cottage

Design V22983 First Floor (Basic Plan): 776 square feet
First Floor (Expanded Plan): 1,072 square feet
Second Floor (Both Plans): 652 square feet
Total: 1,428 (Basic Plan); 1,724 (Expanded Plan)

● This charming gambrel-roofed Colonial cottage is reminiscent of the simple houses built and occupied by seafarers on Cape Ann, Mass. in the 17th and 18th Centuries. However, this adaptation offers a new twist. It is designed to expand as your need and/or budget grows. Of course, building the expanded version first will deliver the bonus livability promised by the formal dining room and quiet study, plus the convenience of the attached garage.

The second floor of each plan is identical. It highlights two bedrooms, and two full baths. In addition, there are two linen closets, double lavatories, built-in vanity, and walk-in wardrobe closet.

54'-0"

28'-0"

TERRACE

DINING RM.
12⁶ x 10⁰ +BAY

COUNTRY KITCHEN
21⁸ x 11⁴

COOK TOP

DW S LS

W.R.

CURB

OVEN REF'G

P'TRY CL.

STUDY
12⁶ x 10⁸

DN.

DN.

GARAGE
12⁸ x 21⁴

LIVING RM.
18⁰ x 12⁸

UP

DN.

FOYER CL.

PORCH

ROOF

MASTER BEDROOM
15⁴ x 11⁴

VANITY

BATH

LINEN

WALK-IN CLOSET

CL.

LINEN

DN.

BEDROOM
13⁸ x 10⁴ +DORMER

CL. BATH

ROOF

The basic unit provides fine livability potential for the small family. The country kitchen is spacious and allows for plenty of dining area. Here, the focal point is the fireplace. The efficient work center is but a few steps from the sliding glass doors to the rear terrace. The living room is of good size and also features a fireplace. The foyer routes traffic efficiently. The open stairwell leads to the basement level for the pursuit of hobbies and recreation. Don't miss the big bay window of the dining room, the pantry, or the handy wash room.

Design V21986 First Floor: 896 square feet
Second Floor: 1,148 square feet; Total: 2,044 square feet

L

● This design with its distinctive Gambrel roof will spell charm wherever it may be situated - far out in the country, or on a busy thoroughfare. Compact and economical to build, it will be easy on the budget. Note the location of the family room. It is over the garage on the second floor.

Design V21777 First Floor: 1,142 square feet
Second Floor: 1,010 square feet; Total: 2,152 square feet

● If it's charm you are after, you'll find this design with a Gambrel roof difficult to top. Its distinctive air is enhanced by the attached family room unit and the two-car garage. The wide vertical siding delightfully contrasts with the narrow horizontal siding.

Design V22531 First Floor: 1,353 square feet
Second Floor: 1,208 square feet; Total: 2,561 square feet

● This design has its roots in the early history of New England. While its exterior is decidedly and purposely dated, the interior reflects an impressive 20th-Century floor plan. All of the elements are present to guarantee outstanding living patterns for today's large, active family.

59

● Efficiently planned, this two-story house will serve the family with ease. Four bedrooms are on the second floor, along with two full baths. Note the attic storage over the projecting garage.

Design V22364
First Floor: 1,440 square feet
Second Floor: 1,206 square feet
Total: 2,646 square feet

Design V21827
First Floor: 1,442 square feet
Second Floor: 1,098 square feet
Total: 2,540 square feet

Design V22131

First Floor: 1,214 square feet
Second Floor: 1,097 square feet
Total: 2,311 square feet

L **D**

● The gambrel-roof home is often the very embodiment of charm from the Early Colonial Period in American architectural history. Fine proportion and excellent detailing were the hallmarks of the era.

Design V22988

First Floor: 1,458 square feet
Second Floor: 1,075 square feet
Total: 2,533 square feet
Optional Loft: 462 square feet

● The Joseph Guyon farmhouse, built in 1740, served as inspiration for this beautiful modern version. Three floors of living space encompass a country kitchen, living room, media room and dining room on the first floor; three bedrooms and two baths on the second floor; and an exercise room and study or sewing room on the third floor. Don't miss the covered porches front and rear, full guest bath near the media room and built-in wet bar.

Design V22995

First Floor: 2,465 square feet

Second Floor: 617 square feet

Total: 3,082 square feet

● This New England Colonial delivers beautiful proportions and great livability on 1½ levels. The main area of the house, the first floor, holds a living room, library, family room, dining room and gourmet kitchen. The master bedroom, also on this floor, features a whirlpool tub and sloped ceiling. A long rear terrace stretches the full width of the house. Two bedrooms on the second floor share a full bath; each has a built-in desk.

Design V22891

First Floor: 1,405 square feet
Second Floor: 1,226 square feet
Total: 2,631 square feet

● Here is a charming two-story house with a Gambrel roof that is very appealing. Entering this home, you will find a large dining room to the right which precedes an efficient kitchen. The adjacent breakfast room makes serving meals easy. The nice sized living room has a fireplace as does the family room. A wet bar and sliding glass doors are also in the family room. A powder room and laundry are on the first floor, too. Upstairs, you will find two bedrooms, a bath and a master bedroom suite with walk-in closet, tub and shower. Note that the second floor hall is open to the first floor.

Design V22897

First Floor: 1,648 square feet
Second Floor: 1,140 square feet
Total: 2,788 square feet

● Second-story dormers pierce the gambrel roof for comfortable window seats in the sleeping area of this comfortable home. An upper family room and all three bedrooms – including a luxurious master bedroom suite, are located upstairs. There's plenty of livability downstairs with a living room, formal dining room, breakfast area, study, and family room with raised hearth. Good zoning allows smooth traffic flow throughout the house.

ROOF

UPPER FAMILY RM.

SLOPED CEILING

MASTER BEDROOM 18⁰x15⁴

SEAT

ROOF

BATH

CL.

BEDROOM 11⁴x11⁴

CL.

ROOF

DN

LINEN

CL.

TUB

GLASS

S

BATH

DRESSING RM.

WALK-IN CLOSET

CL.

BEDROOM 15⁰x11⁴

SEAT

ROOF

SEAT

74'-0"

42'-0"

RAISED HEARTH

FAMILY RM. 20⁰x13⁶

SLOPED CEILING

TERRACE

DISAPPEARING STAIRS

CURB

STUDY 13⁰x13⁴

CL.

DN

RAILING

BRKFST. RM. 10⁰x11⁰

S

D.W.

COOK TOP

KITCHEN 11⁴x13⁴

REF'G

LT.

W.

D.

LAUNDRY

CL.

DN

PDR. RM.

DN

PANTRY

OVENS

BRM CL.

COVERED PORCH

GARAGE 21⁴x21⁴

LIVING RM. 18⁰x13⁴

FOYER

UP

CL.

DINING RM. 12⁸x13⁴

PORCH

Design V21914 First Floor: 1,470 square feet; Second Floor: 888 square feet; Total: 2,358 square feet

● What an interesting facade for passers-by to enjoy. Here, the delightful configuration of the Gambrel roof is fully visible from the road. The interior has all the features to help assure living convenience at its best. What are your favorite features?

Design V21745 First Floor: 1,440 square feet; Second Floor: 1,124 square feet; Total: 2,564 square feet

● A picture of charm. For sheer exterior appeal this house would be difficult to top. And inside there is an abundance of livability. Imagine, four bedrooms, three baths, guest room, family room, separate dining room and first floor laundry.

Design V22224 First Floor: 1,567 square feet
Second Floor: 1,070 square feet; Total: 2,637 square feet

● Certainly reminiscent of the charm of rural New England. The focal point of the first floor is easily the spacious family-kitchen. Formerly referred to as the country-kitchen, this area with its beamed ceiling and fireplace will have a warm and cozy atmosphere, indeed.

Design V21887

First Floor: 1,518 square feet
Second Floor: 1,144 square feet
Total: 2,662 square feet

● This Gambrel roof Colonial is steeped in history. And well it should be, for its pleasing proportions are a delight to the eye. The various roof planes, the window treatment, and the rambling nature of the entire house revive a picture of rural New England. The covered porch protects the front door which opens into a spacious entrance hall. Traffic then flows in an orderly fashion to the end living room, the separate dining room, the cozy family room, and to the spacious country-kitchen. There is a first floor laundry, plenty of coat closets, and a handy powder room. Two fireplaces enliven the decor of the living areas. Upstairs there is an exceptional master bedroom layout, and abundant storage. Note the walk-in closets.

Design V22320 First Floor: 1,856 square feet; Second Floor: 1,171 square feet; Total: 3,027 square feet

● A charming Colonial adaptation with a Gambrel roof front exterior and a Salt Box rear. The focal point of family activities will be the spacious family kitchen with its beamed ceiling and fireplace. Blueprints include details for both three and four bedroom options. In addition to the family kitchen, note the family room with beamed ceiling and fireplace. Don't miss the study with built-in bookshelves and cabinets.

Design V22680 First Floor: 1,707 square feet
Second Floor: 1,439 square feet; Total: 3,146 square feet

D

● This Early American, Dutch Colonial not only has charm, but offers many fine features. The foyer allows easy access to all rooms on the first floor - excellent livability. Note the large country kitchen with beamed ceiling, fireplace and island cook top. A large, formal dining room and powder room are only a few steps away. A fireplace also will be found in the study and living room. The service area, mud room, wash room and laundry are tucked near the garage. Two bedrooms, full bath and master bedroom suite will be found on the second floor. A fourth bedroom and bath are accessible through the master bedroom or stairs in the service entrance.

CAPE COD DESIGNS . . . .

dramatically capture the warmth and charm of an early period of our country's architectural history. The low profile of these 1½- and two-story houses is the result of the necessity of the 17th-Century structures of Cape Cod to be able to withstand the lashing winds that frequently swept across the Cape. The Cape Cod house can be found in three recognizable types: The half house with two windows to one side of the front door; the three-quarter house with two windows to one side and one to the other; the full Cape with a center door flanked by two windows on either side. From these basic main structures, appendages were often added to accommodate the growing family.

Design V22658 First Floor: 1,218 square feet
Second Floor: 764 square feet; Total: 1,982 square feet

● Traditional charm of yesteryear is exemplified delightfully in this 1½-story home. The garage has been conveniently tucked away in the rear of the house which makes this design ideal for a corner lot. Interior livability has been planned for efficient living. The front living room is large and features a fireplace with wood box. The laundry area is accessible by way of both the garage and a side covered porch. Enter the rear terrace from both eating areas, the formal dining room and the informal breakfast room.

Expanding the Half-House

Design V22682

First Floor (Basic Plan): 976 square feet
First Floor (Expanded Plan): 1,230 square feet
Second Floor (Both Plans): 744 square feet
Total: 1,720 Basic Plan; 1,974 Expanded Plan

L **D**

32'-0"

TERRACE

DINING RM.
10⁸ x 12⁰

COUNTRY KITCHEN
20⁰ x 13⁰-15⁸

30'-0"

PDR. RM.

FOYER

LIVING RM.
20⁰ x 13⁰

PORCH

ROOF

BEDROOM
12¹⁰ x 9⁸

BEDROOM
12¹⁰ x 9⁸

BATH

LINEN

BATH

MASTER BEDROOM
11¹⁰ x 14⁰

ROOF

CUSTOMIZABLE

Custom Alterations? See page 413 for customizing this plan to your specifications.

● Here is an expandable Colonial with a full measure of Cape Cod Charm. For those who wish to build the basic house, there is an abundance of low-budget livability. Twin fireplaces serve the formal living room and the informal country kitchen. Note the spaciousness of both areas. A dining room and powder room are also on the first floor of this basic plan. Upstairs three bedrooms and two full baths.

60'-0"

TERRACE

COVERED PORCH

DINING RM.
10⁸ x 12⁰

COUNTRY KITCHEN
20⁰ x 13⁰ - 15⁸

GARAGE
13⁸ x 20⁴

35'-0"

DN

BRM CL

P'TRY

PDR. RM.

CL

STUDY
13⁶ x 18⁰

UP

FOYER

BOOKS

LIVING RM.
20⁰ x 13⁰

PORCH

ATTIC STORAGE
(FUTURE ROOM)

ROOF

BEDROOM
12¹⁰ x 9⁸

BEDROOM
12¹⁰ x 9⁸

ROOF

CL

CL

DN

LINEN

BATH

CL

BATH

S

MASTER BEDROOM
11¹⁰ x 14⁰

ROOF

ROOF

73

Design V22563
First Floor: 1,500 square feet
Second Floor: 690 square feet; Total: 2,190 square feet

L **D**

● You'll have all kinds of fun deciding just how your family will function in this dramatically expanded half-house. There is a lot of attic storage, too. Observe the three-car garage.

Design V22395
First Floor: 1,481 square feet
Second Floor: 861 square feet
Total: 2,342 square feet

● New England revisited. The appeal of this type of home is ageless. As for its livability, it will serve its occupants admirably for generations to come. With two bedrooms downstairs, you may want to finish off the second floor at a later date.

GARAGE
21⁴ x 22⁴

TERRACE

FAMILY-DINING
16⁸ x 11⁶

KIT.
9⁰ x 11⁶

RANGE

BED RM.
10² x 11⁶

BATH

LIVING RM.
18⁶ x 13⁶

FLOWER COURT

ENTRY

UP

DN.

BED RM.
14⁰ x 11⁶

FENCE

22'-0"   8'-0"   45'-0"

75'-0"

37'-0"

24'-0"
26'-0"

Design V23126

First Floor: 1,141 square feet
Second Floor: 630 square feet
Total: 1,771 square feet

L **D**

● This New England adaptation has a lot to offer. There is the U-shaped kitchen, family-dining room, four bedrooms, two full baths, fireplace, covered porch and two-car garage. A delightful addition to any neighborhood.

BED RM.
12⁸ x 12⁰

BATH

CL.

CL.

DN.

STORAGE

BED RM.
14⁰ x 10⁰

Design V21718

First Floor: 2,012 square feet
Second Floor: 589 square feet
Total: 2,601 square feet

L **D**

Second Floor Plan:

MASTER BED RM. 14⁰x16⁰
STUDY-LOUNGE 14⁰x11⁶
BOOKS
CL. CL.
DRESS. RM.
BATH
STORAGE
DN.
WALK-IN CL.
STORAGE
STOR.

First Floor Plan:

100'-0"
26'-0"
52'-0"
22'-0"

GARAGE 25⁴x23⁴
TERRACE
W.R.
CL.
EATING
S.
FAMILY RM. 20⁰x13⁶
BATH
BED RM. 14⁸x11⁶
LAUNDRY
CL.
KITCHEN 13⁶x20⁰
REFG.
DW.
CL.
BRM DESK CL. CHINA
P'TRY
RANGE
O.
RAISED HEARTH
BEAMED CEILING
L/N.
CL.
R.
DINING RM. 11⁸x13⁶
DN.
STUDY-BED RM. 10⁰x10⁰
CL.
BED RM. 11⁴x13⁶
FENCE
LIVING RM. 20⁰x15⁰
UP
ENTRY
CL.
P.
26'-0"
32'-0"

● This house has everything - an extremely attractive exterior and a fine working, convenient floor plan. Don't miss upstairs suite.

Design V21902 First Floor: 1,312 square feet
Second Floor: 850 square feet; Total: 2,162 square feet

● This design has a great deal to offer the prospective home owner. The main living unit has a formal living room with fireplace and wood box, U-shaped kitchen with adjacent dining room, family room with beamed ceiling and sliding glass doors to the terrace, a study with built-in book shelves (or a second bedroom) and a bedroom. Later development of the second floor will create an additional two bedrooms and two full baths. This home offers a lot of livability and many years of enjoyable living.

Design V21987 First Floor: 1,632 square feet
Second Floor: 980 square feet; Total: 2,612 square feet

L D

● The comforts of home will be endless and enduring when experienced and enjoyed in this Colonial adaptation. What's your favorite feature?

Design V22145

First Floor: 1,182 square feet
Second Floor: 708 square feet
Total: 1,890 square feet

L

● Historically referred to as a "half house", this authentic adaptation has its roots in the heritage of New England. With completion of the second floor, the growing family doubles their sleeping capacity. Notice that the overall width of the house is only 44 feet. Take note of the covered porch leading to the garage and the flower court.

Design V22146

First Floor: 1,182 square feet
Second Floor: 708 square feet
Total: 1,890 square feet

L **D**

GARAGE
21⁴ x 21⁴

TERRACE

80'-0"

KITCHEN
9⁰ x 14⁰

FAMILY RM.
16⁶ x 11⁴

BED RM.
10⁰ x 11⁶

BATH

LINEN

COVERED PORCH
14⁰ x 12⁰

OVENS

WOOD BOX

CL.

REFS.

PANTRY

CL.

BOOKS

CABT.

LIN.

CL.

BED RM.
13⁴ x 11⁶

FLOWER COURT

BOOKS

LIVING RM.
19⁰ x 13⁰

ENTRY HALL

UP

CL.

35'-0"

MASTER BED RM.
16⁰ x 13⁰

DESK

BOOKS

PDR. RM.

BATH

LIN.

CL.

ROOF

CLIPPED CEIL'G

STUDY BED RM.
13⁴ x 11⁴

DN.

WALK-IN CLOSET

ROOF

ROOF

● Historically referred to as a "half house", this authentic adaptation has its roots in the heritage of New England. With completion of the second floor, the growing family doubles its sleeping capacity. Notice that both the family and living rooms have a fireplace. Don't overlook the many built-in units featured throughout the plan.

Design V21791 First Floor: 1,157 square feet
Second Floor: 875 square feet; Total: 2,032 square feet

● Wherever you build this moderately sized house an aura of Cape Cod is sure to unfold. The symmetry is pleasing, indeed. The authentic center entrance seems to project a beckoning call.

Design V21870 First Floor: 1,136 square feet
Second Floor: 936 square feet; Total: 2,072 square feet

● Besides an enchanting exterior, this home has formal dining and living rooms, plus informal family and breakfast rooms. Built-ins are located in both of these informal rooms. U-shaped, the kitchen will efficiently service both of the dining areas. Study the sleeping facilities of the second floor.

Design V22396 First Floor: 1,616 square feet
Second Floor: 993 square feet; Total: 2,609 square feet

● Another picturesque facade right from the pages of our Colonial heritage. The authentic features are many. Don't miss the stairs to area over the garage.

Design V21372

First Floor: 768 square feet
Second Floor: 432 square feet
Total: 1,200 square feet

● Low cost livability could hardly ask for more. Here, is an enchanting exterior and a four bedroom floor plan. Note stairs to basement.

Design V22162

First Floor: 741 square feet
Second Floor: 504 square feet
Total: 1,245 square feet

L **D**

● This economical design delivers great exterior appeal and fine livability. In addition to kitchen eating space there is a separate dining room.

Design V21394

First Floor: 832 square feet
Second Floor: 512 square feet
Total: 1,344 square feet

L D

● The growing family with a restricted building budget will find this a great investment - a convenient living floor plan inside an attractively designed facade.

Design V22510

First Floor: 1,191 square feet
Second Floor: 533 square feet
Total: 1,724 square feet

L D

● The pleasant in-line kitchen is flanked by a separate dining room and a family room. The master bedroom is on the first floor with two more bedrooms upstairs.

Design V22655

First Floor: 893 square feet
Second Floor: 652 square feet
Total: 1,545 square feet

● Wonderful things can be enclosed in small packages. This is the case for this two-story design. The total square footage is a mere 1,545 square feet yet its features are many, indeed. Its exterior appeal is very eye-pleasing with horizontal lines and two second story dormers. Livability will be enjoyed in this plan. The front study is ideal for a quiet escape. Nearby is a powder room also convenient to the kitchen and breakfast room. Two bedrooms and two full baths are located on the second floor.

Design V22656 First Floor: 1,122 square feet
Second Floor: 884 square feet; Total: 2,006 square feet

L D

● This charming Cape cottage possesses a great sense of shelter through its gambrel roof. Dormers at front and rear pierce the gambrel roof to provide generous, well-lit living space on the second floor which houses three bedrooms. This design's first floor layout is not far different from that of the Cape cottages of the 18th century. The large kitchen and adjoining dining room recall cottage keeping rooms both in function and in location at the rear of the house.

Design V22852 First Floor: 919 square feet
Second Floor: 535 square feet; Total: 1,454 square feet

L D

● Compact enough for even the smallest lot, this cozy design provides comfortable living space for a small family. At the heart of the plan is a spacious country kitchen. It features a cooking island - snack bar and a dining area that opens to a house-wide rear terrace. The nearby dining room also opens to the terrace. At the front of the plan is the living room, warmed by a fireplace. Across the centered foyer is a cozy study. Two second floor bedrooms are serviced by two baths. Note the first floor powder room and storage closet located next to the side entrance. This home will be a delight.

Design V22571 First Floor: 1,137 square feet
Second Floor: 795 square feet; Total: 1,932 square feet

L D

● Cost-efficient space! That's the bonus with this attractive Cape Cod. Start in the living room. It is spacious and inviting with full-length paned windows. In the formal dining room, a bay window adds the appropriate touch. For more living space, a delightfully appointed family room. The efficient kitchen has a snack bar for casual meals. Three bedrooms are on the second floor.

Design V23189 First Floor: 884 square feet
Second Floor: 598 square feet; Total: 1,482 square feet

D

● A large kitchen/dining area and living room are the living areas of this design. Four bedrooms, two up and two down, compose the sleeping zone. Each floor also has a full bath. A full basement and an attached garage will provide plenty of storage areas.

● Colonial charm could hardly be more appealingly captured than it is by this winsome design. List the features and study the living patterns.

Design V21901
First Floor: 1,200 square feet
Second Floor: 744 square feet
Total: 1,944 square feet

Design V21104
First Floor: 1,396 square feet
Second Floor: 574 square feet
Total: 1,970 square feet

● Here is a home whose front elevation makes one think of early New England. The frame exterior is highlighted by authentic double-hung windows with charming shutters. The attractive front entrance detail, flanked by the traditional side lites, and the projecting two-car garage with its appealing double doors are more exterior features.

● Picturesque, indeed. This L-shaped one-and-a-half story home would attract its full share of attention even on Cape Cod. Study the excellent plan.

Floor Plan Labels

First floor:
- TERRACE
- DINING RM. 12⁰ x 12⁶
- KIT. 15⁰ x 10⁶
- RANGE
- EATING
- PANTRY
- LAUNDRY
- DN.
- ENTRANCE HALL
- BATH
- CL. CL. LIN.
- BED RM. 11⁶ x 14⁰
- FAMILY RM. 20⁰ x 15⁴
- RAISED HEARTH
- BEAM CEILING
- WD. BOX
- STOR.
- GARAGE 21⁴ x 23⁴
- POOL
- FLOWER COURT
- FENCE
- LIVING RM. 15⁶ x 18⁰

Dimensions: 28'-0", 20'-0", 22'-0", 70'-0", 44'-0", 40'-0"

Second floor:
- VANITY
- DRESS. RM.
- BATH
- BATH
- MASTER BED RM. 13⁸ x 14⁴
- DN.
- WALK-IN CL.
- BED RM. 10⁰ x 12⁰
- BED RM. 11⁰ x 14⁴

Design V21903

First Floor: 1,460 square feet
Second Floor: 854 square feet
Total: 2,314 square feet

Design V22921

First Floor: 3,215 square feet
Second Floor: 711 square feet
Total: 3,926 square feet

● This popular traditionally styled house features bay windows, shutters, a fanlight and a cupola on the roof. Interior planning was designed for "empty-nesters," whose children are grown and moved out on their own. Open planning is geared for entertaining and relaxing rather than child-rearing. The major focal point of the interior will be the country kitchen. It has a work island with cook-top and snack bar and a spacious dining area with numerous built-ins. A sun room, 296 sq. ft. not included in the total above, is in the rear corner of the house, adjacent to the kitchen. Its sloped ceiling and glass walls open this room to the outdoors. Also adjacent to the kitchen, there is a "clutter room." It includes a workshop, laundry, pantry and washroom.

A Trend House for "Empty Nesters"

Design V23372

First Floor: 1,259 square feet
Second Floor: 942 square feet
Total: 2,201 square feet

L **D**

● Charm is the key word for this delightful plan's exterior, but don't miss the great floor plan inside. Formal living and dining rooms flank the entry foyer to the front; a family room and breakfast room with beamed ceilings are to the rear. The kitchen and service areas function well together and are near the garage and service entrance for convenience. Upstairs are the sleeping accommodations: two family bedrooms and a master suite of nice proportion.

Design V21196

First Floor: 1,008 square feet
Second Floor: 648 square feet; Total: 1,656 square feet

● This cozy home is ideal for a small family. Upon entering this house, you will find a nice sized living room with a fireplace. Adjacent, the formal dining area has sliding glass doors leading to the terrace. The kitchen and informal eating area are just a few steps away. A full bath and an optional bedroom/study also are on this floor. A full bath and two good sized bedrooms, each with its own dressing area, are on the second floor.

Design V21241

First Floor: 1,064 square feet
Second Floor: 898 square feet
Total: 1,962 square feet

L D

● You don't need a mansion to live graciously. What you do need is a practical floor plan which takes into consideration the varied activities of the busy family. This plan does that! This story-and-a-half design will not require a large piece of property while it returns the maximum per construction dollar. Its living potential is tremendous.

Design V22644

First Floor: 1,349 square feet
Second Floor: 836 square feet
Total: 2,185 square feet

D

● What a delightful, compact two-story this is! This design has many fine features tucked within its framework. The bowed roofline of this house stems from late 17th-Century architecture.

Design V22661

First Floor: 1,020 square feet
Second Floor: 777 square feet
Total: 1,797 square feet

L **D**

● Any other starter house or retirement home couldn't have more charm than this design. Its compact frame houses a very livable plan. An outstanding feature of the first floor is the large country kitchen. Its fine attractions include a beamed ceiling, raised hearth fireplace, built-in window seat and a door leading to the outdoors. A living room is in the front of the plan and has another fireplace which shares the single chimney. The rear dormered second floor houses the sleeping and bath facilities.

CUSTOMIZABLE
Custom Alterations? See page 413 for customizing this plan to your specifications.

Design V23553

First Floor: 2,471 square feet
Second Floor: 1,071 square feet
Total: 3,542 square feet

● Delightful Colonial design makes a fine statement for two-story living. The bay windows, columned front porch and charming dormers are big attractions on the exterior. Inside, a wide entry foyer directs traffic to the left to living areas and to the right to the master bedroom suite and a cozy study. The family room and living room both have fireplaces. The L-shaped kitchen is enhanced by an island cooktop and breakfast room with sliding glass doors to the rear porch. Upstairs are three secondary bedrooms and two full baths.

Design V21967

First Floor: 1,804 square feet
Second Floor: 496 square feet
Total: 2,300 square feet

● You'll always want that first impression your guests get of your new home to be a lasting one. There will be much that will linger in the memories of most of your visitors after their visit to this home. Of course, the impressive exterior will long be remembered. And little wonder with its distinctive projecting garage and bedroom wing, its recessed front porch, its horizontal siding and its interesting roof lines. Inside, there is much to behold. The presence of five bedrooms and three full baths will not be forgotten soon. Formal and informal areas will serve every family occasion.

Design V22500

First Floor: 1,851 square feet
Second Floor: 762 square feet
Total: 2,613 square feet

● The large family will enjoy the wonderful living patterns offered by this charming home. Don't miss the covered rear porch and the many features of the family room.

97

Design V22657

First Floor: 1,217 square feet
Second Floor: 868 square feet
Total: 2,085 square feet

L

● Deriving its design from the traditional Cape Cod style, this facade features clapboard siding, small-paned windows and a transom-lit entrance flanked by carriage lamps. A central chimney services two fireplaces, one in the country-kitchen and the other in the formal living room which is removed from the disturbing flow of traffic. The master suite is located to the left of the upstairs landing. A full bathroom services two additional bedrooms on the second floor.

● Captivating as a New England village! From the weather vane atop the garage to the roofed side entry and paned windows, this home is perfectly detailed. Inside, there is a lot of living space. An exceptionally large family room which is more than 29' by 13' including a dining area. The adjoining kitchen has a laundry just steps away. Two formal rooms are in the front.

Design V22596
First Floor: 1,489 square feet
Second Floor: 982 square feet
Total: 2,471 square feet

L **D**

● A study of the first and second floors of this charming design will reveal that nothing has been omitted to assure convenient living. List your family's living requirements and then observe how this house will proceed to satisfy them. Features galore.

Design V21736 First Floor: 1,618 square feet
Second Floor: 952 square feet; Total: 2,570 square feet

● This cozy home has over 2,600 square feet of livable floor area! And the manner in which this space is put to work to function conveniently for the large family is worth studying. Imagine five bedrooms, three full baths, living, dining and family rooms. Note large kitchen.

Design V21766 First Floor: 1,638 square feet
Second Floor: 1,006 square feet; Total: 2,644 square feet

D

● Surely your list of favorite features will be fun to compile. It certainly will be a long one. The center entry hall helps establish excellent traffic patterns and good zoning. The formal living and dining rooms function well together, as do the kitchen and family room. Note laundry and study.

Design V22124 First Floor: 1,176 square feet
Second Floor: 922 square feet; Total: 2,098 square feet

L D

Design V21701

First Floor: 1,344 square feet
Second Floor: 948 square feet
Total: 2,292 square feet

D

Design V21793 First Floor: 1,986 square feet; Second Floor: 944 square feet; Total: 2,930 square feet

D

● A great plan! The large family will find its living requirements satisfied admirably all throughout those active years of growing up. This would make a fine expansible house. The upstairs may be finished off as the size of the family increases and budget permits. Complete living requirements can be obtained on the first floor.

Design V22569
First Floor: 1,102 square feet
Second Floor: 764 square feet; Total: 1,866 square feet

L D

● What an enchanting updated version of the popular Cape Cod cottage. There are facilities for both formal and informal living pursuits. Note the spacious family area, the formal dining/living room, the first floor laundry and the efficient kitchen. The second floor houses the three bedrooms and two economically located baths.

Design V22559
First Floor: 1,388 square feet
Second Floor: 809 square feet; Total: 2,197 square feet

D

● Imagine, a 26 foot living room with fireplace, a quiet study with built-in bookshelves and excellent dining facilities. All of this, plus much more, is within an appealing, traditional exterior. Study the rest of this plan and list its numerous features.

Design V21365

First Floor: 975 square feet
Second Floor: 583 square feet
Total: 1,558 square feet

● This cozy, story-and-a-half home will suit a small family nicely. Upon entering this home, you will find a good sized living room. A few steps away is the formal dining area which has an excellent view of the backyard. Adjacent is the nice sized kitchen. A bedroom, bath and a study with a built-in desk and bookshelves also will be found on this floor. There are two bedrooms upstairs and a full bath. This home is big on livability; light on your building budget.

Design V22631

First Floor: 1,634 square feet
Second Floor: 1,011 square feet
Total: 2,645 square feet

L D

● Two fireplaces and much more! Notice how all the rooms are accessible from the main hall. That keeps traffic in each room to a minimum, saving you work by preserving your furnishings. There's more. A large family room featuring a beamed ceiling, a fireplace with built-in wood box and double doors onto the terrace. An exceptional U-shaped kitchen is ready to serve you. It has an adjacent breakfast nook. Built-ins, too . . a desk, storage pantry, oven and range. Plus a first floor laundry close at hand.

Design V21970

First Floor: 1,664 square feet
Second Floor: 1,116 square feet
Total: 2,780 square feet

● The prototype of this Colonial house was an integral part of the 18th-Century New England landscape; the updated version is a welcome addition to any suburban scene. The main entry wing, patterned after a classic Cape Cod cottage design, is two stories high but has a pleasing groundhugging look. The steeply pitched roof, triple dormers, and a massive central chimney anchor the house firmly to its site. Entry elevation is symmetrically balanced; doorway, middle dormer, and chimney are in perfect alignment. The one story wing between the main house and the garage is a spacious, beam-ceilinged family room with splay-walled entry porch at the front elevation and sliding glass windows at the rear opening to terrace, which is the full length of the house.

Design V22699

First Floor: 2,188 square feet
Second Floor: 858 square feet
Total: 3,046 square feet

L

ROOF

UPPER
LIVING RM.

BEDROOM
11⁰ x 15⁸

BEDROOM
11⁰ x 12⁰

LOUNGE

RAILING

VANITY

BATH

CL.

BATH

ATTIC

ACCESS
PANEL

DN.

CL.

CL.

BALCONY

LINEN

ROOF

UPPER
FOYER

CL.

ROOF

TERRACE

TERRACE

LIVING RM.
18⁴ x 15⁰

DINING RM.
12⁰ x 13⁰

GARAGE
21⁴ x 29⁴

MASTER
BEDROOM
15⁰ x 18⁰

WHIRLPOOL

LOUNGE ABOVE

EATING

CHINA

P

BATH

36" HIGH CAB'T

B.C.

CL.

W.R.

VANITY

DN

COUNTRY
KITCHEN
15⁸ x 21⁰

DN

MUD AREA

32'-0"

WALK-IN CLOSET

BALCONY
ABOVE

CL.

REF G

COOK
TOP

OVEN

LAUNDRY
11⁴ x 6⁰

W D

LOUNGE
12⁰ x 8⁸

FOYER

DN

TV VCR
HI-FI EQUIP

MEDIA RM.
12⁰ x 10⁰

S

DW

UP

PDR.
RM.

PORCH

106'-8"

The exterior detailing of this design recalls 18th-Century New England architecture. Enter by way of the centered front door and you are greeted into the foyer. Directly to the right is the study or optional bedroom or to the left is the living room. This large formal room features sliding glass doors to the sun-drenched solarium. The beauty of the solarium will be appreciated from the master bedroom and the dining room along with the living room.

Design V22615

First Floor: 2,563 square feet
Second Floor: 552 square feet
Total: 3,115 square feet

L D

Design V23351

First Floor: 1,794 square feet
Second Floor: 887 square feet
Total: 2,681 square feet

L **D**

GARAGE
21⁴ x 31⁸

LAUN.

KITCHEN
10¹⁰ x 9⁴

FAMILY RM
19⁴ x 11⁸

WALK-IN CLOSET

MASTER BEDROOM
11¹⁰ x 15⁰

DW

REF'G

RANGE

MUD RM

WASH'T RM

PANTRY

PDR RM

M. BATH

WHIRLPOOL

VANITY

DN

DINING RM
13⁰ x 11⁸

LIVING RM
17⁶ x 12⁸

DESK

CURB

STORAGE

UP

FOYER

STUDY
11¹⁰ x 12⁰

COVERED PORCH

37'- 4"

90'- 0"

● Home-grown comfort is the key to the appeal of this traditionally styled home. From the kitchen with attached family room to the living room with fireplace and attached formal dining room, this plan has it all. Notice the first-floor master bedroom with whirlpool tub and adjacent study. A nearby powder room turns the study into a convenient guest room. On the second floor are three more bedrooms with ample closet space and a full bath. The two-car garage has a large storage area.

ROOF

ROOF

ATTIC

BEDROOM
11⁰ x 11⁸

BEDROOM
11⁸ x 9⁰

ROOF

ATTIC

ACCESS

DESK

DN

LINEN

ROOF

WALK-IN CLOSET

BATH

WALK-IN CLOSET

BEDROOM
11⁰ x 21⁴

ROOF

ROOF

● Another 1¾-story home - a type of house favored by many of Cape Cod's early whalers. The compact floor plan will be economical to build and surely an energy saver. An excellent house to finish-off in stages.

Design V22636

First Floor: 1,211 square feet
Second Floor: 747 square feet
Total: 1,958 square feet

Design V22521

First Floor: 1,272 square feet
Second Floor: 1,139 square feet
Total: 2,411 square feet

● Here is a house to remind one of the weather-beaten facades of Nantucket. The active family plan is as up-to-date as tomorrow. Along with formal and informal areas on the first floor, there is a music alcove. If a music alcove is not needed, this area would make an ideal intimate sitting area.

THE FARMHOUSE THEME . . .

is one that can be found in abundance throughout the country. It can take many forms and project a limitless variety of faces. It can be a full two-story or feature a partial half-story second floor. It can feature an exterior of wood, stone, brick or a combination of all three materials. Perhaps its most predominant feature is the covered porch. And, of course, this can be executed in numerous ways. The wrap-around porch is once again becoming the favorite of many.

Design V22963

First Floor: 2,046 square feet
Second Floor: 1,644 square feet
Total: 3,690 square feet

● Featuring a gracious foyer and stairway at the entry, this home in the Colonial tradition is actually a modified version of the center-hall classic. Unlike the classic standard, the entrance here is off-center in the facade, with three windows to the left and two to the right of the entry door. Yet the design offers the dignity and grace so readily associated with its center-hall cousin. In addition, the rambling proportions of the house reflect Colonial precedents–as families grew, so did their houses. Both the dining and living rooms boast large fireplaces. Family meals are likely to be served in the cozy nook attached to the kitchen. Ample cabinet, shelf, and pantry space is provided wherever storage space is most needed. To retreat from the clamor of an active household, family members can read a good book in the study tucked in behind the living room, where generous provision is made for an entire library. Upstairs, four bedrooms provide a comfortable arrangement for each family member.

Design V22694

First Floor: 2,026 square feet
Second Floor: 1,386 square feet
Total: 3,412 square feet

L

● This two-story design faithfully recalls the 18th-Century homestead of Sec. of Foreign Affairs John Jay. Downstairs features include a large country kitchen, clutter room, music alcove, and library wing. Upstairs are three sizable bedrooms, including a master suite with whirlpool.

Design V22981

First Floor: 2,104 square feet
Second Floor: 2,015 square feet
Total: 4,119 square feet

● This formal two-story recalls a Louisiana plantation house, Land's End, built in 1857. The Ionic columns of the front porch and the pediment gable echo the Greek Revival style. Highlighting the interior is the bright and cheerful spaciousness of the informal family room area. It features a wall of glass stretching to the second story sloping ceiling. Enhancing the drama of this area is the adjacent glass area of the breakfast room. Note the "His/Her" areas of the master bedroom.

Design V22775

First Floor: 1,317 square feet
Second Floor: 952 square feet
Total: 2,269 square feet

● This front porch Farmhouse adaptation is characteristic of the rolling hills of Pennsylvania. Warm summer evenings will be a delight when the outdoors can be enjoyed in such an impressive manner. You will also be impressed by the interior after the floor plan is reviewed. Double front doors lead the way into this interior. Both the formal and informal areas are outstandingly spacious. There are two eating areas: the formal dining room and the nook with sliding glass doors to a dining terrace. Many built-ins will be found in the nook-kitchen area; including a desk, pantry and more. Notice pass-thru counter. Make special note, there is a covered porch to the side of the family room for more outside enjoyment. Three family bedrooms, bath and master bedroom suite are on the second floor. Years of pleasurable living will be enjoyed in this home.

ROOF

DN.

ATTIC 29⁴ x 26⁴
(HEADROOM 29⁴ x 10⁴)

ROOF

ROOF

BEDROOM / STUDY 11⁰ x 13²

BATH

VANITY

DRESS. RM.

MASTER BEDROOM 13⁰ x 13²

CL.

BATH

DN.

CL.

LIN.

CL.

CL.

UP TO ATTIC

BEDROOM 10⁰ x 10⁶

CL.

BEDROOM 13⁰ x 10⁶

Design V22774

First Floor: 1,370 square feet
Second Floor: 969 square feet
Total: 2,339 square feet

L **D**

● Another Farmhouse adaptation with all the most up-to-date features expected in a new home. Beginning with the formal areas, this design offers pleasures for the entire family. There is the quiet corner living room which has an opening to the sizable dining room. This room will enjoy plenty of natural light from the delightful bay window overlooking the rear yard. It is also conveniently located with the efficient U-shaped kitchen just a step away. The kitchen features many built-ins with pass-thru to the beamed ceiling breakfast room. Sliding glass doors to the terrace are fine attractions in both the sunken family room and breakfast room. The service entrance to the garage is flanked by a clothes closet and a large, walk-in pantry. There is a secondary entrance thru the laundry room. Recreational activities and hobbies can be pursued in the basement area. Four bedrooms, two baths upstairs.

CUSTOMIZABLE

Custom Alterations? See page 413 for customizing this plan to your specifications.

59'-8"

TERRACE

RAISED HEARTH

FAMILY RM. 21⁴ x 13⁶

RAILING

BREAKFAST RM. 14⁰ x 11⁶

KITCHEN 10⁰ x 11⁸

S

D.W.

RANGE

DINING RM. 13⁰ x 11⁶ + BAY

PASS THRU

DN.

DESK

BRM

CL.

REF'G

OVEN

LAUNDRY RM. 10⁰ x 7⁶

DRY.

WASH

L.T.

CL.

PANTRY

DN.

DN.

PDR. RM.

CL.

CURB

FOYER

UP

LIVING RM. 17⁰ x 13⁶

COVERED PORCH

GARAGE 21⁴ x 21⁸

44'-0"

115

Design V22890

First Floor: 1,612 square feet
Second Floor: 1,356 square feet
Total: 2,968 square feet

D

● An appealing Farmhouse that is complimented by an inviting front porch. Many memorable summer evenings will be spent here. Entering this house, you will notice a nice-sized study to your right and spacious living room to the left. The adjacent dining room is enriched by an attractive bay window. Just a step away, an efficient kitchen will be found. Many family activities will be enjoyed in the large family room. The tavern/snack bar will make entertaining guests a joy. A powder room and laundry are also on the first floor. Upstairs you'll find a master bedroom suite featuring a bath with an oversized tub and shower and a dressing room. Also on this floor; two bedrooms, full bath and a large attic.

CUSTOMIZABLE
Custom Alterations? See page 413 for customizing this plan to your specifications.

Design V22776

First Floor: 1,134 square feet
Second Floor: 874 square feet
Total: 2,008 square feet

L D

● This board-and-batten farmhouse design has all of the country charm of New England. The large front covered porch surely will be appreciated during the beautiful warm weather months. Immediately off the front entrance is the delightful corner living room. The

dining room with bay window will be easily served by the U-shaped kitchen. Informal family living enjoyment will be obtained in the family room which features a raised hearth fireplace, sliding glass doors to the rear terrace and easy access to the work center of powd-

er room, laundry and service entrance. The second floor houses all of the sleeping facilities. There is a master bedroom with a private bath and walk-in closet. Two other bedrooms share a bath. This is an excellent one-and-a-half story design.

Design V22946 First Floor: 1,590 square feet; Second Floor: 1,344 square feet; Total: 2,934 square feet

L **D**

● Here's a traditional design that's made for down-home hospitality, the pleasures of casual conversation, and the good grace of pleasant company. The star attractions are the large covered porch and terrace, perfectly relaxing gathering points for family and friends. Inside, though, the design is truly a hard worker; separate living room and family room, each with its own fireplace; formal dining room; large kitchen and breakfast area with bay windows; separate study; workshop with plenty of room to maneuver; mud room; and four bedrooms up, including a master suite. Not to be overlooked are the curio niches, the powder room, the built-in bookshelves, the kitchen pass-thru, the pantry, the planning desk, the workbench, and the stairs to the basement.

Design V22865

First Floor: 1,703 square feet
Second Floor: 1,044 square feet
Total: 2,747 square feet

D

● Here's a cozy traditional farmhouse with a big wrap-around covered porch. Up front, flanking the entry foyer, are a living room with fireplace, and formal dining room. To the rear are a study, that could be used as a guest room, and the family room with another fireplace. The kitchen/breakfast room combination is conveniently located near the service entrance off the garage. Note three bedrooms with dormer windows upstairs.

119

Design V22945

First Floor: 1,644 square feet
Second Floor: 971 square feet
Total: 2,615 square feet

CUSTOMIZABLE

Custom Alterations? See page 413 for customizing this plan to your specifications.

● Here is a new floor plan designed to go with the almost identical exterior of one of Home Planners' most popular houses. A masterfully affordable design, this plan manages to include all the basics - and then adds a little more. Note the wraparound covered porch, large family room with raised-hearth fireplace and wet bar, spacious kitchen with island cook top, formal dining room, rear terrace, and extra storage on the first floor. Upstairs, the plan's as flexible as they come: three or four bedrooms (the fourth could easily be a study or playroom) and lots of unfinished attic just waiting for you to transform it into living space. This could make a fine studio, sewing room, home office, or just a place for the safe, dry storage of the family's paraphernalia, Christmas decorations, etc.

Design V22650

First Floor: 1,451 square feet
Second Floor: 1,091 square feet; Total 2,542 square feet

L **D**

● The dormers and the covered porch with pillars introduce this house to the on-lookers. Inside, the appeal is also outstanding. Note the size (18 x 25 foot) of the gathering room which is open to the dining room. Kitchen-nook area is very spacious and features a cooking island, built-in desk and more. Great convenience having the laundry and the service area close to the kitchen. Imagine, a fireplace in both the gathering room and the master bedroom! Make special note of the service entrance doors leading to both the front and back of the house.

Floor plan labels

82'-8"
34'-0"

TERRACE

DINING RM. 10⁰ x 13⁶
NOOK 10⁴ x 13⁶
KITCHEN 11⁰ x 13⁶
RANGE
PORCH
LAUNDRY
SERVICE ENTRANCE
DESK
OVEN
POWDER RM.
GATHERING RM. 18⁰ x 25⁴
UP
ENTRANCE
STUDY 12⁰ x 11⁶
GARAGE 23⁴ x 21⁴
PORCH

WALK-IN CLOSET
DRESSING RM.
BATH
BED RM. 11⁴ x 10⁰
BATH
SHELVES
MASTER BED RM. 18⁰ x 14¹⁰
LINEN
SHELVES
BED RM. 17⁰ x 12⁶

Design V21239
First Floor: 1,822 square feet
Second Floor: 1,419 square feet
Total: 3,241 square feet

Design V21955
First Floor: 1,192 square feet
Second Floor: 1,192 square feet
Total: 2,384 square feet

● Here is a design with all of the features a home-owner would want most in a new house. It abound in exterior appeal and will be a neighborhood show place. Picture yourself relaxing on the front, covere porch after a hard day of work.

Design V21728
First Floor: 1,942 square feet
Second Floor: 2,224 square feet
Total: 4,166 square feet

Design V22907 First Floor: 1,546 square feet; Second Floor: 1,144 square feet; Total: 2,690 square feet

● This traditional L-shaped farmhouse is charming, indeed, with gambrel roof, dormer windows, and covered porch supported by slender columns and side rails. A spacious country kitchen with a bay provides a cozy gathering place for family and friends, as well as convenient place for food preparation with its central work island and size. There's a formal dining room also adjacent to the kitchen. A rear family room features its own fireplace, as does a large living room in the front. All four bedrooms are isolated upstairs, away from other household activity and noise. Included is a larger master bedroom suite with its own bath, dressing room, and abundant closet space. This is a comfortable home for the modern family who can appreciate the tradition and charm of the past.

CUSTOMIZABLE

Custom Alterations? See page 413 for customizing this plan to your specifications.

Custom Alterations? See page 413

Design V22908

First Floor: 1,427 square feet
Second Floor: 1,153 square feet
Total: 2,580 square feet

L **D**

● This Early American farmhouse offers plenty of modern comfort with its covered front porch with pillars and rails, double chimneys, building attachment, and four upstairs bedrooms. The first floor attachment includes a family room with bay window. It leads from the main house to a two-car garage. The family room certainly is the central focus of this fine design, with its own fireplace and rear entrance to a laundry and sewing room behind the garage. Disappearing stairs in the building attachment lead to attic space over the garage. The upstairs also is accessible from stairs just off the front foyer. Included is a master bedroom suite. Downstairs one finds a modern kitchen with breakfast room, dining room, and front living room.

Design V21996

First Floor: 1,056 square feet
Second Floor: 1,040 square feet
Total: 2,096 square feet

L **D**

BED RM. 14⁴ x 11⁴
BATH
BATH
WALK-IN CL.
CL.
CL.
STORAGE
DN.
BED RM. 11⁰ x 13⁸
LIN.
CL.
BED RM. 10⁸ x 10⁰
WALK-IN CL.
MASTER BED RM. 11⁴ x 17⁰

62'-0"
40'-0"
22'-0"
TERRACE
DINING 12⁰ x 11⁸
KIT. 10⁴ x 11⁸
REF'G.
BREAKFAST 8⁴ x 11⁸
PDR. RM.
LAUND.
32'-0"
26'-0"
PANTRY
SLIDING DOOR
RANGE
OVEN
DN.
WOOD GRILLE
CL.
LIVING 18⁸ x 13⁴
ENTRY HALL
FAMILY RM. 11⁴ x 17⁴
STORAGE
GARAGE 21⁸ x 23⁴
PORCH

126

Design V21304

First Floor: 1,120 square feet
Second Floor: 1,120 square feet
Total: 2,240 square feet

Design V21339

First Floor: 1,292 square feet
Second Floor: 1,232 square feet
Total: 2,524 square feet

Design V21354

First Floor: 644 square feet
Second Floor: 572 square feet
Total: 1,216 square feet

L **D**

● Livability galore for the 50 foot building site. The homemaker will enjoy the U-shaped work center with the extra washroom, laundry equipment nearby.

OPTIONAL BASEMENT

Design V21361

First Floor: 965 square feet
Second Floor: 740 square feet
Total: 1,705 square feet

L **D**

● An abundance of livability is in this charming, traditional adaptation. It will be most economical to build. Count the numerous features.

Design V21723

First Floor: 888 square feet
Second Floor: 970 square feet
Total: 1,858 square feet

● You'll not need a large parcel of property to accommodate this home. Neither will you need too large a building budget. Note fourth bedroom.

Design V21368

First Floor: 728 square feet
Second Floor: 728 square feet
Total: 1,456 square feet

● Study this outstanding layout. All of the elements are present for fine family living. Four bedrooms, family room, first floor laundry and more are available.

Design V21905

First Floor: 1,596 square feet
Second Floor: 1,574 square feet
Total: 3,170 square feet

● A pleasing Farmhouse adaptation that just looks like it should be catering to the needs of a big, active family. What makes this house so interesting are the various roof lines and projecting wings. The covered front porch and the double front doors add their full measure of charm, too. The traffic patterns of this plan will be a favorite feature for a long time. One whole wing is devoted to living activities. Off the formal entrance hall is the quiet living room. Behind, and functioning with the covered rear porch, is the beamed ceiling family room. It has fine blank wall space and a raised hearth fireplace. The kitchen looks out upon the rear yard and efficiently serves the eating areas. Observe the laundry area with the powder room. Upstairs, four bedrooms!

Design V22223 First Floor: 1,266 square feet; Second Floor: 1,232 square feet; Total: 2,498 square feet
L D

● The appealing double front doors of this home open wide to fine livability for the large, growing family. The spacious entrance hall is flanked by the formal, end living room and the all-purpose, beamed ceiling family room. Both rooms have a commanding fire-place. The U-shaped kitchen overlooks the rear yard and is but a step, or two, from the breakfast nook and the formal dining room. The mud room controls the flows of traffic during the inclement weather. Observe the laundry equipment and the washroom. Five bedrooms, two full baths, and plenty of closets are what make the second floor truly outstanding. There are a number of other convenient living features that make this design distinctive. How many of these can you list?

Design V21318

First Floor: 854 square feet
Second Floor: 896 square feet
Total: 1,750 square feet

● Imagine! Five bedrooms, 2½ baths, informal family room, formal living and dining rooms, excellent kitchen, snack bar and a big two-car garage.

CUSTOMIZABLE

Custom Alterations? See page 413 for customizing this plan to your specifications.

OPTIONAL 3 BEDROOM PLAN

Design V21956

First Floor: 990 square feet
Second Floor: 728 square feet
Total: 1,718 square feet

L **D**

● The blueprints for this home include details for both the three bedroom and four bedroom options. The first floor livability does not change.

Design V22172
First Floor: 1,618 square feet
Second Floor: 1,205 square feet
Total: 2,823 square feet

Design V21868

First Floor: 1,190 square feet
Second Floor: 1,300 square feet
Total: 2,490 square feet

● A five-bedroom Farmhouse adaptation that is truly a home for family living. The big family room will be everyone's favorite area. Note the master bedroom suite, located over the garage.

Design V21285

First Floor: 1,202 square feet
Second Floor: 896 square feet
Total: 2,098 square feet

L **D**

● Such a pretty traditional Farmhouse design — and with so much to offer in the way of floor planning. From the front entry, turn left into a good-sized living room with attached dining room. A right turn leads to a well-placed powder room and laundry or farther back to the beamed-ceiling family room (note the fireplace with wood box here). The kitchen and adjacent breakfast nook will make mealtimes a pleasure. Upstairs, four symmetrically laid-out bedrooms share space with two baths.

Design V21933

First Floor: 1,184 square feet
Second Floor: 884 square feet
Total: 2,068 square feet

Design V21269

First Floor: 1,232 square feet
Second Floor: 1,232 square feet
Total: 2,464 square feet

Design V21082

First Floor: 1,254 square feet
Second Floor: 1,096 square feet
Total: 2,350 square feet

● Here are three homes of modest size each one completely capable of catering most successfully to the living requirements of the large family. There is no lack of sleeping space. Bath facilities are excellent. Eating potential is outstanding. Formal and informal living space is exceptional. As for exterior design appeal - unsurpassed. Don't miss the laundries, fireplaces, number of closets and oversized garages. Each design has a big basement.

Design V21787

First Floor: 2,656 square feet
Second Floor: 744 square feet
Total: 3,400 square feet

D

● Can't you picture this dramatic home sitting on your property? The curving front drive is impressive as it passes the walks to the front door and the service entrance. The roof masses, the centered masonry chimney, the window symmetry and the 108 foot expanse across the front are among the features that make this a distinctive home. Of interest are the living and family rooms — both similar in size and each having its own fireplace.

Design V22225
First Floor: 2,683 square feet
Second Floor: 1,167 square feet
Total: 3,850 square feet

● The exterior of this house will give you the feeling that it came from the pages of our Colonial heritage. Its configuration is pleasing and its interior will be efficient. Study each area carefully for its great number of features. Your list might begin with the large coat closet and adjacent powder room off the foyer. Then you could add the island cook top in the kitchen, three first-floor bedrooms, second-floor dormitory and spacious sauna. Be sure you don't miss a single highlight of this outstanding home.

BED RM.
11⁰ x 11⁶

CL.

SEAT

BATH

BED RM.
9⁸ x 11⁶

CL.

DN.

LINEN

CL.

WALK-IN
CLOSET

CL.

MASTER
BED RM.
11⁴ x 17⁶

BATH

BED RM.
12⁰ x 12¹⁰

66'-8"

TERRACE

DINING RM.
11⁴ x 11²

KITCHEN
10⁰ x 11²

RANGE

S.

D.W.

NOOK
9⁰ x 11²

FAMILY RM.
12⁰ x 20⁴

B.CL.

REF'G.

OVEN

PANTRY

DN.

RAISED HEARTH

CURB

32'-4"

LIVING RM.
20⁸ x 13²

CL.

ENTRY

UP

CL.

PORCH

PDR.
RM.

LAUNDRY

LT.

WASH.

DRY.

GARAGE
22⁰ x 21⁴

Design V22752

First Floor: 1,209 square feet
Second Floor: 960 square feet
Total: 2,169 square feet

● This impressive two-story home is sure to catch the eye of even the most casual of on-lookers. The extended one-story wing adds great appeal to the exterior. The covered porch with pillars also is a charming feature. Now take a walk through the efficient floor plan. The living/dining room is L-shaped with the dining room being convenient to the kitchen. The U-shaped kitchen has a pass-thru to the breakfast nook plus has many built-ins to help ease kitchen duties. The nook, along with the family room, has sliding glass doors to the terrace. Also on the first floor is a powder room and laundry. The second floor houses the three family bedrooms, bath and the master bedroom suite with all the extras. Note the extra curb area in the garage.

Design V22585

First Floor: 990 square feet
Second Floor: 1,011 square feet
Total: 2,001 square feet

L D

● An elegant Colonial! This
is a version of a front porch
type house. The exterior is
highlighted with seven large
paned-glass windows and
pillars. Note that the second
floor overhangs in the front
to extend the size of the master bedroom. After entering
through the front door one
can either go directly to the
formal area of the living room
and dining room or to the informal area which is the front
family room with fireplace.
No matter which direction
you choose, satisfaction will
be found. The U-shaped kitch-
en will serve the nook area
orderly and is just a step
away from the wash room.
Upstairs one will find all of
the sleeping facilities.

BED RM. 10⁰ x 10⁸

BED RM. 12⁴ x 10⁸

BATH

LINEN

CL

DN.

MASTER BED RM. 13⁴ x 16⁸

BATH

BED RM. 13⁰ x 12⁰

58'-0"

TERRACE

DINING RM. 12⁰ x 11²

NOOK 7⁴ x 11²

KITCHEN 9⁶ x 11²

WASH RM.

D.W.

REFG.

WASH. DRY.

B.CL.

DN.

CL.

UP

CURB

ENTRY

FAMILY RM. 12⁴ x 13²

LIVING RM. 13⁰ x 17²

PORCH

GARAGE 21⁸ x 24⁸

31'-4"

141

Design V23397

First Floor: 1,855 square feet

Second Floor: 1,241 square feet

Total: 3,096 square feet

● Five second-story dormers and a wide covered front porch add to the charm of this farmhouse design. Inside, the entry foyer opens to the left to a formal living room with fireplace and attached dining room. To the right is a private study. The back of the plan is dominated by a huge country kitchen featuring an island cook top. On this floor is the master suite with a large walk-in closet. The second floor holds three bedrooms (or two and a sitting room) with two full baths.

Design V23399

First Floor: 1,716 square feet
Second Floor: 2,102 square feet
Total: 3,818 square feet

L **D**

● This is the ultimate in farmhouse living —
six dormer windows and a porch that stretches
essentially around the entire house. Inside, the
plan is open and inviting. Besides the large
country kitchen with fireplace, there is a small
game room with attached tavern, a library with
built-in bookshelves and a fireplace, and a
formal living room. The second floor has four
bedrooms and three full baths. The service
entrance features a laundry area conveniently
just off the garage.

Design V23396

First Floor: 1,829 square feet
Second Floor: 947 square feet
Total: 2,776 square feet

L **D**

● Rustic charm abounds in this pleasant farm-house rendition. Covered porches to the front and rear enclose living potential for the whole family. Flanking the entrance foyer are the living and dining rooms. To the rear is the L-shaped kitchen with island cook top and snack bar. A small family room/breakfast nook is attached. A private study is tucked away on this floor next to the master suite. On the second floor are three bedrooms and a full bath. Two of the bedrooms have charming dormer windows.

Design V23398
First Floor: 1,533 square feet
Second Floor: 1,288 square feet
Total: 2,821 square feet

L **D**

● With its classic Farmhouse good-looks and just-right floor plan, this country residence has it all. The wraparound covered porch at the entry gives way to a long foyer with open staircase. To the right and left are the formal dining room and the living room. More casual living areas are to the rear: a family room, and U-shaped kitchen with attached breakfast room. The second floor holds sleeping areas — two family bedrooms and a huge master suite with walk-in closet and pampering master bath.

145

Design V22633

First Floor: 1,338 square feet
Second Floor: 1,200 square feet
Third Floor: 506 square feet
Total: 3,044 square feet

● This is certainly a pleasing Georgian. Its facade features a front porch with a roof supported by 12'' diameter wooden columns. The garage wing has a sheltered service entry and brick facing which complements the design. Sliding glass doors link the terrace and family room, providing an indoor/outdoor area for entertaining as pictured in the rear elevation. The floor plan has been designed to serve the family efficiently. The stairway in the foyer leads to four second-floor bedrooms. The third floor is windowed and can be used as a studio and study.

GEORGIAN HOUSES . . .

are noted for the many fine characteristics that first graced these popular homes: perfect proportions, eye-pleasing symmetry, massive chimneys, tasteful detailing, and classic entries. The well-designed Georgian epitomizes quiet strength, restrained beauty, and gracious living.

Design V21858

First Floor: 1,794 square feet
Second Floor: 1,474 square feet
Studio: 424 square feet
Total: 3,692 square feet

D

● You'll never regret your choice of this Georgian design. Its stately facade seems to foretell all of the exceptional features to be found inside. From the delightful spacious front entry hall, to the studio or maid's room over the garage, this home is unique all along the way. Imagine four fireplaces, three full baths, two extra washrooms, a family room, plus a quiet library. Don't miss the first floor laundry. Note the separate set of stairs to the studio or maid's room. The center entrance leads to the vestibule and entry hall. All the major areas are but a step or two from this formal hall. The kitchen is well planned and strategically located between the separate dining room and the breakfast room. Sliding glass doors permit easy access to the functional rear terraces.

Design V22683 First Floor: 2,126 square feet; Second Floor: 1,882 square feet; Total: 4,008 square feet

L **D**

● This historical Georgian home has its roots in the 18th Century. Dignified symmetry is a hallmark of both front and rear elevations. The full two-story center section is delightfully complemented by the 1½-story wings. Interior livability has been planned to serve today's active family. The elegant gathering room, three steps down from the rest of the house, has ample space for entertaining on a grand scale. It fills an entire wing and is dead-ended so that traffic does not pass through it. Guests and family alike will enjoy the two rooms flanking the foyer, the study and formal dining room. Each of these rooms will have a fireplace as its highlight. The breakfast room, kitchen, powder room and laundry are arranged for maximum efficiency. This area will always have that desired light and airy atmosphere with the sliding glass door and the triple window over the kitchen sink. The second floor houses the family bedrooms. Take special note of the spacious master bedroom suite. It has a deluxe bath, fireplace and sunken lounge with dressing room and walk-in closet. Surely an area to be appreciated.

Georgian Elegance from the Past

Design V22638

First Floor: 1,836 square feet
Second Floor: 1,323 square feet
Total: 3,159 square feet

● The brick facade of this two-story represents the mid-18th-Century design concept. Examine its fine exterior. It has a steeply pitched roof which is broken by two large chimneys at each end and by pedimented dormers. Inside Georgian details lend elegance. Turned balusters and a curved banister ornament the formal staircase. Blueprints include details for both three and four bedroom options.

Design V22132

First Floor: 1,958 square feet
Second Floor: 1,305 square feet
Total: 3,263 square feet

L

● Another Georgian adaptation with a great heritage dating back to 18th-Century America. Exquisite and symmetrical detailing set the character of this impressive home. Don't over-look such features as the two fireplaces, the laundry, the beamed ceiling, the built-in china cabinets and the oversized garage.

Design V22975 First Floor: 1,656 square feet
Second Floor: 1,440 square feet; Third Floor: 715 square feet
Total: 3,811 square feet

Design V22662 First Floor: 1,735 square feet
Second Floor: 1,075 square feet; Third Floor: 746 square feet
Total: 3,556 square feet

L

GARAGE
22⁸ x 22⁸

TERRACE

LAUNDRY

MUD RM.

COVERED PORCH

GATHERING RM.
20⁴ x 13²

KITCHEN
16⁴ x 13²

POWDER RM.

PANTRY

STUDY
10⁴ x 16⁸ BAY

OVENS

BREAKFAST RM.
10⁴ x 16⁸ BAY

PARLOR
14⁴ x 13²

FOYER

DINING RM.
14⁴ x 13²

PORCH

64'-0"

64'-0"

BATH

ROOF

LINEN

BEDROOM
11¹⁰ x 14⁰

BEDROOM
11¹⁰ x 14⁰

ROOF

BATH

DRESSING RM.

BATH

LINEN

BEDROOM
13⁴ x 10⁶

ROOF

MASTER BEDROOM
14⁴ x 17⁶

BEDROOM
14⁴ x 13⁶

Design V22192

First Floor: 1,884 square feet
Second Floor: 1,521 square feet
Total: 3,405 square feet

L **D**

● This is surely a fine adaptation from the 18th-Century when formality and elegance were by-words. The authentic detailing of this design centers around the fine proportions, the dentils, the window symmetry, the front door and entranceway, the massive chimneys and the masonry work. The rear elevation retains all the grandeur exemplary of exquisite architecture. The appeal of this outstanding home does not end with its exterior elevations. Consider the formal living room with its corner fireplace. Also, the library with its wall of bookshelves and cabinets. Further, the dining room highlights corner china cabinets. Continue to study this elegant plan.

Design V22982

First Floor: 1,584 square feet
Second Floor: 1,513 square feet
Total: 3,097 square feet

● An early 18th Century Georgian so common to Williamsburg, Va. and environs. Observe the massive twin chimneys, the cornice ornamentation, and the wrought iron balcony sheltering the front panelled door. The rectangular shape of this house will lead to economical construction costs. The 30 foot, beamed-ceiling country kitchen with its commanding corner fireplace and rear yard access is outstanding. Notice the fireplaces for the country kitchen, living, dining and master bedrooms.

● A big, end living room featuring a fireplace and sliding glass doors is the focal point of this Georgian design. Adjacent is the formal dining room strategically located but a couple of steps from the efficient kitchen. Functioning closely with the kitchen is the family room.

Design V22176

First Floor: 1,485 square feet
Second Floor: 1,175 square feet
Total: 2,660 square feet

L **D**

Design V21767

First Floor: 1,510 square feet
Second Floor: 1,406 square feet
Total: 2,916 square feet

GARAGE 21⁸ x 25⁴

OFFICE-HOBBY RM. 9⁸ x 10⁴

LAUND.

KIT. 13⁰ x 13⁶

BREAKFAST 8⁴ x 11⁶

DINING RM. 13⁴ x 11⁶

TERRACE

W.R.

WOOD BOX

SHELVES

SHELVES

CL.

PANTRY

RANGE

OVEN

BUFFET

CHINA

B.M.

FAMILY RM. 18⁰ x 15⁶

CL.

POR. RM.

ENTRY

UP

LIVING RM. 21⁸ x 13⁶

22'-0"   32'-0"   22'-0"
76'-10"

26'-0"   30'-10"

Design V22139

First Floor: 1,581 square feet
Second Floor: 991 square feet
Total: 2,572 square feet

BED RM. 11⁴ x 13⁶

BATH

CL.

CL.

BED RM. 9⁶ x 13⁶

POR. RM.

LIN.

LIN.

DN.

CL.

BOOKS

MASTER BED RM. 11⁴ x 15⁶

DRESS. RM.

BATH

CL.

BED RM. 12⁰ x 9⁸

● Four bedrooms and two baths make-up the second floor of this two-story design. The first floor has all of the living areas and work center. Note the convenience of the powder room at the entry.

● A Georgian Colonial adaptation on the grand scale. The authentic front entrance is delightfully detailed. Two massive end chimneys, housing four fireplaces, are in keeping with the architecture of its day.

Design V22221 First Floor: 1,726 square feet
Second Floor: 1,440 square feet; Total: 3,166 square feet

Design V21852 First Floor: 1,802 square feet
Second Floor: 1,603 square feet; Total: 3,405 square feet

● This is an impressive Georgian adaptation. The front entrance detailing, the window treatment and the masses of brick help put this house in a class of its own.

This stately home, whose roots go back to an earlier period in American architecture, will forever retain its aura of distinction. The spacious front entry effectively separates the formal and informal living zones. Four bedrooms on second floor.

Design V22250

First Floor: 1,442 square feet
Second Floor: 1,404 square feet
Total: 2,846 square feet

Design V22980 First Floor: 1,648 square feet
Second Floor: 1,368 square feet; Third Floor: 567 square feet
Total: 3,583 square feet

● This late Georgian adaptation is reminiscent of the Cowles house built in Farmington, Conn. around 1786. The formal symmetry and rich ornamentation were typical of houses of this period. Ionic columns, a Palladian window, and a pedimented gable are among the details that set the character of this historic house. Inside there are three floors of livability. And, of course, there is no hint of antiquity here. The centered foyer is flanked by wonderfully spacious living areas which flow around the fireplaces. Note the sun room, laundry, and bonus space of the third floor where there is all kinds of livability.

● This Cape Cod Georgian recalls the Julia Wood House built approximately 1790 in Falmouth, Mass. Such homes generally featured a balustraded roof deck or "widow's walk" where wives of captains looked to sea for signs of returning ships. Our updated floor plans include four bedrooms including master suite on the second floor and country kitchen, study, dining room, and living room on the first floor. A third floor makes a fine 15 x 10 studio, with ladder leading up to the widow's walk.

Design V22690 First Floor: 1,559 square feet
Second Floor: 1,344 square feet; Third Floor: 176 square feet
Total: 3,079 square feet

● Here is a New England Georgian adaptation with an elevated doorway highlighted by pilasters and a pediment. It gives way to a second-story Palladian window, capped in turn by a pediment projecting from the hipped roof. The interior is decidely up-to-date with even an upstairs lounge.

Design V22639 First Floor: 1,556 square feet; Second Floor: 1,428 square feet; Total: 2,984 square feet

L D

Design V23349

First Floor: 2,807 square feet
Second Floor: 1,363 square feet
Total: 4,170 square feet

L **D**

● Grand traditional design comes to the forefront in this elegant two-story. From the dramatic front entry with curving double stairs to the less formal gathering room with fireplace and terrace access, this plan accommodates family lifestyles. Notice the split-bedroom plan with the master suite on the first floor and family bedrooms upstairs. A four-car garage handles the largest of family fleets.

Design V22556

First Floor: 1,675 square feet
Second Floor: 1,472 square feet
Total: 3,147 square feet

D

78'-4"

44'-4"

STORAGE
18⁴ x 18⁸

POTENTIAL PLAYROOM, STUDIO, GUEST ROOM
22⁸ X 18⁸

ROOF

DN.

BED RM.-SITTING RM.
15⁴ x 10²

BED RM.
16⁰ x 10²

BATH

SEAT

CL.

CL.

CL.

DRESSING RM.

LIN.

LIN.

VANITY

BATH

SEAT

DN.

MASTER BED RM.
18⁴ x 12¹⁰

HALL

UP

CL.

BED RM.
16⁰ x 12¹⁰

TERRACE

FAMILY RM.
18⁴ x 15⁶

NOOK
12⁰ x 13²

BEAMED CEILING

KITCHEN
14⁶ x 13²

RANGE

DW

CL.

WASH

DRY.

OVENS

REFR.

LAUNDRY

B.CL.

PORCH

DISAPPEARING STAIR

CABINET

BOOKS

BOOKS

CABINET

RAISED HEARTH

DN.

PDR. RM.

PANTRY

CHINA

CABINET

DN.

CL.

SERV. ENT.

SEAT

GARAGE
23⁴ x 21⁴

LIVING RM.
18⁴ x 12¹⁰

UP

ENTRY

CL.

CHINA

CHINA

DINING RM.
16⁰ x 12¹⁰

PORCH

PORCH

Design V22600

First Floor: 1,408 square feet
Second Floor: 1,408 square feet
Total: 2,816 square feet

● Here are two full stories of excellently planned living space. A third floor is available if the extra space is needed.

67'-8"

40'-0"

TERRACE

DINING RM.
13⁰ x 13⁴

KITCHEN
12⁰ x 11⁰

BREAKFAST RM.
10⁰ x 11⁰

LAUNDRY

PANTRY OVENS

PDR. RM. HALL

LIVING RM.
17⁴ x 15⁴

ENTRANCE
HALL

BEAMED
CEILING

RAISED HEARTH

WOOD BOX

FAMILY RM.
15⁴ x 20⁰

GARAGE
23⁴ x 23⁴

PORCH

MASTER
BED RM.
17⁴ x 14⁴

BATH

BED RM.
12⁰ x 14⁴

VANITY

BATH

WALK-IN CLOSET

BOOKS
CABINET

STAIR HALL

ATTIC
STORAGE

BED RM.
17⁴ x 12⁰

BED RM.
15⁵ x 13⁴

Design V23367

First Floor: 3,634 square feet
Second Floor: 1,450 square feet
Total: 5,084 square feet

● This may be the perfect plan for you if your proposed building site is narrow but quite deep. Notice that the entire width of the home is only 64', while the depth is over 100'. The floor plan loses nothing to this unusual scheme. First-floor living areas include a two-story gathering room, more casual keeping room (note fireplaces in both rooms), media room (another fireplace!), dining room with bow window, and kitchen with butler's pantry. The handy service entrance off the garage has a huge walk-in closet, washroom, and laundry area. The master bedroom on this level has a sloped ceiling and His and Hers walk-ins. Three family bedrooms are upstairs. One of these has its own private bath; the other two share a full bath.

● One of the most popular home renditions is the two-story four-bedroom, and few designs of this type offer as much as the one shown here. The gracious entry opens to the right to a media room and to a living room with fireplace. On the left is a formal dining room. At the back, find the kitchen with attached breakfast room and just a step down is everyone's favorite family room. All four bedrooms are located on the second floor. The master suite features a double-size walk-in closet and bumped-out window in the bath. Three family bedrooms share a full bath.

Design V23365 First Floor: 1,731 square feet
Second Floor: 1,248 square feet; Total: 2,979 square feet

Design V22695 First Floor: 2,058 square feet
Second Floor: 1,181 square feet; Total: 3,239 square feet

● This is a house style that was common to Tidewater, Virginia during the 18th Century. The gambrel roof, projecting dormers, and end chimneys were highly indentifiable architectural features of the period. This house takes a huge leap from the past with the addition of a first floor master bedroom suite. With three bedrooms upstairs, one with private bath, the first floor could accommodate a live-in relative in fine fashion. The projecting rear bay windows add an extra measure of light and livability.

Design V22520
First Floor: 1,419 square feet
Second Floor: 1,040 square feet
Total: 2,459 square feet

L D

● From Tidewater Virginia comes this historic adaptation, a positive reminder of the charm of Early American architecture. Note how the center entrance gives birth to fine traffic circulation. List the numerous features.

● The memory of Noah Webster's house, built in 1823, in New Hampshire is recalled by this Greek Revival adaptation. A picture home for a narrow site, it delivers big-house livability. In addition to the formal living and dining rooms, there is the huge country kitchen and handy mud room. There is also a study. Upstairs, four bedrooms and three full baths. Don't miss the four fireplaces or the outdoor balcony of the master bedroom. A basement provides additional space for recreation and the pursuit of hobbies.

Design V22979 First Floor: 1,440 square feet
Second Floor: 1,394 square feet; Total: 2,834 square feet

SOUTHERN COLONIAL VERSIONS . . .

and more Georgian adaptations are featured in this section. Stately Greek Revival columns supporting projecting pediment gables have become symbols of gracious living. Other variations of this theme are hardly less dramatic as evidenced by winged two-story houses. (The formal Georgian designs are enhanced by the massive twin chimneys, symmetrical window arrangement, and appealing front entrance detailing. Brick quoins, dentils, carriage lamps, recessed entrances, and cupolas are among the other attractive features.)

Design V22889

First Floor: 2,529 square feet
Second Floor: 1,872 square feet
Total: 4,401 square feet

● This is truly classical, Georgian design at its best. Some of the exterior highlights of this two-story include the pediment gable with cornice work and dentils, the beautifully proportioned columns, the front door detailing and the window treatment. These are just some of the features which make this design so unique and appealing. Behind the facade of this design is an equally elegant interior. Imagine greeting your guests in the large receiving hall. It is graced by two curving staircases and opens to the formal living and dining rooms. Beyond the living room is the study. It has access to the rear terrace. Those large, informal occasions for family get-togethers or entertaining will be enjoyed in the spacious gathering room. It has a centered fireplace flanked by windows on each side, access to the terrace and a wet bar. Your appreciation for this room will be never-ending. The work center is efficient: the kitchen with island cook top, breakfast room, washroom, laundry and service entrance. The second floor also is outstanding. Three family bedrooms and two full baths are joined by the feature-filled master bedroom suite. Study this area carefully. If you like this basic floor plan but would prefer a French exterior, see Design V22543 on page 215. 171

Design V22987

First Floor: 2,822 square feet
Second Floor: 1,335 square feet
Total: 4,157 square feet

● Andrew Jackson's dream of white-pillared splendor resulted in the building of The Hermitage. The essence of that grand dream is recaptured in this modern variation. One wing of the first floor contains a luxurious master suite which accommodates everyone's needs gracefully. The opposite wing features a country kitchen, laundry, washroom and two-car garage. The family room, dining room and living room are centrally located. On the second floor are three bedrooms (one a guest room) and one and a half baths.

Design V22993

First Floor: 2,440 square feet
Second Floor: 2,250 square feet
Total: 4,690 square feet

● This dramatically columned home delivers beautiful proportions and great livability on two levels. The main area of the house, the first floor, holds a gathering room, library, family room, dining room and gourmet kitchen. The master bedroom features a whirlpool tub and through fireplace. Two family bedrooms on the second floor share a full bath. A fourth bedroom is the perfect guest bedroom with its own private bath.

Design V22984

First Floor: 3,116 square feet
Second Floor: 1,997 square feet
Total: 5,113 square feet

● An echo of Whitehall, built in 1765 in Anne Arundel County, Maryland, resounds in this home. Its classic symmetry and columned facade herald a grand interior. There's no lack of space whether entertaining formally or just enjoying a family get-together, and all are kept cozy with fireplaces in the gathering room, study, and family room. An island kitchen with attached breakfast room handily serves the nearby dining room. Four second floor bedrooms include a large master suite with another fireplace, a whirlpool, and His and Hers closets in the bath. Three more full baths are found on this floor.

Design V22283

First Floor: 1,559 square feet
Second Floor: 1,404 square feet
Total: 2,963 square feet

L D

● Reminiscent of the stately character of Federal architecture during an earlier period in our history, this two-story is replete with exquisite detailing. The cornice work, pediment gable, dentils, brick quoins at the corners, beautifully proportioned columns, front door detailing, window treatment and massive twin chimneys are among the features which make this design so unique and appealing.

Design V22696 First Floor: 2,217 square feet
Second Floor: 1,962 square feet; Total: 4,179 square feet

● This gracious Greek Revival design features a white classic portico with six Doric columns. It is reminiscent of plantation homes built in the South between 1820 and 1860. The interior is no less impressive. The foyer highlights an open curving staircase to the four bedroom, three bath second floor. The formal living and dining rooms are large and each features a fireplace. The big morning room with its wall of windows will be just the place from which to start the day. Notice the media room with its fireplace. Don't miss the two upstairs fireplaces.

Design V22230

First Floor: 2,288 square feet
Second Floor: 1,863 square feet
Total: 4,151 square feet

● The gracefulness and appeal of this southern adaptation will be everlasting. The imposing two-story portico is truly dramatic. Notice the authentic detailing of the tapered Doric columns, the balustraded roof deck, the denticulated cornice, the front entrance and the shuttered windows. The architecture of the rear is no less appealing with its formal symmetry and smaller Doric portico. The impressive exterior of this two-story houses a total of 4,151 square feet. The spacious, formal front entrance hall provides a fitting introduction to the scale and elegance of the interior.

Design V23320

First Floor: 2,337 square feet
Second Floor: 1,232 square feet
Total: 3,569 square feet

● What a grand impression this home makes! A spacious two-story foyer with circular staircase greets visitors and leads to the dining room, media room and two-story gathering room with fireplace. The well-equipped kitchen includes a snack bar for informal meals. A luxurious master suite downstairs and four bedrooms upstairs complete this impressive plan.

ATTIC 29² x 26⁴
(HEADROOM 29² x 10⁴)

ROOF

BEDROOM
11⁰ x 10⁸

BATH   DRESS RM   VANITY

MASTER
BEDROOM
13⁴ x 13⁴

BATH

LINEN

BEDROOM
10⁸ x 9²

BEDROOM
12⁰ x 10⁶

UPPER PORTICO

Design V23339

First Floor: 1,460 square feet
Second Floor: 1,014 square feet
Total: 2,474 square feet

● This Colonial four-bedroom features the livable kind of plan you're looking for. A formal living room extends from the front foyer and leads to the formal dining area and nearby kitchen. A sunken family room has a raised-hearth fireplace. Three family bedrooms share a bath and are joined by the master bedroom with its own full bath.

60'-4"

TERRACE

RAISED HEARTH

FAMILY RM
21⁰ x 13⁴

BRKFST RM
14⁰ x 11⁴

KITCHEN
10⁰ x 11⁴

DINING RM
12¹⁰ x 11⁴

GATE

LAUNDRY
10⁸ x 7⁴

DESK

PDR
RM

REF'G   OVEN

COURTYARD

SEAT

46'-8"

CURB

FOYER

UP

LIVING RM
16¹⁰ x 14⁸

GARAGE
21⁴ x 21⁴

PORTICO

Design V23337

First Floor: 2,167 square feet
Second Floor: 1,992 square feet
Total: 4,159 square feet

● The elegant facade of this design with its columned portico, fanlights, and dormers houses an amenity-filled interior. The gathering room, study and dining room, each with fireplace, provide plenty of room for relaxing and entertaining. A large work area contains a kitchen with breakfast room and snack bar, laundry room and pantry. The four-bedroom upstairs includes a master suite with a sumptuous bath and an exercise room.

Design V23303

First Floor: 2,563 square feet
Second Floor: 1,496 square feet
Total: 4,059 square feet

● With its stately columns and one-story wings, this design is a fine representation of 18th Century adaptations. Formal living and dining areas flank the entry foyer at the front of the home. Look for a fireplace in the living room, china cabinet built-ins in the dining room. More casual living dominates the back section in a family room and kitchen/breakfast room combination that features access to the rear terrace and plenty of space for cooking and informal dining. The left wing garage is connected to the main structure by a service entrance adjacent to the laundry. The right wing contains the private master suite. Four second floor bedrooms share two full baths and each has its own walk-in closet.

A Mount Vernon Reminiscence

● This magnificent manor's streetview illustrates a centralized mansion connected by curving galleries to matching wings. What a grand presentation this home will make! The origin of this house dates back to 1787 and George Washington's stately Mount Vernon. The underlying aesthetics for this design come from the rational balancing of porticoes, fenestration and chimneys. The rear elevation of this home also deserves mention. Six two-story columns, along with four sets of French doors, highlight this view. Study all of the intricate detailing that is featured all around these exteriors.

The flanking wings create a large formal courtyard where guests of today can park their cars. This home, designed from architecture of the past, is efficient and compact enough to fit many suburban lots. Its interior has been well planned and is ready to serve a family of any size.

Design V22665 First Floor: 1,152 square feet; Second Floor: 1,152 square feet
Total: 2,304 square feet (Excludes Guest Suite and Galleries)

● The main, two-story section of this home houses the living areas. First - there is the large, tiled foyer with two closets and powder room. Then there is the living room which is the entire width of the house. This room has a fireplace and leads into the formal dining room. Three sets of double French doors lead to the rear portico from this formal area. The kitchen and breakfast room will function together. There is a pass-thru from the kitchen to the keeping room. All of the sleeping facilities, four bedrooms, are on the second floor. The gallery on the right leads to the garage; the one on the left, to a lounge and guest suite with studio above. The square footage quoted above does not include the guest suite or gallery areas. The first floor of the guest suite contains 688 sq. ft.; the second floor studio, 306 sq. ft. The optional plan shows a game room with a loft above having 162 sq. ft.

Design V22899

First Floor: 1,685 square feet
Second Floor: 1,437 square feet
Total: 3,122 square feet

● This impressive Georgian home with massive twin chimneys and slender Roman Doric columns is authentic in its 18th-Century detailing. Inside, the home offers comfort and elegance with living room, study, large formal dining room, breakfast room, and even a butler's pantry. Smooth traffic flow is enhanced by a central foyer that opens to stairs leading to the second story. Downstairs there's also a mud room adjacent to the laundry. Upstairs is thoughtfully zoned, too, with a central bath to accommodate a master bedroom and three other bedrooms there.

Design V22898

First Floor: 1,619 square feet
Second Floor: 1,723 square feet
Total: 3,342 square feet

● Four soaring Doric columns highlight the exterior of this Greek Revival dwelling. The elevation reflects a balanced design that incorporates four bedrooms and a two-car garage in one central unit. The stylish heart of this dwelling is a two-story gathering room. A balcony lounge on the second floor offers a quiet aerie overlooking this living area. Both of these areas will have sunlight streaming through the high windows. A second living area is the parlor. It could serve as the formal area whereas the gathering room could be considered informal. Entrance to all of these areas will be through the foyer. It has an adjacent powder room and spacious walk-in closet. The U-shaped kitchen will conveniently serve the breakfast and dining rooms. Second floor livability is outstanding. Study all of the features in the master bedroom: dressing room, tub and shower, large vanity and exercise area. Three more bedrooms, another has a private bath which would make it an ideal guest room.

Design V22184

First Floor: 1,999 square feet
Second Floor: 1,288 square feet
Total: 3,287 square feet

Design V22185 First Floor: 1,916 square feet
Second Floor: 1,564 square feet; Total: 3,480 square feet

● The elements of Greek Revival architecture when adapted to present day standards can be impressive, indeed. A study of this floor plan will reveal its similarity to that on the opposite page. There is a vestibule which leads to a wonderfully spacious entrance hall. The open stairwell is most dramatic. As it affords a view of the four bedroom, two bath second floor. The study and family room will be favorite spots for family relaxation. Both the dining and living rooms can be made to function as formally as you wish.

Design V22668 First Floor: 1,206 square feet
Second Floor: 1,254 square feet; Total: 2,460 square feet

L

● This elegant exterior houses a very livable plan. Every bit of space has been put to good use. The front country kitchen is a good place to begin. It is efficiently planned with its island cook top, built-ins and pass-thru to the dining room. The large great room will be the center of all family activities. Quiet times can be enjoyed in the front library. Study the second floor sleeping areas.

Design V22667

First Floor: 1,827 square feet
Second Floor: 697 square feet
Total: 2,524 square feet

● Two one-story wings flank the two-story center section of this design which echoes the architectural forms of 18th-Century Tidewater Virginia. The left wing is a huge living room; the right, the master bedroom suite, service area and garage. Kitchen, dining room and family room are centrally located with the three bedrooms above. Study both plans and envision your family occupying them.

Design V22924

First Floor: 1,520 square feet
Second Floor: 1,352 square feet
Total: 2,872 square feet

● Southern Colonial architecture makes a delightful statement here. It is not often that you'll find an attached two-car garage included in the overall 46 foot width of a house. And it isn't often you'll find such interesting, enjoyable and workable living patterns as those found here. There are formal and informal living areas, a separate formal dining room and an informal snack bar. Then there is the fine laundry room with the handy powder room. A curving open stairway leads to the upstairs. Here three large bedrooms are to be found. The master bath has an impressive whirlpool plus a stall shower. A second bath with twin lavatories serve the two children's bedrooms. The master bedroom has its own fireplace. This design also has a basement for recreation space.

Design V23333

First Floor: 1,584 square feet
Second Floor: 1,344 square feet
Total: 2,928 square feet

● This Southern Colonial adaptation boasts an up-to-date floor plan which caters to the needs of today's families. The entrance hall is flanked by formal and informal living areas: to the left a spacious living room and connecting dining room, to the right a cozy study and family room. A large kitchen with bay-windowed morning room is convenient to both the dining and family rooms. The upstairs sleeping area includes four bedrooms.

Second Floor (plan labels)

BEDROOM 11⁶ x 14²
BATH
WSHR TOOL
MASTER BATH
VANITY
HER WALK-IN CLOSET
HIS WALK-IN CLOSET
LINEN
ROOF
METAL ROOF
ROOF
LINEN
RAILING
DN
BEDROOM 13⁴ x 14²
BEDROOM 13⁸ x 10⁰
MASTER BEDROOM 13⁴ x 19⁶
UPPER PORTICO
RAILING

First Floor (plan labels)

TERRACE
DN
RAILING
TERRACE
MORNING RM 13⁸ x 8¹⁰
FAMILY RM 13⁴ x 20⁰
WASH RM
LAUNDRY 7⁸ x 8⁰
LT
W
D
STORAGE
DINING RM 13⁴ x 11⁰
RAILING
KITCHEN 13⁸ x 10⁸
DW
PASS THRU
COOK TOP
DN
RAILING
REFR
P'TRY
BOOKS BOOKS BOOKS
LIVING RM 13⁴ x 19⁸
DN
UP
FOYER
PDR RM
STUDY 10⁰ x 10⁸
GARAGE 25⁸ x 21⁸
PORTICO
RAILING
RAILING
UP

54'-5"
70'-6"

● The exterior of this full two-story is highlighted by the covered porch and balcony. Many enjoyable hours will be spent at these outdoor areas. The interior is highlighted by a spacious country kitchen. Be sure to notice its island cook-top, fireplace and the beamed ceiling. A built-in bar is in the family room.

Design V22664 First Floor: 1,308 square feet
Second Floor: 1,262 square feet; Total: 2,570 square feet

D

GUEST BEDROOM 11⁰ x 20⁶

WALK-IN CLOSET

BATH

LINEN

DN

STUDY 11⁰ x 13⁰

BASEMENT

WASH RM

GAME STOR.

WINE CELLAR

UP

RAISED HEARTH

ACTIVITIES RM. 17⁸ x 21¹⁰

● Here is an adaptation of the 18th Century "Single House" so popular in Charleston, SC. In its original form, the house was but a single room wide. This up-dated version features the kitchen/garage wing.

PIAZZA

MASTER BEDROOM 19⁴ x 13⁰

BATH

BEDROOM 13⁴ x 11⁸

BATH

ROOF

ATTIC

CL

BEDROOM 14⁰ x 13⁰

LINEN

BATH

ATTIC

DN

UP

ROOF

BEDROOM 19⁴ x 13⁰

90'-0"

40'-0"

50'-0"

TERRACE

PIAZZA

GATHERING RM. 19⁴ x 15⁰

COVERED PORCH

KITCHEN 12⁰ x 12⁰

BRKFST. RM. 9⁸ x 12⁰

DINING RM. 13⁴ x 12⁰

PANTRY **DESK** **PANTRY**

OVEN

CURB

PDR RM.

CL

LAUNDRY

68'-0"

FOYER

OPEN

GARAGE 21⁸ x 22⁰

COURTYARD

FOUNTAIN

UP

PARLOR 19⁴ x 13⁰

PORCH

Design V22660 First Floor: 1,479 square feet
Second Floor: 1,501 square feet; Third Floor: 912 square feet
Activities Room Area: 556 square feet; Total: 4,448 square feet

● A Southern Colonial adaptation under 2,000 square feet. The two projecting, one-story wings are devoted to the living room and garage. The two-story portion houses three bedrooms, 2½ baths, study, laundry, dining room and kitchen with eating area.

Design V22107

First Floor: 1,020 square feet
Second Floor: 720 square feet
Total: 1,740 square feet

Design V21773

First Floor: 1,546 square feet
Second Floor: 1,040 square feet
Total: 2,586 square feet

Design V21208

First Floor: 1,170 square feet
Second Floor: 768 square feet
Total: 1,938 square feet

Design V22996 First Floor: 2,191 square feet
Second Floor: 1,928 square feet; Total: 4,119 square feet

● Covered porches upstairs and down are charming additions to the well appointed two-story. Four chimney stacks herald four hearths inside: living room, dining room, family room and study. The second floor holds four bedrooms including a master suite with its own fireplace and a huge walk-in closet.

Design V22762

First Floor: 2,345 square feet
Second Floor: 1,016 square feet
Total: 3,361 square feet

● This home features a full apartment to the side to accommodate a live-in relative. The main house has all the features to ensure happiness for years to come. The three-car garage is sure to come in handy.

Design V22553

First Floor: 2,065 square feet
Second Floor: 1,612 square feet
Total: 3,677 square feet

● A stately Southern Colonial that could hardly be more impressive, or offer more pleasurable livability. The massive columns and the pediment gable are dramatic.

Design V22673

First Floor: 1,895 square feet
Second Floor: 1,661 square feet
Total: 3,556 square feet

● A two-story pillared entrance portico and tall multi-paned windows, flanking the double front doors, together accentuate the facade of this Southern Colonial design. This brick home is stately and classic in its exterior appeal. The three-car garage opens to the side so it does not disturb the street view. This is definitely a charming home that will stand strong for many years into the future. Not only is the exterior something to talk about, but so is the interior. Enter into the extremely spacious foyer and begin to discover what this home has to offer in the way of livability. Front, living and dining rooms are at each end of this foyer. The living room is complimented by a music room, or close it off and make it a bedroom. A full bath is nearby. The formal dining room will be easily served by the kitchen as will the breakfast room and snack bar. The family room is spacious and features a built-in wet bar which can be closed off by doors. An open, staircase leads to the second floor, four bedroom sleeping area.

Design V22700 First Floor: 1,640 square feet; Second Floor: 1,129 square feet; Total: 2,769 square feet

● Southern Colonial grace! And much more. An elegant gathering room, more than 21' by 23' large. . . with sloped ceilings and a raised-hearth fireplace. Plus two sets of sliding glass doors that open onto the terrace. Correctly appointed formal rooms! A living room with full length paned windows. And a formal dining room that features a large bay window. Plus a contemporary kitchen. A separate dining nook that includes another bay window. Charming and sunny! Around the corner, a first floor laundry offers more modern conveniences. Four large bedrooms! Including a master suite with two walk-in closets and private bath. This home offers all the conveniences that make life easy! And its eminently suited to a family with traditional tastes. List your favorite features.

Design V22839 First Floor: 1,565 square feet; Second Floor: 1,120 square feet; Total: 2,685 square feet

● Bay windows highlight the front and side exteriors of this three-bedroom Colonial. For energy efficiency, this design has an enclosed garden room that collects free solar energy. This area opens to the family room, breakfast room and second floor master suite. The solar garden room includes 576 sq. ft. This figure is not included in the above total.

Design V22140 First Floor: 1,822 square feet; Second Floor: 1,638 square feet; Total: 3,460 square feet

L

● The grandeur of this Southern Colonial adaptation is almost breathtaking. The stately columns supporting the distinctive pediment gable are truly impressive. The proportions and the symmetry of the windows and the entranceway are delightful. The double front doors enter to a spacious hall. Among the noteworthy features are the library, the powder room and the spacious kitchen area. Also, the second floor has three baths and a lounge or fifth bedroom. An outdoor balcony is accessible from each of the three rear bedrooms. What other features does your family like? Why not make a list?

Design V22693
3,462 square feet

● This elegant Georgian manor is reminiscent of historic Rose Hill, built 1818 in Lexington, Kentucky. It is typical of the classic manors with Greek Revival features built in Kentucky as the 19th Century dawned. Note the classical portico of four Ionic columns plus the fine proportions. Also noteworthy is the updated interior, highlighted by a large country kitchen with fireplace and an efficient work center that includes an island cooktop. The country kitchen leads directly into a front formal dining room, just off the foyer. On the other side of the foyer is a front living room. A large library is located in the back of the house. It features built-in bookcases plus a fireplace, one of four fireplaces.

Design V22977 First Floor: 4,104 square feet; Second Floor: 979 square feet; Total: 5,083 square feet

L

● Both front and rear facades of this elegant brick manor depict classic Georgian symmetry. A columned, Greek entry opens to an impressive two-story foyer. Fireplaces, built-in shelves, and cabinets highlight each of the four main gathering areas: living room, dining room, family room, and library.

Design V22686 First Floor: 1,683 square feet
Second Floor: 1,541 square feet; Total: 3,224 square feet

L D

● This design has its roots in the South and is referred to as a raised cottage. This adaptation has front and rear covered porches whose columns reflect a modified Greek Revival style. Flanking the center foyer are the formal living areas of the living room and library and the informal country kitchen.

Design V22697

First Floor: 1,764 square feet
Second Floor: 1,506 square feet
Total: 3,270 square feet

● This two-story design with Gambrel roof is reminiscent of the historic home of Robert Nicolson, Williamsburg tailor and merchant. He built his house around 1751. Our updated floor plans include a large rear family room with raised-hearth fireplace and a large front living room with fireplace. A convenience kitchen offers pass-thru to an informal eating area off the family room. The house includes a formal dining room, as well. Upstairs are four bedrooms, including a master suite.

Design V22688 First Floor: 1,588 square feet
Second Floor: 1,101 square feet; Total: 2,689 square feet

● Here are two floors of excellent livability. Start at the country kitchen. It will be the center for family activities. It has an island, desk, raised hearth fireplace, conversation area and sliding glass doors to the terrace. Adjacent to this area is the washroom and laundry. Quieter areas are available in the living room and library. Three bedrooms are housed on the second floor.

Design V22684
First Floor: 1,600 square feet
Second Floor: 1,498 square feet; Total: 3,098 square feet

L **D**

● Highlighting this plan is the spacious, country kitchen. Its features are many, indeed. Also, worth a special note is the second floor studio/office. It is accessible by way of a staircase in the back of the plan. Just imagine the many uses for this area. There is a great deal of livability in this plan.

VANITY
BATH
CL
DRESSING RM.
CL
LINEN
BRM. CL
BEDROOM 16⁰×11⁴
ROOF
ATTIC
STUDIO/ OFFICE 18⁰×13⁰
DN
BOOKS
DN
MASTER BEDROOM 12⁰×16⁸
BATH
CAB'T
BEDROOM 11⁴×13⁴
ATTIC
ROOF
BOOKS
CL
ROOF
34'-0"

66'-0"
TERRACE
DINING RM. 13⁰×11⁴
REF'G
DW
COUNTRY KITCHEN 24⁰×17⁴
WOOD BOX
UP
BATH
MUD RM.
LAUNDRY 8⁰×8⁸
CHINA
PANTRY
OVENS
COOK TOP
DN
WOOD BOX
PDR. RM.
BRM. CL.
UP
LIVING RM. 14¹⁰×19⁴
FOYER
CL
STUDY 14¹⁰×13⁴
GARAGE 23⁸×20⁰
COVERED PORCH

Design V22133 First Floor: 3,024 square feet; Second Floor: 826 square feet; Total: 3,850 square feet

L **D**

● A country-estate home which will command all the attention it truly deserves. The projecting pediment gable supported by the finely proportioned columns lends an aura of elegance. The window treatment, the front door detailing, the massive, capped chimney, the cupola, the brick veneer exterior and the varying roof planes complete the characterization of an impressive home. Inside, there are 3,024 square feet on the first floor. In addition, there is a two bedroom second floor should its development be necessary. However, whether called upon to function as one, or 1-1/2 story home it will provide a lifetime of gracious living. Don't overlook the compartment baths, the big library, the coat room, the beamed ceiling family room, the two fireplaces, the breakfast room and the efficient kitchen. Note pass-thru to breakfast room.

Design V21711 First Floor: 2,580 square feet; Second Floor: 938 square feet; Total: 3,518 square feet

● If the gracious charm of the Colonial South appeals to you, this may be just the house you've been waiting for. There is something solid and dependable in its well-balanced facade and wide, pillared front porch. Much of the interest generated by this design comes from its interesting expanses of roof and angular projection of its kitchen and garage. The feeling of elegance is further experienced upon stepping inside, through double doors, to the spacious entrance hall where there is the separate coat room. Adjacent to this is the powder room, also convenient to the living areas. The work area of the kitchen and laundry room is truly outstanding. Designed as a five bedroom house, each is large. Storage and bath facilities are excellent.

Design V22991

First Floor: 2,658 square feet
Second Floor: 1,429 square feet
Total: 4,087 square feet

L **D**

● This antebellum Greek Revival manor represents the grace of Southern plantation style. Between covered front and rear verandas lies a floor plan for great livability. Flanking a wide entry foyer are the formal living and dining rooms. Each has its own fireplace. Less formal activities take place in the family room which is conveniently open to the island kitchen. A handy cook top with snack bar island serves both areas. Separating living areas from the master suite is a quiet study. On the second floor are three bedrooms and three full baths. There's also a small sitting room and a storage area.

● This Southern Colonial adaptation is certainly one of a kind. It will forever foster the feeling of distinctiveness as well as individuality. The second floor porches provide the shelter for the porticos. The solidly proportioned pillars of the porticos are delightful, indeed. The center entry introduces one to a very orderly and formal interior, which is planned to assure each room its full measure of privacy. If desired, however, the family room may easily be opened up to function directly with the kitchen-nook area. The library will be a favorite spot for retreat. Four large bedrooms and three full baths are the highlights of the upstairs. Notice the complete accessibility of the two porches. The garage is attached and has a generous bulk storage area. Ideal for garden, lawn equipment.

Design V22336

First Floor: 1,872 square feet
Second Floor: 1,872 square feet
Total: 3,744 square feet

Design V21816 First Floor: 2,036 square feet
Second Floor: 1,836 square feet; Total: 3,872 square feet

● The influence of the Colonial South is delightfully apparent in this gracious design. The stately
columns of the front porch set the stage for a
memorable visit. The entry hall is impressive
with its open stairway. The large, country kitchen
will be a sheer delight in which to work and, yes,
even congregate.

Design V22524 First Floor: 994 square feet
Second Floor: 994 square feet; Total: 1,988 square feet

D

● This small two-story, with a modest investment,
will result in an impressive exterior and an
outstanding interior which will provide exceptional
livability. Your list of features will be long and
surely impressive.

Design V22627 First Floor: 845 square feet
Second Floor: 896 square feet; Total: 1,741 square feet

● This charming, economically built, home with its stately two-story porch columns is reminiscent of the South. The efficient interior features bonus space over garage and in the third-floor attic which may be developed into another livable room. The U-shaped kitchen offers many built-ins and is conveniently located to serve the nook and the dining room with ease. Sliding glass doors in both these eating areas lead to the terrace.

Design V22663 First Floor: 1,344 square feet
Second Floor: 947 square feet; Total: 2,291 square feet

● Reminiscent of the past, this home reflects the Greek Revival heritage. This is demonstrated in its front and rear porticoes which have graceful columns. While the exterior comes from yesteryear, the floor plan is designed to serve today's active family. Imagine the activities that can be enjoyed in the huge gathering room. It stretches from the front to the rear of the house. Three bedrooms are on the second floor.

FRENCH FACADES . . .

and the pleasing formality they successfully project, are featured in this section by a variety of adaptations. The Mansard roof lends itself to many floor plan configurations. The hip-roof is also highly identifiable with the French style. Brick quoins at the corners, dentils, casement windows, arched window openings and shutters, raised molding doors, carriage lamps, and wrought iron grillwork complete the picture. Center entrances, large foyers, formal living and dining rooms, family rooms and abundant second floor sleeping facilities are among the floor plan features of these French Facades. Don't miss the extra baths, studies, and first floor laundries.

Design V22543 First Floor: 2,345 square feet
Second Floor: 1,687 square feet; Total: 4,032 square feet

L **D**

● Certainly a dramatic French adaptation highlighted by effective window treatment, delicate cornice detailing, appealing brick quoins and excellent proportion. Stepping through the double front doors the drama is heightened by the spacious entry hall with its two curving staircases to the second floor. The upper hall is open and looks down to the hall below. There is a study and a big gathering room which look out on the raised terrace. The work center is outstanding. The garage will accommodate three cars.

Design V22222

First Floor: 1,485 square feet
Second Floor: 1,175 square feet
Total: 2,660 square feet

● Gracious, formal living could hardly find a better backdrop than this two-story French adaptation. The exterior is truly exquisite. Inside, living patterns will be most enjoyable.

Design V22281 First Floor: 1,961 square feet; Second Floor: 1,472 square feet; Total: 3,433 square feet

D

● Regal in character, this French design is a fine example of excellent proportion and perfect symmetry. The distinctiveness of this home continues right through the front doors into the spacious entrance hall with its curving staircase.

Design V22326

First Floor: 1,674 square feet
Second Floor: 1,107 square feet
Total: 2,781 square feet

● If your family enjoys the view of the backyard, then this is the design for you. The main rooms, family, dining and living, are all in the back of the plan, each having sliding glass doors to the terrace. They are away from the confusion of the work center, yet easily accessible. A study and separate office are also available. Four bedrooms are on the second floor. Be sure to note all of the features in the master bedroom suite.

Design V21228

First Floor: 2,583 square feet
Second Floor: 697 square feet
Total: 3,280 square feet

[L] [D]

● This beautiful house has a wealth of detail taken from the rich traditions of French Regency design. The roof itself is a study in pleasant dormers and the hips and valleys of a big flowing area. A close examination of the plan shows the careful arrangement of space for privacy as well as good circulation of traffic. The spacious formal entrance hall sets the stage for good zoning. The informal living area is highlighted by the updated version of the old country kitchen. Observe the fireplace, built-in wood box, and china cabinet. While there is a half-story devoted to the master bedroom suite, this home functons more as a one-story country estate design than as a 1½ story.

Design V22342

First Floor: 2,824 square feet
Second Floor: 1,013 square feet
Total: 3,837 square feet

● A distinctive exterior characterized by varying roof planes, appealing window treatment, attractive chimneys and a covered front porch with prominent vertical columns. The main portion of the house is effectively balanced by the master bedroom wing on the one side and the garage wing on the other. As a buffer between house and garage is the mud room and the laundry. The kitchen is U-shaped, efficient and strategically located to serve the breakfast and dining rooms. Notice how the rooms at the rear function through sliding glass doors with the outdoor terrace areas. Fireplaces highlight both the spacious living room and the large library. The big family room features a built-in bookshelf and cabinet. Upstairs, two bedrooms and a study alcove will be found.

Design V22503

First Floor: 1,847 square feet
Second Floor: 1,423 square feet
Total: 3,270 square feet

Design V22507

First Floor: 1,529 square feet
Second Floor: 1,206 square feet
Total: 2,735 square feet

Design V21260

First Floor: 1,318 square feet
Second Floor: 989 square feet
Total: 2,307 square feet

● The elegance of pleasing proportion and delightful detailing has seldom been better exemplified than by this classic French country manor adaptation. Approaching the house across the drive court, the majesty of this multi-roofed structure is breathtaking, indeed. An outstanding feature is the maid's suite. It is located above the garage and is easily reached by use of the covered porch connecting the laundry room's service entrance to the garage. If desired, it would make an excellent studio, quiet retreat or even a game room.

Design V21993

First Floor: 2,658 square feet
Master Suite: 840 square feet
Maid's Suite: 376 square feet
Total: 3,874 square feet

Design V23380

First Floor: 3,350 square feet
Second Floor: 1,298 square feet
Total: 4,648 square feet

● Reminiscent of a Mediterranean villa, this grand manor is a showstopper on the outside and a comfortable residence on the inside. An elegant receiving hall boasts a double staircase and is flanked by the formal dining room and the library. A huge gathering room is found to the back. The master bedroom is found on the first floor for privacy. Upstairs are four additional bedrooms and two full baths.

50'- 0"

TERRACE

TERRACE

DINING RM.
11⁰ x 12⁶

KITCHEN
9⁸ x 12⁶

BRKFST RM.
8⁰ x 12⁶

FAMILY RM.
19⁴ x 16⁶

38'- 8"

BRM. OVENS
CL.

POWDER RM.

DN

DESK

CURB

LIVING RM.
16⁰ x 12⁶ + BAY

CL.

FOYER

DN

UP

PORCH

GARAGE
19⁴ x 20⁶

MASTER BEDROOM
11⁰ x 16⁸

BATH

BEDROOM/ STUDY
10² x 11⁰

CL.

CL.

BATH

CL.

HALL

LINEN

CL.

DN

BEDROOM
13⁸ x 10⁴

CL.

BEDROOM
9³ x 10⁴

Design V22798

First Floor: 1,149 square feet
Second Floor: 850 square feet
Total: 1,999 square feet

● An island range in the kitchen is a great feature of the work center in this two-story French designed home. The breakfast room has an open railing to the sunken family room so it can enjoy the view of the family room's fireplace.

Sliding glass doors in each of the major rear rooms, dining, breakfast and family rooms, lead to the terrace for outdoor enjoyment. The front, formal living room is highlighted by a bay window. A powder room is conven-

iently located on the first floor near all of the major areas. All of the sleeping facilities are housed on the second floor. Each of the four bedrooms will serve its occupants ideally. A relatively narrow lot can house this design.

VICTORIAN HOUSES . . .

extend from a pointed, exuberant expression of America's prominent place in the world late in the 19th Century. Today, they are every bit as lively, dressed in all the spectacular finery so typical of the style. Spindlework details, expansive porches, towers, turrets, grand chimneys, and varied exterior materials combine to create our fine collection of Victorian adaptations.

Design V22971 First Floor: 1,766 square feet
Second Floor: 1,519 square feet; Total: 3,285 square feet

● The stately proportions and the exquisite detailing of Victorian styling are exciting, indeed. Like so many Victorian houses, interesting roof lines set the character with this design. Observe the delightful mixture of gable roof, hip roof, and the dramatic turret. Horizontal siding, wood shingling, wide fascia, rake and corner boards make a strong statement. Of course, the delicate detailing of the windows, railings, cornices and front entry is most appealing to the eye. Inside, a great four-bedroom family living plan.

Design V22973

First Floor: 1,269 square feet
Second Floor: 1,227 square feet
Total: 2,496 square feet

L

● A most popular feature of the Victorian house has always been its covered porches. In addition to being an appealing exterior design feature, covered porches have their practical side, too. They provide wonderful indoor-outdoor living relationships. Notice sheltered outdoor living facilities for the various formal and informal living and dining areas of the plan. This home has a myriad of features to cater to the living requirements of the growing, active family.

Design V22972

First Floor: 1,432 square feet
Second Floor: 1,108 square feet
Total: 2,540 square feet

L

● The spacious foyer of this Victorian is prelude to a practical and efficient interior. The formal living and dining area is located to one side of the plan. The more informal area of the plan includes the fine U-shaped kitchen which opens to the big family room. Just inside the entrance from the garage is the laundry; a closet and the powder room are a few steps away. The library will enjoy its full measure of privacy. Upstairs is the three-bedroom sleeping zone with a fireplace.

226

Design V22969

First Floor: 1,618 square feet
Second Floor: 1,315 square feet
Third Floor: 477 square feet
Total: 3,410 square feet

L **D**

● What could beat the charm of a tur-
reted Victorian with covered porches
to the front, side and rear? This delicately detailed exterior houses an
outstanding family oriented floor plan.
Projecting bays make their contribution
to the exterior styling. In addition, they
provide an extra measure of livability

to the living, dining and family rooms,
plus two of the bedrooms. The efficient
kitchen, with its island cooking station,
functions well with the dining and
family rooms. A study provides a quiet
first floor haven for the family's less
active pursuits. Upstairs there are three
big bedrooms and a fine master bath.

The third floor provides a guest suite
and huge bulk storage area (make it a
cedar closet if you wish). This house
has a basement for the development of
further recreational and storage facilities. Don't miss the two fireplaces,
large laundry and attached two-car
garage. A great investment.

Design V23308

First Floor: 2,515 square feet
Second Floor: 1,708 square feet
Third Floor: 1,001 square feet
Total: 5,224 square feet

L **D**

● Uniquely shaped rooms and a cache of amenities highlight this three-story beauty. Downstairs rooms can accommodate both formal and informal entertaining and also provide a liberal share of work space in the kitchen and laundry. Notice the abundance of built-ins and the butler's pantry. A four-car garage easily holds the family fleet. The second floor has two bedrooms and a full bath plus a master suite with His and Hers closets and whirlpool bath. An exercise room on the third floor has its own sauna and bath, while the large guest room on this floor is complemented by a charming alcove and another full bath.

Design V23386

First Floor: 1,683 square feet
Second Floor: 1,388 square feet
Third Floor: 808 square feet
Total: 3,879 square feet

L D

● This beautiful Folk Victorian has all the properties of others in its class. Living areas include a formal Victorian parlor, a private study and large gathering room. The formal dining room has its more casual counterpart in a bay-windowed breakfast room. Both are near the well-appointed kitchen. Five bedrooms serve family and guest needs handily. Three bedrooms on the second floor include a luxurious master suite. For outdoor entertaining, there is a covered rear porch leading to a terrace.

Design V23388

First Floor: 1,517 square feet
Second Floor: 1,267 square feet
Third Floor: 480 square feet
Total: 3,264 square feet

L D

● This delightful home offers the best in
thoughtful floor planning. The home opens to a
well-executed entry foyer. To the left is the
casual family room with fireplace. To the right
is the formal living room which connects to the
formal dining area. The kitchen/breakfast room
combination features an island cook top and
large pantry. Second-floor bedrooms include a
master suite and two family bedrooms served
by a full bath. A guest room dominates the third
floor.

Design V23394

First Floor: 1,531 square feet
Second Floor: 1,307 square feet
Third Floor: 664 square feet
Total: 3,502 square feet

L D

● The Folk Victorian is an important and
delightful interpretation. And this version
offers the finest in modern floor plans. The
formal living areas are set off by a family room
which connects the main house to the service
areas. The second floor holds three bedrooms
and two full baths. A sitting area in the master
suite separates it from family bedrooms. On the
third floor is a guest bedroom with gracious
bath and large walk-in closet.

230

Design V22829 First Floor: 2,044 square feet
Second Floor: 1,962 square feet; Total: 4,006 square feet

L **D**

● The architecture of this design is Post-Modern with a taste of Victorian styling. Detailed with gingerbread woodwork and a handsome double-width chimney, this two-story design is breathtaking. Enter this home to the large, tiled receiving hall and begin to explore this very livable floor plan. Formal areas consist of the front living room and the dining room. Each has features to make it memorable. The living room is spacious, has a fireplace and access to the covered porch; the dining room has a delightful bay window and is convenient to the kitchen for ease in meal serving. The library is tucked between these two formal areas. Now let's go to the informal area. The family room will welcome many an explorer. It will be a great place for many family activities. Note the L-shaped snack bar with cabinets below. Onward to the second floor, where the private area will be found. Start with the two bedrooms that have two full bathrooms joining them together. The older children will marvel at this area's efficiency and privacy. A third family bedroom is nearby. Then, there is the master bedroom suite. Its list of features is long, indeed. Begin with the "his" and "her" baths and see how many features you can list. A guest bedroom and bath are on the first floor.

Design V22646
First Floor: 1,274 square feet
Second Floor: 1,322 square feet; Total: 2,596 square feet

L **D**

● What a stylish departure from today's usual architecture. This refreshing exterior may be referred to as Neo-Victorian. Its vertical lines, steep roofs and variety of gables remind one of the old Victorian houses of yesteryear. Inside, there is an efficiently working floor plan that is delightfully spacious.

Design V22645
First Floor: 1,600 square feet
Second Floor: 1,305 square feet
Third Floor: 925 square feet
Total: 3,830 square feet

L

Design V22647 First Floor: 2,104 square feet; Second Floor: 1,230 square feet; Total: 3,334 square feet

L

● Another Neo-Victorian, and what an impressive and unique design it is. Observe the roof lines, the window treatment, the use of contrasting exterior materials and the arched, covered front entrance.

● Reminiscent of the Gothic Victorian style of the mid-19th Century, this delightfully detailed, three-story house has a wraparound veranda for summertime relaxing. The parlor and family room, each with fireplaces, provide excellent formal and informal living facilities. The third floor houses two more great areas plus bath.

233

● A grand facade makes this Victorian stand out. Inside, guests and family are well accommodated: gathering room with terrace access, fireplace and attached formal dining room; split-bedroom sleeping arrangements. The master suite contains His and Hers walk-in closets, a separate shower and whirlpool tub and a delightful bay-windowed area. Upstairs there are three more bedrooms (one could serve as a study, one as a media room), a full bath and an open lounge area overlooking the gathering room.

Design V23393
First Floor: 1,449 square feet
Second Floor: 902 square feet
Total: 2,351 square feet

L **D**

Design V23389
First Floor: 1,161 square feet
Second Floor: 1,090 square feet
Third Floor: 488 square feet
Total: 2,739 square feet

L **D**

● A Victorian turret accents the facade of this compact three-story. Downstairs rooms include a grand-sized living room/dining room combination. The U-shaped kitchen has a snack-bar pass-through to the dining room. Just to the left of the entry foyer is a private study. On the second floor are three bedrooms and two full baths. The master bedroom has a whirlpool spa and large walk-in closet. The third floor is a perfect location for a guest bedroom with private bath.

Design V22970 First Floor: 1,538 square feet
Second Floor: 1,526 square feet; Third Floor: 658 square feet
Total: 3,722 square feet

L

● A porch, is a porch, is a porch. But, when it wraps around to a side, or even two sides, of the house, we have called it a veranda. This charming Victorian features a covered outdoor living area on all four sides! It even ends at a screened porch which features a sun deck above. This interesting plan offers three floors of livability. And what livability it is! Plenty of formal and informal living facilities to go along with the potential of five bedrooms. The master suite is just that. It is adjacent to an interesting sitting room. It has a sun deck and excellent bath/personal care facilities. The third floor will make a wonderful haven for the family's student members.

Design V23383

First Floor: 995 square feet
Second Floor: 1,064 square feet
Third Floor: 425 square feet
Total: 2,484 square feet

L D

● This delightful Victorian cottage features exterior details that perfectly complement the convenient plan inside. Note the central placement of the kitchen, near to the dining room and the family room. Two fireplaces keep things warm and cozy. Three second-floor bedrooms include a master suite with bay window and two family bedrooms, one with an alcove and walk-in closet. Use the third-floor studio as a study, office or playroom for the children.

Design V23384

First Floor: 1,399 square feet
Second Floor: 1,123 square feet
Total: 2,522 square feet

L D

● Classic Victorian styling comes to the forefront in this Queen Anne. The interior boasts comfortable living quarters for the entire family. On opposite sides of the foyer are the formal dining and living rooms. To the rear is a country-style island kitchen with attached family room. A small library shares a covered porch with this informal gathering area and also has its own fireplace. Three bedrooms on the second floor include a master suite with grand bath. The two family bathrooms share a full bath.

Design V23391

First Floor: 1,230 square feet
Second Floor: 991 square feet
Total: 2,221 square feet

L **D**

● Detailing is one of the characteristic features of Queen Anne Victorians and this home has no lack of it. Interior rooms add special living patterns. Features include a powder room for guests in the front hallway, a through-fireplace between the ample gathering room and cozy study, an efficient U-shaped kitchen with pantry, and a full-width terrace to the rear. On the second floor are three bedrooms — one a master suite with walk-in closet and amenity-filled bath. An open balcony overlooks the gathering room.

Design V23382

First Floor: 1,366 square feet
Second Floor: 837 square feet
Third Floor: 363 square feet
Total: 2,566 square feet

L **D**

MASTER BATH

WHIRLPOOL

DN

UP

MASTER BEDROOM
16⁰ X 11¹⁰

WALK-IN CLOSET

LINEN

CL

BATH

BEDROOM
14⁶ X 9⁸

COVERED BALCONY

RAILING

BATH

WALK-IN CLOSET

DN

CEILING CLP

GUEST BEDROOM
12² X 14⁶

ROOF

50'2"

RAILING

UP

RAILING

GAZEBO

VERANDA

EATING

RAISED HEARTH

RAILING

FAMILY KITCHEN
29⁶ X 14⁸

RAILING

69'3"

UP

REF'S

OVEN

PANTRY

BC

WET BAR

PDR RM

CL

DN

UP

RAILING

FOYER

DINING RM
12⁰ X 16²

ENTRY

LIVING RM
14⁰ X 15⁶ BAY

VERANDA

RAILING

RAILING

UP

● A simple but charming Queen Anne Victorian, this enchanting three-story home boasts delicately turned rails and decorated columns on its covered front porch. Inside is a floor plan that includes a living room with fireplace and dining room that connects to the kitchen via a wet bar. The adjoining family room contains another fireplace. The second floor holds two bedrooms, one a master suite with grand bath. A tucked-away guest suite on the third floor has a private bath.

Design V22974 First Floor: 911 square feet
Second Floor: 861 square feet; Total: 1,772 square feet

L

● Victorian houses are well known for their orientation on narrow building sites. And when this occurs nothing is lost to captivating exterior styling. This house is but 38 feet wide. Its narrow width belies the tremendous amount of livability found inside. And, of course, the ubiquitous porch/veranda contributes mightily to style as well as livability. The efficient, U-shape kitchen is flanked by the informal breakfast room and formal dining room. The rear living area is spacious and functions in an exciting manner with the outdoor areas. Bonus recreational, hobby and storage space is offered by the basement and the attic.

● This two-story farmhouse will be a delight for those who work at home. The second floor has a secluded master bedroom and a studio. A U-shaped kitchen with snack bar and breakfast area with bay window are only the first of the eating areas, which extend to a formal dining room and a covered rear porch for dining al fresco. The two-story living room features a cozy fireplace. A versatile room to the back could serve as a media room or a third bedroom.

Design V23390

First Floor: 1,508 square feet
Second Floor: 760 square feet
Total: 2,268 square feet

Design V23385

First Floor: 1,096 square feet
Second Floor: 900 square feet
Total: 1,996 square feet

● Covered porches front and rear are complemented by a grand plan for family living. A formal living room and attached dining room provide space for entertaining guests. The large family room with fireplace is a gathering room for everyday use. Four bedrooms occupy the second floor. The master suite features two lavatories, a window seat and three closets. One of the family bedrooms has its own private balcony and could be used as a study.

Design V23307

First Floor: 1,765 square feet
Second Floor: 1,105 square feet
Total: 2,870 square feet

L **D**

● This charming design brings together the best in historical styling and modern floor planning. Inside, the first-floor plan boasts formal living and dining areas on either side of the entry foyer, a study that could double as a guest room, a large family room with raised-hearth fireplace and snack bar pass-through, and a U-shaped kitchen with attached breakfast room. Two family bedrooms on the second floor share a full bath; the master bedroom has a thoughtfully appointed bath and large walk-in closet.

Design V23392

First Floor: 1,405 square feet
Second Floor: 1,430 square feet
Third Floor: 624 square feet
Total: 3,459 square feet

L **D**

● Named for the architect, Henry Hobson Richardson, the Richardson Romanesque is known for being ample in size. This three-story example has complementary arched turrets on the outside which give way to a convenient floor plan. Formal and informal living areas occupy the first floor in a living room, dining room, family room and grand country kitchen. Upstairs are two family bedrooms and a master suite with sitting area. The third floor contains another bedroom and private bath that could serve guests.

Design V23387

First Floor: 2,393 square feet
Second Floor: 1,703 square feet
Third Floor: 716 square feet
Total: 4,812 square feet

L **D**

● Another design that borrows from the forceful style of Henry Hobson Richardson, this home features a rounded turret. The interior allows room for family living. Besides formal living and dining rooms and a casual family room, there is a study with corner fireplace. Three bedrooms are found on the second floor along with two full baths. The third floor contains another bedroom with full bath and small alcove. Wide verandas both front and rear and a screened porch allow good indoor/outdoor living relationships.

Design V23309

First Floor: 1,375 square feet
Second Floor: 1,016 square feet
Total: 2,391 square feet

L **D**

● Covered porches, front and back, are a fine preview to the livable nature of this Victorian. Living areas are defined in a family room with fireplace, formal living and dining rooms, and a kitchen with breakfast room. An ample laundry room, garage with storage area, and powder room round out the first floor. Three second floor bedrooms are joined by a study and two full baths.

ENGLISH TUDOR HOUSES . . . .

have enjoyed a long and varied history in America. Recent years have seen a growth in popularity of this pleasing exterior style. From a purist standpoint, what is called Tudor today should really be referred to as Elizabethan. The many variations on the following pages are highlighted by simulated half-timber work, stucco, diamond-paned casement windows, massive sculptured chimneys, brick, stone and frame exterior walls, panelled doors, and varied roof planes. Note wavy siding and extra beam work. Of particular interest are the Cotswold Cottage/1½-story variations which project a low profile and retain a full measure of English charm.

Design V22356

First Floor: 1,969 square feet
Second Floor: 1,702 square feet
Total: 3,671 square feet

L **D**

● Here is truly an exquisite Tudor adaptation. The exterior, with its interesting roof lines, window treatment, stately chimney and its appealing use of brick and stucco, could hardly be more dramatic. Inside, the drama really begins to unfold as one envisions his family's living patterns. The delightfully large receiving hall has a two story ceiling and controls the flexible traffic patterns. The living and dining rooms, with the library nearby, will cater to the formal living pursuits. The guest room offers another haven for the enjoyment of peace and quiet. Observe the adjacent full bath. Just inside the entrance from the garage is the laundry room. For the family's informal activities there are the interactions of the family room - covered porch - nook - kitchen zone. Notice the raised hearth fireplace, the wood boxes, the sliding glass doors, built-in bar and the kitchen pass-thru. Adding to the charm of the family room is its high ceiling. From the second floor hall one can look down and observe the activities below.

Design V22794

First Floor: 1,680 square feet
Second Floor: 1,165 square feet
Apartment: 867 square feet
Total: 3,712 square feet

● This exceptionally pleasing Tudor design has a great deal of interior livability to offer its occupants. Use the main entrance, enter into the foyer and begin your journey throughout this design. To the left of the foyer is the study, to the right, the formal living room. The living room leads to the rear, formal dining room. This room has access to the outdoors and is conveniently located adjacent to the kitchen. A snack bar divides the kitchen from the family room which also has access to outdoors plus it has a fireplace as does the living room. The second floor houses the family's four bedrooms. Down six steps from the mud room is the laundry and entrance to the garage, up six steps from this area is a complete apartment. This is an excellent room for a live-in relative. It is completely private by gaining access from the outdoor balcony.

Design V22957

First Floor: 2,557 square feet
Second Floor: 1,939 square feet
Total: 4,496 square feet

L **D**

● The decorative half timbers and stone wall-cladding on this manor are stately examples of Tudor architecture. A grand double staircase is the highlight of the elegant, two-story foyer that opens to each of the main living areas. The living and gathering rooms are anchored by impressive central fireplaces. Handy built-ins, including a lazy susan and desk, and an island workstation with sink and cooktop, are convenient amenities in the kitchen. The adjacent breakfast room opens to the terrace for a sunny start to the day. Functioning with both the kitchen and the formal dining room is the butler's pantry. It has an abundance of cabinet and cupboard space and even a sink for a wet bar. Accessible from both the gathering and living rooms is the quiet study. If desired this could become a media center, sewing room or home office. The outstanding master suite features a cozy bedroom fireplace, picturesque whirl-pool bath, and a convenient walk-in closet. Three additional second-floor bedrooms include a guest suite with dressing room and walk-in closet. Every part of this house speaks elegance, formality and the time-honored values for which Tudor is renowned.

247

Design V22960

First Floor: 1,372 square feet
Second Floor: 1,245 square feet
Total: 2,617 square feet

● The swooping roof of the projecting front gable results in a sheltered entrance to the foyer of this unique design. It would be difficult to imagine more appealing roof lines than this Tudor has to offer. Roof, exterior wall, and window treatment all blend together to present a harmonious facade. The two chimneys with their massive caps add their appeal, too. Once inside your guests will be impressed again. They will delight to find two such large living areas - one for formal and another for informal living. They will enjoy further the eating facilities - a formal dining room and informal breakfast room. The L-shaped kitchen will be a charm in which to work. It has an island cooking station, plenty of cupboard and counter space and a pantry nearby. The homemaker will love the strategic location of the mud room. It is just inside the entrance from the garage and is directly accessible from the rear yard. The covered porch is a nice feature. And don't miss the two fireplaces - one with a raised hearth. Upstairs there are four bedrooms, two baths and good storage facilities.

CUSTOMIZABLE

Custom Alterations? See page 413
for customizing this plan to your
specifications.

Design V22855

First Floor: 1,372 square feet
Second Floor: 1,245 square feet
Total: 2,617 square feet

L D

● This elegant Tudor house is perfect for the family who wants to move-up in living area, style and luxury. As you enter this home you will find a large living room with a fireplace on your right. Adjacent, the formal dining room has easy access to both the living room and the kitchen. The kitchen/ breakfast room has an open plan and access to the rear terrace. Sunken a few steps, the spacious family room is highlighted with a fireplace and access to the rear, covered porch. Note the optional planning of the garage storage area. Plan this area according to the needs of your family. Upstairs, your family will enjoy three bedrooms and a full bath, along with a spacious master bedroom suite. Truly a house that will bring many years of pleasure to your family.

Design V22508
First Floor: 1,692 square feet
Second Floor: 1,445 square feet; Total: 3,137 square feet

● Dramatic, indeed. Both exterior and interior. Note that the living room has a two-story ceiling so it can be viewed from the second floor study. The cooking island in the kitchen is very efficient.

Design V22128
First Floor: 1,152 square feet
Second Floor: 896 square feet; Total: 2,048 square feet

L D

● Here is proof that your restricted building budget can return to you wonderfully pleasing design and loads of livability. This is an English Tudor adaptation that will surely become your subdivision's favorite facade. Its mark of individuality is obvious to all.

● Imagine, six bedrooms on the second floor. The first floor houses the living areas: family room, living room, dining areas plus a library. Not much more livability could be packed into this spaciously designed home.

Design V22141 First Floor: 1,490 square feet
Second Floor: 1,474 square feet; Total: 2,964 square feet

Design V22967

First Floor: 1,877 square feet
Second Floor: 467 square feet
Total: 2,344 square feet

● Special interior amenities abound in this unique 1½-story Tudor. Living areas include an open gathering room/dining room area with fireplace and pass-through to the breakfast room. Quiet time can be spent in a sloped-ceiling study. Look for plenty of workspace in the island kitchen and workshop/storage area. Sleeping areas are separated for utmost privacy: an elegant master suite on the first floor, two bedrooms and a full bath on the second. Note the unusual curved balcony seat in the stairwell and the second floor ledge—a perfect spot for displaying plants or collectibles.

Design V22965

First Floor: 2,313 square feet
Second Floor: 1,314 square feet
Total: 3,627 square feet

● An appealing mix of contrasting exterior materials go well together to help create this distinctive Tudor. Brick, quarried stone and stucco will result in a pleasingly colorful facade. The varying heights of the gabled roof planes add their measure of drama. But that is not all that helps set the character of this stylish house. The window and door treatments add their exquisite appeal too. As one passes through the double front door he is welcomed by a delightfully spacious foyer. It has a sloping two-story ceiling which fosters a view upward to the overlooking balcony and the expanse of window-wall. To the right of the foyer is a fine-functioning kitchen which conveniently opens to the breakfast room. It is strategically located to serve both the formal dining room and the informal family room equally well. The mud room with laundry and washroom is but a step or two away. The sunken living room could hardly be more inviting. It has a high sloping ceiling, a view of the overhanging balcony, a wall of windows, a fireplace and a wet bar. Access to the terrace is through two sets of sliding glass doors. Imagine, four baths serving the four bedrooms. Don't miss the three-car garage.

Design V22242 First Floor: 1,327 square feet
Second Floor: 832 square feet; Total: 2,159 square feet

● Here, the main two-story section of this house is flanked by two, one-story wings. The roof, projecting from the second floor, results in a pleasant, covered front porch. This home gives the appearance of being much larger than it really is with the garage opening to the side.

Design V22732

First Floor: 1,071 square feet
Second Floor: 1,022 square feet
Total: 2,093 square feet

● The two-story front entry hall will be dramatic indeed. Note the efficient kitchen adjacent to informal family room, formal dining room. Upstairs, three big bedrooms, two baths.

72'-10"

36'-10"

OFFICE DEN 11⁰ x 9⁶   W.R.
CL.
DISAPPEARING STAIR
LAUNDRY
NOOK 9⁰ x 10⁰
DINING RM. 13⁸ x 13⁶
LIVING RM. 13⁰ x 22⁰
TERRACE
KIT. 11⁰ x 13⁶
PANTRY
DWH. OVEN RANGE
RAISED HEARTH
BEAMED CEILING
FAMILY RM. 20⁰ x 13⁶
SLDG DOOR
FOYER
UP
CL.
GARAGE 23⁴ x 21⁶
PORCH
PDR. RM.
LIBRARY 13⁰ x 13⁰

BED RM. 10⁸ x 13⁶   CL.   BED RM. 12⁰ x 10⁰   BATH   CL.   BED RM. 11⁴ x 13⁶
LINEN
LINEN
BED RM. 14⁰ x 13⁶   LIN.   DN.   CL.   BED RM. STUDY 13⁰ x 9⁶   CL.
DRESS. RM.   BATH
MASTER BED RM. 17⁴ x 13⁰

● Not only does the first floor of this plan contain formal and informal living areas, but it also houses a library and a rear office, plus two washrooms and a first floor laundry. Now that is a lot of living space! Imagine a second floor with five bedrooms and a study. Or make it six bedrooms.

Design V22239

First Floor: 1,797 square feet
Second Floor: 1,514 square feet
Total: 3,311 square feet

Design V23335

First Floor: 1,504 square feet
Second Floor: 1,348 square feet
Total: 2,852 square feet

● This is a first-rate Tudor with three bedrooms upstairs and casual and formal living downstairs. Corner fireplaces in the family room and living room will be favorite gathering spots. From the efficient U-shaped kitchen move to a convenient service area and two-car garage.

Design V23342 First Floor: 1,467 square feet
Second Floor: 715 square feet; Total: 2,182 square feet

● Just the right amount of living space is contained in this charming traditional house and it's arranged in a great floor plan. The split-bedroom configuration, with two bedrooms (or optional study) on the first floor and the master suite on the second floor with its own studio, assures complete privacy. The living room has a second-floor balcony overlook and a warming fireplace. The full-width terrace in back is counter-balanced nicely by the entry garden court.

68'-10"

51'-6"

TERRACE

FAMILY RM.
19⁴x13⁰

BATH

BATH

LINEN

WALK-IN CLOSET

MASTER BEDROOM
13⁰x13⁰

KITCHEN
10⁰x10⁴

RANGE

BEDROOM
11⁰x10⁰

BEDROOM
11⁰x10⁰

DINING RM.
12⁰x10²

BUFFET

CHINA

FOYER

SLOPED   CEILING

LIVING RM.
19⁴x13⁸

GATES

GARDEN COURT

COVERED   PASSAGE

GARAGE
19⁴x21⁴

Design V22127 First Floor: 1,712 square feet
Second Floor: 450 square feet; Total: 2,162 square feet

LOUNGE
13⁸x12⁰

BATH

DN

LINEN

MASTER BEDROOM
16⁸x14⁴

● The second floor of this delightful Tudor design can be used in a variety of ways. It can be used as a suite for the live-in relative or for the parents. Either way, the two rooms with a full bath will function nicely together. The first floor is also very livable. Both the formal and informal living areas have a beamed ceiling. The living room's ceiling is also sloped. The overall configuration of this design creates a U-shape. This makes a delightful garden court and a covered passage from the garage.

Design V22586

First Floor: 991 square feet
Second Floor: 1,003 square feet
Total: 1,994 square feet

● A stately Tudor! With four large bedrooms. And lots of living space . . . formal living and dining rooms, a family room with a traditional fireplace, a spacious kitchen with nook.

Design V22190
First Floor: 1,221 square feet; Second Floor: 884 square feet; Total: 2,105 square feet

● Here is a Tudor adaptation with a popular floor plan. The open planning of the formal living/dining area results in a spacious atmosphere. Sliding glass doors and a bowed bay window foster an awareness of the rear yard.

Design V23302

First Floor: 1,326 square feet
Second Floor: 542 square feet
Total: 1,868 square feet

● A cottage fit for a king! Appreciate the highlights: a two-story foyer, a rear living zone (gathering room, terrace, and dining room), pass-through snack bar in kitchen, a two-story master bedroom. Two upstairs bedrooms share a full bath.

CUSTOMIZABLE

Custom Alterations? See page 413 for customizing this plan to your specifications.

Design V22491

First Floor: 1,060 square feet
Second Floor: 580 square feet
Total: 1,640 square feet

L **D**

● This modest-looking plan surprises everyone with its wealth of amenities inside. Look for a U-shaped kitchen with snack bar, morning room, sunken gathering room (note fireplace with wood box), and abundant built-ins. The master suite on the second floor is a true eye-catcher.

CUSTOMIZABLE
Custom Alterations? See page 413 for customizing this plan to your specifications.

Design V22568

First Floor: 1,512 square feet
Second Floor: 1,480 square feet
Total: 2,992 square feet

● Here's an English version with a hip-roof and an overhanging second story. As with all these designs, the distinctive exterior beam-work is simulated and built-up of readily available and conventional framing members. This is a great plan. Study it carefully.

Design V22618

First Floor: 1,269 square feet
Second Floor: 1,064 square feet
Total: 2,333 square feet

● This four bedroom Tudor design is the object of an outstanding investment for a lifetime of proud ownership and fine, family living facilities. Note that the family room is sunken and it, along with the nook, has sliding glass doors.

Design V22637

First Floor: 1,308 square feet
Second Floor: 1,063 square feet
Total: 2,371 square feet

● A generous, centered entrance hall routes traffic efficiently to all areas. And what wonderfully spacious areas they are. Note living, dining, sleeping and bath facilities. Don't miss first floor laundry.

Design V22959

First Floor: 1,003 square feet
Second Floor: 1,056 square feet
Total: 2,059 square feet

● Here the stateliness of Tudor styling is captured in a design suited for a narrow building site. This relatively low-budget two-story delivers all the livability found in many much larger homes. Imagine, a 31 foot living-dining area that stretches across the entire rear of the house and functions with the big terrace. Then, there is the efficient U-shaped kitchen with built-in cooking facilities and a pass-thru to the snack bar. Just inside the entrance from the garage is the mud room with its adjacent wash room. Enhancing first floor livability is the study with its big walk-in closet. An open staircase leads to the basement recreation area. Upstairs, three bedrooms, two baths and an outdoor balcony.

Design V22964

First Floor: 1,441 square feet
Second Floor: 621 square feet
Total: 2,062 square feet

55'-0"

TERRACE

LIVING RM.
14⁰ x 17⁸

DINING RM.
10⁴ x 15⁰

BRKFST. RM.
11⁰ x 10⁴

MASTER BEDROOM
14⁴ x 16⁰

BALCONY OVER

SNACK BAR

KITCHEN
11⁰ x 13⁰

VANITY

WALK-IN CLOSET

DN   UP

OPEN ABOVE

CL.

FOYER

PDR. RM.

LAUND.
6⁴ x 10⁰

OVENS

DW.

REF'G   COOK TOP

BATH

WHIRLPOOL

COVERED PORCH

59'-8"

GARAGE
21⁸ x 22⁸

STORAGE

UPPER LIVING RM.

BEDROOM
10⁰ x 10⁶

BEDROOM
11⁴ x 16²

LOUNGE
14⁰ x 6⁸

RAILING

BALCONY

CL.

DN

RAILING

LINEN

BATH

WALK-IN CLOSET

OPEN BELOW

STORAGE

ACCESS PANEL

● Tudor houses have their own unique exterior design features. They include: gable roofs, simulated beam work, stucco and brick surfaces, diamond-lite windows, muntins, panelled doors, varying roof planes and hefty cornices. This outstanding two-story features a first-floor master bedroom, plus two more with lounge upstairs. The living room is dramatically spacious. It has a two-story sloping ceiling which permits it to look upward to the lounge. Large glass areas across the rear further enhance the bright, cheerful atmosphere of this area as well as the bedroom, dining and breakfast rooms. The open staircase to the upstairs has plenty of natural light as does the stairway to the basement recreation area.

Design V22939 First Floor: 1,409 square feet; Second Floor: 1,020 square feet; Total: 2,429 square feet

● Here's a Tudor adaptation with plenty of warmth and comfort for the entire family! Start with the big wrap-around covered porch in front. Then there's a large attic with headroom, a bonus for bulk storage and even possible expansion. An efficient U-shaped kitchen features many built-ins with also a pass-thru to a beamed-ceiling breakfast room. Sliding glass doors to a terrace are highlights in both the sunken family room and the breakfast room. A service entrance to the garage has a storage closet on each side, plus a secondary entrance through the laundry area. Recreational activities and hobbies can be enjoyed in the basement area. There are four bedrooms plus two baths upstairs, isolated from household noise and activity. A quiet corner living room opens to a sizable formal dining room. This room enjoys natural light from a bay window that overlooks the backyard.

Design V22148

First Floor: 1,656 square feet
Second Floor: 1,565 square feet
Total: 3,221 square feet

● The charm of this Tudor adaptation could hardly be improved upon. Its fine proportion and exquisite use of materials result in a most distinctive home. However, the tremendous exterior appeal tells only half of the story. Inside there is a breathtaking array of highlights which will cater to the whims of the large family. Imagine six large bedrooms, two full baths and plenty of closets on the second floor! The first floor has a formal living zone made up of the big living room, the separate dining room and the sizeable library. A second zone is comprised of the U-shaped kitchen, the breakfast room and the family room — all contributing to fine informal family living patterns. Behind the garage is the mud room, washroom and the practical equipment storage room. Don't miss beamed ceiling, powder room, two fireplaces and two flights of stairs to the basement.

Design V22324 First Floor: 1,256 square feet
Second Floor: 1,351 square feet; Total: 2,607 square feet

● Dramatic, indeed! Both the interior and the exterior of these three Tudor designs deserve mention. Study each of them closely. The design featured here has a simple rectangular plan which will be relatively economical to build. This design is ideal for a corner lot.

Design V22274

First Floor: 1,941 square feet
Second Floor: 1,392 square feet
Total: 3,333 square feet

Design V22276

First Floor: 1,273 square feet
Second Floor: 1,323 square feet
Total: 2,596 square feet

Design V23369

First Floor: 2,740 square feet
Second Floor: 2,257 square feet
Total: 4,997 square feet

● In magnificent Tudor style, this home delivers a stunning facade complemented by a most livable floor plan. The living areas include a library, a great hall and a family room (both with fireplaces) and a formal dining room. The island kitchen has an attached breakfast room. Connecting the main body of the house to the garage is a service area with full bath and laundry/hobby room. Upstairs, there are four bedrooms with walk-in closets and four full baths. The master has a fireplace and His and Hers walk-ins.

Design V23554

First Floor: 3,275 square feet
Second Floor: 2,363 square feet
Total: 5,638 square feet

● A splendid garden entry greets visitors to this regal Tudor home. Past the double doors is a two-story foyer that leads to the various living areas of the home. A quiet library is secluded directly off the foyer and has a box bay window, private powder room and sloped ceiling. Formal living takes place to the right of the foyer—an attached garden room shares a through fireplace with this area. Formal dining is found to the left of the foyer, accessed from the kitchen via a butler's pantry. The gathering room handles casual occasions and is just across the hall from the wet bar. Upstairs there is a grand master suite with lavish bath and sitting room and three secondary bedroom, each with private bath.

271

Design V22629

First Floor: 1,555 square feet
Second Floor: 1,080 square feet
Total: 2,635 square feet

● This home will really be fun in which to live. In addition to the sizeable living, dining and family rooms, many extras will be found. There are two fireplaces one to serve each of the formal and the informal areas. The back porch is a delightful extra. It will be great to relax in after a long hard day. Note two half baths on the first floor and two full baths on the second floor to serve the three bedrooms. Count the number of closets in the spacious upstairs. The door from the bedroom leads to storage over garage.

Design V22630

First Floor: 1,491 square feet
Second Floor: 788 square feet
Total: 2,279 square feet

● This distinctive version of Tudor styling will foster many years of prideful ownership and unique, yet practical living patterns. The main portion of the facade is delightfully symmetrical. Inside, the family living will focus on the 29 foot great room with its dramatic fireplace and beamed ceiling. The kitchen is outstanding with snack bar and dining nook nearby. Note the three large bedrooms each having its own dressing room. Extra storage space is available above the garage or may be developed into another room. Oversized garage includes a built-in workbench. Study plan carefully. It has much to offer.

Design V23354

First Floor: 3,556 square feet
Second Floor: 684 square feet
Total: 4,240 square feet

L **D**

● Tudor styling forms the basis
for this comfortable home. Stone
and half-timbering provide the
structure, multi-paned windows
and window boxes provide the
accent. The livability inside is
designed for empty-nesters: the
main living areas and the master
suite are on the first floor; secondary bedrooms are on the second floor. Special features such as
a clutter room, an island kitchen
and bay or boxed windows provide added attraction. Note the
bonus room that can be developed into additional sleeping
space or used for storage.

Design V23371

First Floor: 2,486 square feet
Second Floor: 1,553 square feet
Total: 4,039 square feet

L **D**

● Dramatic and bold, the Tudor reigns supreme among housing styles. This one combines all the favorite elements—stone, brick and half-timbering—on the outside with great livability. This is a perfect family plan. It contains formal and informal living spaces, indoor/outdoor areas, work spaces, spacious bedrooms and plenty of storage. The garage allows space for three cars. Note the extras: four fireplaces, sloped beamed ceilings in the living room and maser bedroom, and an island kitchen.

Design V22541

First Floor: 1,985 square feet
Second Floor: 1,659 square feet
Total: 3,644 square feet

● Here is English Tudor styling at its stately best. The massive stone work is complemented by stucco and massive beams. The diamond lite windows, the projecting bays, the carriage lamps and the twin chimneys add to the charm of this exterior. The spacious center entrance routes traffic effectively to all areas. Worthy of particular note is the formal living room with its fireplace, the adjacent family room overlooking the terrace, the quiet study with fireplace, two sizeable dining areas and an excellent master suite. Plus two more sizeable bedrooms.

Design V22391

First Floor: 2,496 square feet
Second Floor: 958 square feet
Total: 3,454 square feet

● Here is a stately English adaptation that is impressive, indeed. The two-story octagonal foyer strikes a delightfully authentic design note. The entrance hall with open staircase and two-story ceiling is spacious. Clustered around the efficient kitchen are the formal living areas and those catering to informal activities. The family room with its beamed ceiling and raised-hearth fireplace functions like the formal living/dining zone, with the partially enclosed outdoor terrace. Three bedrooms with two baths comprise the first floor sleeping zone. Each room will enjoy its access to the terrace. Upstairs there are two more bedrooms and a study. Notice the sliding glass doors to the balcony and how the study looks down into the entrance hall. The three-car garage is great. Your own list of favorite features will surely be lengthy.

Design V21991

First Floor: 1,262 square feet
Second Floor: 1,108 square feet
Total: 2,370 square feet

● Put yourself and your family in this English cottage adaptation and you'll all rejoice over your new home for many a year. The pride of owning and living in a home that is distinctive will be a constant source of satisfaction. Count the features that will serve your family well for years.

Design V22175
First Floor: 1,206 square feet
Second Floor: 1,185 square feet; Total: 2,391 square feet

● An English adaptation with all the amenities for gracious living. Note built-ins.

277

Design V22674
First Floor: 1,922 square feet
Second Floor: 890 square feet; Total: 2,812 square feet

● This delightful Tudor design's configuration permits a
flexible orientation on its site with either the garage doors or
the front doors facing the street. One-and-a-half-story designs offer great flexibilty in their livability. Complete livability is offered on the first floor then by utilizing the second
floor another three bedrooms and bath are available. First
floor features include a sunken family room with fireplace
and built-in bookshelves, rear living room with sliding glass
doors to the terrace, large formal dining room, first floor
laundry and two washrooms.

Design V22286
First Floor: 1,496 square feet
Second Floor: 751 square feet; Total: 2,247 square feet

● This charming home has a hint of
Tudor styling. It will offer you and your
family lots of livability. Take note of the
spacious living room with fireplace. Just a
few steps away, you can easily entertain
family and friends in the sizable family-
dining room. It is attractively highlighted
with a beamed ceiling. Access to the rear
terrace is obtained from both family room
and nook area. A nice sized kitchen overlooks the terrace. Two bedrooms and a
full bath also are on this floor. The development of the second floor adds two more
bedrooms and another bath.

Design V22278 First Floor: 1,804 square feet; Second Floor: 939 square feet; Total: 2,743 square feet

● This cozy Tudor adaptation is surely inviting. Its friendly demeanor seems to say, "welcome". Upon admittance to the formal front entrance hall, even the most casual of visitors will be filled with anticipation at the prospect of touring the house. And little wonder, too. Traffic patterns are efficient. Room relationships are excellent. A great feature is the location of the living, dining, kitchen and family rooms across the back of the house. Each enjoys a view of the rear yard and sliding glass doors provide direct access to the terrace. Another outstanding feature is the flexibility of the sleeping patterns. This may be a five bedroom house, or one with three bedrooms with study and lounge. Don't miss the three fireplaces and three baths.

Design V22373 First Floor: 1,160 square feet; Second Floor: 1,222 square feet; Total: 2,382 square feet

● Finding more livability wrapped in such an attractive facade would be difficult, indeed. This charming Tudor adaptation will return big dividends per construction dollar. It is compact and efficient. And, of course, it will not require a big, expensive piece of property. The location of the two-car garage as an integral part of the structure has its convenience and economic advantages, too. The living room is sunken and is divided from the dining room by a railing which helps maintain the desirable spacious atmosphere. The family room with its beamed ceiling, attractive fireplace wall, built-in storage and snack bar functions well with both the kitchen and the outdoor terrace. Four bedrooms, two baths, plenty of closets and built-in vanities.

Design V23331

First Floor: 1,115 square feet
Second Floor: 690 square feet
Total: 1,805 square feet

● Who could guess that this compact design contains three bedrooms and two full baths? The kitchen has indoor eating space in the dining room and outdoor eating space in an attached deck. A fireplace in the two-story gathering room welcomes company.

DINING
10¹⁰ x 11⁶

DECK

BATH

LINEN LINEN

KITCHEN
9⁰ x 12⁶

PTRY

REFG

GATHERING RM
15⁴ x 15⁰

SLOPED CEILING

SLOPED CEILING

DN UP

MASTER BEDROOM
11⁴ x 16⁶

FOYER

LOUNGE ABOVE

30'-6"

COVERED PORCH

UP

42'-0"

ROOF

ROOF

BEDROOM
16⁴ x 10⁶

ATTIC ACCESS

BATH

ATTIC

ROOF

BEDROOM
11⁰ x 10⁶

DN

LOUNGE
11⁰ x 17⁰

UPPER GATHERING RM

RAILING

RAILING

ROOF

ROOF

BALCONY

RAILING

● This Tudor design has many fine features. The exterior is enhanced by front and side bay windows in the family and dining rooms. Along with an outstanding exterior, it also contains a modern and efficient floor plan within its modest proportions. Flanking the entrance foyer is a comfortable living room. The U-shaped kitchen is conveniently located between the dining and breakfast rooms.

Design V22800 First Floor: 999 square feet
Second Floor: 997 square feet; Total: 1,996 square feet

L **D**

● The charm of old England has been captured in this outstanding one-and-a-half story design. Interior livability will efficiently serve the various needs of all family members. The first floor offers both formal and informal areas along with the work centers. Features include: a wet-bar in the dining room, the kitchen's snack bar, first floor laundry and rear covered porch.

Design V22854 First Floor: 1,261 square feet
Second Floor: 950 square feet; Total: 2,211 square feet

L **D**

THE SIGNATURE SERIES . . . *is a superior selection of first-quality*

homes. Each plan embodies an admirable assortment of amenities that signal luxury living at its finest. Appreciable features include interior balcony overlooks, unconventional shapes, dramatic styling, and abundant space for living and entertaining. Styles vary from Contemporary to the stately Tudor manor to the charming Victorian estate.

Design V23395

First Floor: 2,248 square feet
Second Floor: 2,020 square feet
Third Floor: 1,117 square feet
Total: 5,385 square feet

L D

● This home is a lovely example of classic Queen Anne architecture. Its floor plan offers: a gathering room with fireplace, a study with an octagonal window area, a formal dining room and a kitchen with attached breakfast room. Bedrooms on the second floor include three family bedrooms and a grand master suite. On the third floor are a guest room with private bath and sitting room and a game room with attached library.

Design V22954

First Floor: 3,079 square feet
Second Floor: 1,461 square feet
Total: 4,540 square feet

L

● This enchanting manor displays architectural elements typical of the Victorian style: asymmetrical facade, decorative shingles and gables, and a covered porch. The two-story living room with fireplace and wet bar is located at the rear of this home where it opens to the glass-enclosed porch with skylights. A spacious kitchen is filled with amenities including an island cooktop, built-in desk, and butler's pantry connecting to the dining room. The master suite, adjacent to the study, opens to a rear deck, perfect for taking in the night air before retiring. A cozy fireplace keeps the room warm on chilly evenings. Separate His and Hers dressing rooms are outfitted with vanities and walk-in closets, and a luxurious whirlpool tub connects the baths. The second floor opens to a large lounge with built-in cabinets and bookshelves ideal for study or peaceful relaxation. Three bedrooms and two full baths complete the second-floor livability. A three-car garage with disappearing stairs to a huge attic storage area makes this home as practical as it is charming.

● A magnificent, finely wrought covered porch wraps around this impressive Victorian estate home. The gracious two-story foyer provides a direct view past the stylish bannister and into the great room with large central fireplace. To the left of the foyer is a bookshelf-lined library and to the right is a dramatic, octagonal-shaped dining room. The island cooktop completes a convenient work triangle in the kitchen, and a pass-through connects this room with the Victorian-style morning room. A butler's pantry, walk-in closet, and broom closet offer plenty of storage space. A luxurious master suite is located on the first floor and opens to the rear covered porch. A through-fireplace warms the bedroom, sitting room, and dressing room, which includes His and Hers walk-in closets. The step-up whirlpool tub is an elegant focal point to the master bath. Four uniquely designed bedrooms, three full baths, and a restful lounge with fireplace are located on the second floor. Who says you can't combine the absolute best of today's amenities with the quaint styling and comfortable warmth of the Victorian past!

Design V22953

First Floor: 2,991 square feet
Second Floor: 1,802 square feet
Total: 4,793 square feet

L **D**

Design V22951

First Floor: 4,195 square feet
Second Floor: 2,094 square feet
Total: 6,289 square feet

● A single prominent turret with two-story divided windows draws attention to this stately Tudor home. The open foyer allows an uninterrupted view into the impressive, two-story great room with wet bar, where a fireplace with raised hearth runs the entire length of one wall. The expansive kitchen, conveniently located near the service entrance, has a U-shaped work area and a snack bar that opens to the morning room. The adjacent sloped-ceiling family room has an additional fireplace and a comfortable window seat. A Victorian-inspired, octagon-shaped sitting room is tucked into the corner of the unique master bedroom. His and Hers baths and walk-in closets complete the impressive first-floor suite. Two bedrooms, a study, and a guest suite with private sitting room are located on the second floor. A magnificent second-floor bridge overlooks foyer and gathering room and provides extraordinary views to guests on the way to their bedroom.

● Cross gables, decorative half-timbers, and three massive chimneys mark the exterior of this magnificent baronial Tudor. A circular staircase housed in the turret makes an impressive opening statement in the two-story foyer. A powder room and telephone center are located off the foyer for easy use by guests. Two steps down lead to the elegant living room with music alcove or the sumptuous library with wet bar. The kitchen is a chef's delight with large work island, full cooking counter, snack bar, and a butler's pantry leading to a formal dining room with bow window. The second floor features four bedrooms, two with fireplaces, and each with private bath and abundant closet space. The master suite has an additional fireplace, His and Hers walk-in closets, whirlpool bath and separate shower, and a private sitting room in a windowed alcove. Adjacent to the master suite is a nursery that would also make an ideal exercise room.

Design V22955
First Floor: 4,274 square feet
Second Floor: 3,008 square feet; Total: 7,282 square feet

Design V22940 First Floor: 4,786 square feet; Second Floor: 1,842 square feet; Total: 6,628 square fe

D

● Graceful window arches soften the massive chimneys and steeply gabled roof of this grand Norman manor. A two-story gathering room is two steps down from the adjacent lounge with impressive wet bar and semi-circular music alcove perfect for private concerts. The highly efficient galley-style kitchen overlooks the family room fireplace and spectacular windowed breakfast room. Bookshelves line an entire wall of the media room. The master suite is a private retreat equal to any of the best hotels. A fireplace and woodbox are tucked into a corner of the curved sitting room. Separate His and Hers baths and dressing rooms guarantee plenty of space and privacy while bathing and dressing. A large, built-in whirlpool tub adds the final touch of luxury to this personal spa. Upstairs, a second-floor balcony overlooks the gathering room below. Four additional bedrooms, each with a private bath, are located on the second floor, making every room of this house unique and memorable.

Design V22968 First Floor: 3,736 square feet; Second Floor: 2,264 square feet; Total: 6,000 square feet

● The distinctive covered entry to this stunning manor, flanked by twin turrets, leads to a gracious foyer with impressive, two-story semi-circular fan lights. Using "clustered rooms" and minimal hallways, the plan opens from the foyer to a formal dining room, master study and step-down gathering room. The spacious kitchen has numerous amenities including an island workstation and built-in desk. The adjacent morning room and gathering room with wet bar and raised-hearth fireplace are bathed in light and open to the terrace for outdoor entertaining. The luxurious master suite, secluded in its own wing, is complete with raised-hearth fireplace, His and Hers walk-in closets, whirlpool bath, spa-exercise room, and private courtyard. The second floor, accessed by foyer or utility area stairways, features four bedrooms, and an oversized activities room with fireplace and balcony. Unfinished attic space for maid's quarters, artist's retreat or storage, completes this extraordinary home.

Design V22952

First Floor: 2,870 square feet
Second Floor: 2,222 square feet
Total: 5,092 square feet

● Semi-circular arches complement the strong linear roof lines and balconies of this exciting contemporary. The first floor is filled with well-planned amenities for entertaining and relaxing. The foyer opens to a step-down living room with a dramatic sloped ceiling, fireplace, and three sliding glass doors that access the front courtyard and terrace. A tavern with built-in wine rack and an adjacent butler's pantry are ideal for entertaining. The family room features a fireplace, sliding glass door, and a handy snack bar. The kitchen allows meal preparation, cooking and storage within a step of the central work island. Three second-floor bedrooms, each with a private bath and balcony, are reached by either of two staircases. The master suite, with His and Hers baths and walk-in closets, whirlpool, and fireplace, adds the finishing touch to this memorable home.

Design V22956

First Floor: 4,222 square feet
Second Floor: 1,762 square feet
Total: 5,984 square feet

● Tall windows and two-story arches emphasize the soaring height of this elegant, northwest contemporary. A curved staircase is the focal point of the foyer. Two steps down from the foyer or dining room is the comfortable, two-story gathering room featuring a fireplace and two sliding glass doors. A large walk-in pantry, work island, snack bar, and view of the family room fireplace make the kitchen functional and comfortable. The master suite is secluded in its own wing. The bedroom, with a curved-hearth fireplace, and exercise room open to the terrace through sliding glass doors. His and Hers walk-in closets and baths (Hers with whirlpool tub) are added luxuries. A media room with wet bar, accessible from master bedroom and foyer, is the perfect place to relax. The second floor stairs open to a lounge which overlooks the gathering room. Three additional bedrooms and a quiet study alcove on the second floor round out the living area of this gracious and functional home.

291

Design V23300

First Floor: 3,202 square feet
Second Floor: 3,612 square feet
Total: 6,814 square feet

● Magnificent detailing accentuates this home's exterior – a dramatic roof line, soaring columns and chimneys, and a grand entryway. Inside, none of the splendor is lost. Each of five bedrooms, one a private in-law suite, has its own full bath.

Design V23305

First Floor: 3,644 square feet
Second Floor: 2,005 square feet
Total: 5,649 square feet

● A steeply pitched roof, a generous supply of multi-paned windows, and fanlights and glass side panels accenting the front entry signal the grand design of this home. Highlights include an elegant first-floor master suite, two-story foyer and living room, and bonus storage over the garage.

Design V23301

First Floor: 3,425 square feet
Second Floor: 2,501 square feet
Total: 5,926 square feet

● Masterful use of space with a profusion of windows and terrace access are all employed in this Tudor treasure. A two-story foyer points the way directly to the living room which features a raised-hearth fireplace, huge bay window, and curved bar. The angular kitchen has a center island and is strategically placed with relationship to the formal dining room, the family room and its gracious fireplace, and a captivating breakfast room. A media room to the left of the foyer provides built-in space for an entertainment system. The sloped-ceiling master bedroom contains a third fireplace and another gigantic bay window. Its adjoining bath is divided into His and Hers dressing areas and closets, and centers around a relaxing whirlpool spa. Guests are easily accommodated in a full suite with its own living room and bath on the second floor. Three other bedrooms and a lounge on this floor share a balcony overlook to the living room below.

Design V23304

First Floor: 2,102 square feet
Second Floor: 1,971 square feet
Total: 4,073 square feet

L **D**

● Victorian style is displayed in most exquisite proportions in this three-bedroom, four-bath home. From verandas, both front and rear, to the stately turrets and impressive chimney stack, this is a beauty. Inside is a great lay-out with many thoughtful amenities. Besides the large living room, formal dining room, and two-story family room, there is a cozy study for private time. A gourmet kitchen with built-ins has a pass-through counter to the breakfast room. The master suite on the second floor includes many special features: whirlpool spa, His and Hers walk-in closets, exercise room, and fireplace. There are two more bedrooms, each with a full bath, on the second floor.

Design V23364

First Floor: 2,883 square feet
Second Floor: 1,919 square feet
Total: 4,802 square feet

● The impressive stonework facade of this contemporary home is as dramatic as it is practical — and it contains a grand floor plan. Notice the varying levels — a family room, living room, media room, and atrium are down a few steps from the elegant entry foyer. The large L-shaped kitchen is highlighted by an island work center and a pass-through snack bar. A double curved staircase leads to a second floor where four bedrooms and three full baths are found.

TRADITIONAL VARIATIONS . . .

includes the incorporation of traditional design features such as muntined windows, shutters, panelled doors, glass side lights, gabled roofs, horizontal siding, stone chimneys, bay windows, dovecotes, cupolas, carriage lamps, and cornice brackets. All are tastefully blended to result in an appealing and distinctive facade. The examples on the following pages include Spanish, Victorian, Tudor, French, and Georgian adaptations.

Design V22883 First Floor: 1,919 square feet
Second Floor: 895 square feet; Total: 2,814 square feet

● A country-style home is part of America's fascination with the rural past. This home's emphasis of the traditional home is in its gambrel roof, dormers and fanlight windows. Having a traditional exterior from the street view, this home has window walls and a greenhouse, which opens the house to the outdoors in a thoroughly contemporary manner. The interior meets the requirements of today's active family. Like the country houses of the past, it has a gathering room for family get-togethers or entertaining. The adjacent two-story greenhouse doubles as the dining room. There is a pass-through snack bar to the country kitchen here. This country kitchen just might be the heart of the house with its two areas — work zone and sitting room. There are four bedrooms on the two floors — the master bedroom suite on the first floor; three more on the second floor. A lounge, overlooking the gathering room and front foyer, is also on the second floor.

Design V23338

First Floor: 1,314 square feet
Second Floor: 970 square feet
Total: 2,284 square feet

● For the new parents or empty-nesters, this plan's master suite has an attached nursery or sitting room. Downstairs there's a formal living room and dining room and the more casual family room with snack bar eating area. A front study is near the powder room.

Design V22722

First Floor: 2,330 square feet
Second Floor: 921 square feet
Total: 3,251 square feet

Design V22927

First Floor: 1,425 square feet
Second Floor: 704 square feet
Total: 2,129 square feet

D

Design V22909 First Floor: 1,221 square feet
Second Floor: 767 square feet; Total: 1,988 square feet

D

● This charming traditional home with striking good looks offers the modern family plenty of contemporary amenities. The first floor features a large gathering room with fireplace, media room for stereos and VCRs, a convenient kitchen with breakfast room, plus a dining room. The second floor includes an upper gathering room, spacious master bedroom suite, and a second bedroom. Notice columns that support a covered porch and window treatments.

Design V22826
First Floor: 1,112 square feet
Second Floor: 881 square feet; Total: 1,993 square feet

D

● This is an outstanding example of the type of informal, traditional-style architecture that has captured the modern imagination. The interior plan houses all of the features that people want most - a spacious gathering room, formal and informal dining areas, efficient, U-shaped kitchen, master bedroom, two children's bedrooms, second floor lounge, entrance court and rear terrace and deck. Study all areas of this plan carefully.

ALTERNATE KITCHEN / DINING RM /
BREAKFAST RM. FLOOR PLAN

Design V22724

First Floor: 2,543 square feet
Second Floor: 884 square feet
Total: 3,427 square feet

● Impressive at first glance! The interior of this one-and-a-half story home offers an abundance of livability. The master bedroom suite is on the first floor and has a private terrace. The second floor houses two more bedrooms and a bath. A design sure to provide enjoyment.

Design V22676

First Floor: 1,889 square feet
Second Floor: 872 square feet; Total: 2,761 square feet

● Here is the perfect home for those who want lots of livability. Note the easy access to each room. A luxurious master bedroom suite will provide all of the comforts you deserve. Take note of the sitting room, his/her dressing and closet areas and the raised tub. Upstairs, two nice sized bedrooms and a full bath.

● The inviting warmth of this delightful home catches the eye of even the most casual observer. Imagine, four big bedrooms! Formal and informal living can be enjoyed throughout this charming plan. A private, formal dining room is available for those very special occasions.

Design V21794 First Floor: 2,122 square feet
Second Floor: 802 square feet; Total: 2,924 square feet

Pleasing appearance, with an excellent floor plan. Notice how all the rooms are accessible from a hall. That's a plus for easy housekeeping. Some other extras: an exceptionally large family room which is more than 20' x 15', a gracious living room, formal dining room adjacent to the kitchen/nook area, four large bedrooms, a secluded guest suite plus a huge storage area.

Note that the large guest suite, featuring a full bath, is only accessible by the back stairs in the family room. You could use it as a spacious library, playroom, or a hobby area. Two fireplaces (one with a built-in wood box), walk-in closets, covered front porch and rear terrace also highlight this home.

Design V22614

First Floor: 1,701 square feet
Second Floor: 1,340 square feet
Total: 3,041 square feet

D

MASTER BED RM. 13⁰ x 17²

BED RM. 13⁶ x 13²

BATH

CL.

CL.

LINEN

HIS WALK-IN CL. SHLVS.

HER WALK-IN CL. SHLVS.

BATH

DN.

RAILING

CLG. CLIP

BED RM. 13² x 20⁰

STOR.

Design V23363

First Floor: 1,926 square feet
Second Floor: 1,189 square feet
Total: 3,115 square feet

● Timeless traditional style and 1½-story design are highlights in this lovely home. On the first floor, formal living areas are found to the right; more casual living to the left. The spacious family room devotes one full wall to a raised-hearth fireplace with built-in wood box and a built-in barbecue and bookshelves. Just off the dining room is a screened porch, perfect for outdoor eating. Examine the three upstairs bedrooms and you'll find two adjoining baths. His and Hers walk-in closets enhance the master suite.

62'-4"

73'-4"

FAMILY RM. 21¹⁰ x 14²

SCREENED PORCH

BKS.

BAR-B-Q

RAISED HEARTH

WOOD BOX

CABINET

BOOKS

BRKFST. RM. 8⁰ x 13²

D.W.

KIT. 10² x 13²

RANGE

DINING RM. 12⁰ x 13²

DESK

REF'G.

P'TRY.

PDR. RM.

D. W.

LAUND.

CL.

DN.

UP

FOYER

CURIOS

CL.

BKS.

LIVING RM. 12¹⁰ x 20⁴

MEDIA RM. 16⁰ x 11⁴

SER. ENT.

WALK-IN CL.

P.

BOOKS

PORCH

P.

GARAGE 24⁰ x 23⁰

CEILING CLIP

CURB

STORAGE

305

Design V23341 First Floor: 1,055 square feet
Second Floor: 981 square feet; Total: 2,036 square feet

● Designed for the empty-nester, small family, or as a second home, this appealing Tudor adaptation holds a most livable floor plan. Besides the 31' gathering room/dining room area and U-shaped kitchen with nearby washroom, there is a front study with large storage closet on the first floor. Three bedrooms on the second floor meet sleeping needs without a hitch. Notice the walk-in closets and the master-bedroom balcony.

Design V23343

First Floor: 1,953 square feet; Second Floor: 895 square feet
Total: 2,848 square feet

● Beyond the simple traditional styling of this home's exterior are many of the amenities required by today's lifestyles. Among them: a huge country kitchen with fireplace, an attached greenhouse/dining area, a media room off the two-story foyer, split-bedroom planning, and a second-floor lounge. There are three bedrooms upstairs, which share a full bath.

Design V23330

First Floor: 1,394 square feet
Second Floor: 320 square feet
Total: 1,714 square feet

● Outdoor living and open floor planning are highlights of this moderately sized plan. Amenities include a private hot tub on a wooden deck that is accessible via sliding glass doors in both bedrooms, and a two-story gathering room. An optional second-floor plan allows for a full 503 square feet of space with a balcony.

OPTIONAL FLOOR PLAN

Design V23334

First Floor: 2,193 square feet
Second Floor: 831 square feet
Total: 3,024 square feet

● A traditional favorite, this home combines classic style with progressive floor
planning. Four bedrooms are split — master suite and one bedroom on the first
floor, two more bedrooms upstairs. The
second-floor lounge overlooks a large,
sunken gathering room near the formal
dining area. A handy butler's pantry connects the dining room and kitchen.

● You and your family will love the new living patterns you'll experience in this story-and-a-half home. The front entry hall features an impressive open staircase to the upstairs and basement. Adjacent is the master bedroom which has a compartmented bath with both tub and stall shower. The spacious dressing room steps down into a unique, sunken conversation pit. This cozy area has a planter, built-in seat and a view of the thru-fireplace, opening to the gathering room as well. Here, the ceiling slopes to the top of the second floor lounge which looks down into the gathering room.

Design V22718 First Floor: 1,941 square feet
Second Floor: 791 square feet; Total: 2,732 square feet

D

Design V22513
First Floor: 1,799 square feet
Second Floor: 1,160 square feet
Total: 3,101 square feet

● What an appealing story-and-a-half design. Delightful, indeed, is the colonial detailing of the garage. The large entry hall with its open curving staircase is dramatic.

66'-8"

TERRACE

TERRACE

FAMILY RM.
13⁸ x 20⁰

RAISED HEARTH

NOOK
8⁰ x 13⁰

KITCHEN
10⁰ x 13⁶

D.W.

COOK TOP

DINING RM.
13⁰ x 13⁶

FLUSH HEARTH

DESK

OVEN

P'TRY

REF.

BOOKS

CAB'T

HALL

DN.

UP

STUDY
15⁸ x 11⁶

ENTRY

LIVING RM.
15⁸ x 27⁴

DRY. WASH

LAUNDRY

WASH RM.

STO.

HTR.

SERVICE ENTRANCE

SEAT

CL.

PORCH

CL.

PORCH

CL.

CL.

62'-8"

CURB

GARAGE
25⁴ x 23⁴

Design V22757

First Floor: 2,052 square feet
Second Floor: 1,425 square feet
Total: 3,477 square feet

● An L-shaped story-and-a-half with a traditional facade is hard to beat for pure charm. Here, the use of contrasting exterior materials - fieldstone, brick, vertical siding - along with delightful window treatment, recessed front door, carriage lamps, two massive chimneys and a cupola all make a contribution to outright appeal.

ROOF

ROOF

S

MASTER BED RM.
13⁰ x 20⁴

BATH

BED RM.
11⁴ x 11²

LOUNGE / BED RM.
13⁰ x 13⁶

BED RM.
9⁰-16⁰ x 20⁸

CL.

CL.

DRESSING ROOM

UNIT SEAT

LINEN

CL.

WALK-IN CLOSET

CL.

CL.

TUB

BATH

DN.

SITTING RM.
9⁰ x 5⁰

ATTIC

Design V22923

First Floor: 1,100 square feet
Second Floor: 970 square feet
Total: 2,070 square feet

● This Trend Home is as charming on the outside as it is comfortable on the inside. Note the Early American window treatments, second-story overhang, central fireplace, and textured look of stone and board siding. Inside one finds a large rear gathering room with fireplace, efficient U-shaped kitchen, formal dining room, study, and foyer on the first floor. Upstairs are three bedrooms plus an upper gathering room. The two-car garage includes storage space. Note the view windows and covered porch in the rear.

Design V23550

First Floor: 2,328 square feet
Second Floor: 712 square feet
Total: 3,040 square feet

● A transitional 1½-story home combines the best of contemporary and traditional elements. This one uses vertical wood siding, stone and multi-paned windows to beautiful advantage. The floor plan makes great use of space with first-floor living and dining areas and a first-floor master suite. Two secondary bedrooms, a full bath and an open lounge area are found on the second floor. The garage is accessed from the island kitchen through the laundry.

Design V23555

First Floor: 1,948 square feet
Second Floor: 1,669 square feet
Total: 3,617 square feet

● Round-top windows add elegance to the interior and exterior of this traditional home. Large gathering areas on the first floor flow together for ease in entertaining. The sunken gathering room stretches from the front of the house to the back, with a terrace at each end and a fireplace in the middle. Another fireplace is found in the conversation area adjoining the kitchen. The formal dining room features a bay window. Sleeping areas upstairs include a master bedroom with spacious bath and walk-in closet, three family bedrooms and two full baths.

Design V23356

First Floor: 1,610 square feet
Second Floor: 1,200 square feet
Total: 2,810 square feet

L **D**

● Traditionally speaking, this home takes blue ribbons. Its family room has a raised-hearth fireplace and there's a covered porch reached through sliding glass doors for informal eating. The living room also has a fireplace and is near the boxed-windowed dining room. A clutter room off the garage could be turned into a hobby or sewing room. Three bedrooms on the second floor include a master suite with His and Hers walk-in closets and three family bedrooms.

Design V23370

First Floor: 2,055 square feet
Second Floor: 1,288 square feet
Total: 3,343 square feet

L **D**

● The combination of stone and brick allow an impressive facade on this traditional two-story. The symmetrically designed interior will provide efficient traffic patterns. Note the formal living and dining areas to the right and huge family room to the rear. The U-shaped kitchen has an attached breakfast room and built-ins. There are four bedrooms on the second floor. The master features a walk-in closet, double vanity and whirlpool tub.

Design V23381

First Floor: 2,485 square feet
Second Floor: 1,864 square feet
Total: 4,349 square feet

● A place for everything and everything in its place. If that's your motto, this is your house. A central foyer allows access to every part of the home. To the left sits the spacious gathering room with fireplace and music alcove. Straight ahead, the open living and dining rooms offer sweeping views of the back yard. The modern kitchen and conversation area are situated to the right of the home. Near the entrance, a library with bay window and built-in bookcase is found. Look for extra amenities throughout the home: curio cabinets in the foyer, stairwell, conversation area and hall; built-in desk; walk-in closet and a second fireplace. Upstairs, the master suite features an enormous walk-in closet and a pampering bath. Another bedroom has a private bath, while the remaining two bedrooms share a bath with dual lavs.

Design V23551

First Floor: 1,575 square feet
Second Floor: 1,501 square feet
Total: 3,076 square feet

● Efficient floor planning provides a spacious, yet economical home. The large kitchen adjoins a breakfast/family room combination with fireplace. A butler's pantry connects the kitchen to the formal dining room with terrace access. A second fireplace is found in the living room. Also on the first floor: a library and convenient powder room. The master bedroom features His and Hers walk-in closets and a grand bath with whirlpool tub. The bedroom next door would make a fine nursery or office. A large bonus room over the garage offers many optional uses.

Design V21907 First Floor: 1,448 square feet
Second Floor: 1,248 square feet; Total: 2,696 square feet

● Here's an L-shaped, two-story which will lend itself to flexible orientation on your building site. You may face the garage doors toward the street, or if you prefer, the double front doors of the house itself may face the street. Whichever you choose, you'll not require a very wide building site. A particularly noteworthy feature is the covered, service entry. This leads to the extra first floor room which would be ideal for a home office.

Design V22540
First Floor: 1,306 square feet
Second Floor: 1,360 square feet; Total: 2,666 square feet

L **D**

● This efficient Colonial abounds in features. A spacious entry flanked by living areas. A kitchen flanked by eating areas. Upstairs, four bedrooms including a sitting room in the master suite.

Design V21966
First Floor: 1,244 square feet
Second Floor: 1,232 square feet
Total: 2,476 square feet

Design V22599

First Floor: 2,075 square feet
Second Floor: 1,398 square feet
Total: 3,473 square feet

D

● This traditional two-story with its projecting one-story wings is delightfully proportioned. The symmetrical window treatment is most appealing. The massive field-stone arch projects from the front line of the house providing a sheltered front entrance. Inside, there is the large foyer with the curving, open staircase to the second floor. Flexibility will be the byword to describe the living patterns. Not only are there the formal living and informal family rooms, but there is the quiet study and the upstairs sitting room. As for eating, there is a sizeable breakfast nook and a separate dining room. The second floor offers the option to function as either a three, or four, bedroom sleeping zone. That's a fine master bedroom suite when the sitting room is included.

Design V22325

First Floor: 1,154 square feet
Second Floor: 1,188 square feet
Total: 2,342 square feet

● Here is a modest package which will build economically on a relatively small site. All the elements are present to guarantee tremendous livability. Your family is not likely to outgrow this house. Imagine, four bedrooms, 2½ baths!

Design V21972

First Floor: 1,286 square feet
Second Floor: 960 square feet
Total: 2,246 square feet

● What an appealingly different type of two-story home! It is one whose grace and charm project an aura of welcome. The large entry hall routes traffic efficiently to all areas. Don't miss the covered porch.

321

Design V21715 First Floor: 1,276 square feet; Second Floor: 1,064 square feet; Total: 2,340 square feet

L **D**

● The blueprints you order for this design show details for building each of these three appealing exteriors. Which do you like best? Whatever your choice, the interior will provide the growing family with all the facilities for fine living.

Design V21957 First Floor: 1,042 square feet; Second Floor: 780 square feet; Total: 1,822 square feet

L **D**

● When you order your blueprints for this design you will receive details for the construction of each of the three charming exteriors pictured above. Whichever the exterior you finally decide to build, the floor plan will be essentially the same except the location of the windows. This will be a fine home for the growing family. It will serve well for many years. There are four bedrooms and two full baths (one with a stall shower) upstairs.

Design V23318

First Floor: 1,557 square feet
Second Floor: 540 square feet
Total: 2,097 square feet

● Details make the difference in this darling two-bedroom (or three-bedroom if you choose) bungalow. From covered front porch to covered rear porch, there's a fine floor plan. Living areas are to the rear: a gathering room with through-fireplace and pass-through counter to the kitchen and a formal dining room with porch access. To the front of the plan are a family bedroom and bath and a study. The study can also be planned as a guest bedroom with bath. Upstairs is the master bedroom with through-fireplace to the bath and a gigantic walk-in closet.

CUSTOMIZABLE

Custom Alterations? See page 413 for customizing this plan to your specifications.

BATH
LINEN
CL

GUEST BEDROOM
13⁶ X 11⁸

ALTERNATE 1ST FLOOR PLAN

WHIRLPOOL
S
MASTER BATH
LINEN   OPEN THRU   AUDIO/VISUAL

MASTER BEDROOM
19⁴ X 13²

WALK-IN CLOSET

HALF WALL   RAILING   DN

48'-0"

43'-8"

DN   COVERED PORCH   RAILING   DN

GATHERING RM
18¹⁰ X 16⁴

PASS THRU   PTRY OVEN

KITCHEN
14⁰ X 16⁴

DINING RM
11¹⁰ X 16⁴

OPEN THRU

COOK TOP

REF'G   DW

EATING

HALF WALL

BATH
LINEN   CL

FOYER   RAILING   DN   LT   W D

LAUNDRY   LINEN   CL

UP   CL   UP

COVERED PORCH

BEDROOM
13⁶ X 11⁴

STUDY
13⁶ X 11⁴

UP

Design V22488

First Floor: 1,113 square feet
Second Floor: 543 square feet
Total: 1,656 square feet

D

● A cozy cottage for the young at heart! Whether called upon to serve the young, active family as a leisure-time retreat at the lake, or the retired couple as a quiet haven in later years, this charming design will perform well. As a year round second home, the upstairs with its two sizable bedrooms, full bath and lounge area, looking down into the gathering room below, will ideally accommodate the younger generation.

CUSTOMIZABLE
Custom Alterations? See page 413 for customizing this plan to your specifications.

Design V22853
First Floor: 1,161 square feet
Second Floor: 475 square feet; Total: 1,636 square feet

● Natural stone, board-and-batten, multi-paned windows, overhanging eaves and the covered front porch highlight the exterior of this two-story home. Not only is the exterior well designed, but so is the interior. The sunken gathering room's ceiling is open to the second floor and is sloped for an even more dramatic appeal.

Design V22490

First Floor: 1,414 square feet
Second Floor: 620 square feet
Total: 2,034 square feet

● Split-bedroom planning makes the most of this contemporary plan. The master suite pampers with a lavish bath and a fireplace. The living areas are open and have easy access to the rear terrace.

CUSTOMIZABLE

Custom Alterations? See page 413 for customizing this plan to your specifications.

Design V23321

First Floor: 1,705 square feet
Second Floor: 572 square feet
Total: 2,277 square feet

● Cozy and completely functional, this 1½-story bungalow has many amenities not often found in homes its size. The covered porch at the front opens at the entry to a foyer with angled staircase. To the left is a media room, to the rear the gathering room with fireplace. Attached to the gathering room is a formal dining room with rear terrace access. The kitchen features a curved casual eating area and island work station. The right side of the first floor is dominated by the master suite. It has access to the rear terrace and a luxurious bath. Upstairs are two family bedrooms connected by a loft area overlooking the gathering room and foyer.

CUSTOMIZABLE

Custom Alterations? See page 413 for customizing this plan to your specifications.

Design V23313

First Floor: 1,482 square feet
Second Floor: 885 square feet
Total: 2,367 square feet

● Cozy living abounds in a
first-floor living room and
family room, dining room,
and kitchen with breakfast
room. Two fireplaces keep
things warm. Three bed-
rooms upstairs have more
than adequate closet space.

Design V23316

First Floor: 1,111 square feet
Second Floor: 886 square feet
Total: 1,997 square feet

● Don't be fooled by a small-looking exterior. This plan offers three bedrooms and plenty of living space. Notice that the screened porch leads to a rear terrace with access to the breakfast room. A living room/dining room combination adds spaciousness to the first floor.

32'-8"

TERRACE

UP

UP

BREAKFAST RM.
16⁸ x 10⁶

SCREENED
PORCH
11¹⁰ x 11²

SNACK BAR

DESK

RANGE

BC

DINING RM.
12⁰ x 12⁸

KITCHEN
16⁸ x 11²

FLOWER BOX

DW S

REF'S

PANTRY

PDR RM

DN

DN

50'-0"

OPEN ABOVE

CL

CURIO

UP

FOYER

CURIO

LIVING RM.
18⁴ x 14⁰

VERANDA

RAILING

RAILING

UP

ROOF

ROOF

WALL BELOW

RECESSED ROOF

UPPER BREAKFAST RM

BEDROOM
11¹⁰ x 11⁴

BEDROOM
11⁴ x 11⁴

WALK-IN CLOSET

LINEN

CL

BATH

WHIRLPOOL

DN

RAILING

BATH

OPEN BELOW

DRESS. RM

UPPER FOYER

MASTER BEDROOM
12⁴ x 16⁰

WALK-IN CLOSET

RECESSED ROOF

ROOF

ROOF

● This house combines the best of both worlds: a traditional look and a contemporary feel. Inside, the master bedroom provides many modern amenities, including a study, walk-in closet and deluxe bath with whirlpool tub and dual vanities. The traditional country kitchen with fireplace and built-in desk is spacious and yet cozy. A second fireplace is found in the expansive living room. Each of two bedrooms on the second floor has its own full bath.

Design V23353

First Floor: 2,191 square feet
Second Floor: 874 square feet
Total: 3,065 square feet

WIDTH 106'-8"
DEPTH 32'

CONTEMPORARY HOMES . . .

are known for, and often identified by, their lack of exterior adornment. Simple, uncluttered lines generally highlight their exteriors. Often, irregular shapes and soaring roof lines achieve a visual impact that is, indeed, dramatic. And as appealing as many of these contemporary forms are, so too are their accompanying, refreshing living patterns. Open planning, dual and multi-use space, sunken living areas, indoor balconies and lounges, cathedral ceilings, effective uses of glass, and functional indoor-outdoor living relationships can all complement one another to assure outstanding family living patterns. The contemporary home can offer an exciting break from the conventions of the past.

Design V22379 First Floor: 1,525 square feet; Second Floor: 748 square feet; Total: 2,273 square feet

L D

● A house that has "everything" may very well look just like this design. Its exterior is well-proportioned and impressive. Inside the inviting double front doors there are features galore. The living room and family room level are sunken. Separating these two rooms is a dramatic thru fireplace. A built-in bar, planter and beamed ceiling highlight the family room. Nearby is a full bath and a study which could be utilized as a fourth bedroom. The fine functioning kitchen has a pass-thru to the snack bar in the breakfast nook. The adjacent dining room overlooks the living room and has sliding doors to the covered porch. Upstairs three bedrooms, two baths and an outdoor balcony. Blueprints for this design include optional basement details.

Design V22711 First Floor: 975 square feet
Second Floor: 1,024 square feet; Total: 1,999 square feet

L **D**

● Special features! A complete master suite with a private balcony plus two more bedrooms and a bath upstairs. The first floor has a study with a storage closet. A convenient snack bar between kitchen and dining room. The kitchen offers many built-in appliances. Plus a gathering room and dining room that measures 31 feet wide. Note the curb area in the garage and fireplace in gathering room.

Design V22748

First Floor: 1,232 square feet
Second Floor: 720 square feet
Total: 1,952 square feet

● This four bedroom contemporary will definitely have appeal for the entire family. The U-shaped kitchen-nook area with its built-in desk, adjacent laundry/wash room and service entrance will be very efficient for the busy kitchen activities. The living and family rooms are both sunken one step.

55'-4"

TERRACE

COVERED PORCH

DINING RM.
11'⁴ x 14'⁰

GATHERING RM.
19'⁴ x 19'⁴

RAISED HEARTH

THRU-FIREPLACE

STUDY
10'⁰ x 12'⁶

NOOK
9'⁸ x 11'¹⁰

PDR. RM.

BAR

PANTRY

BOOKS

BOOKS
CL.

SNACK BAR

KITCHEN
12'⁰ x 11'⁶

CL.

LAUNDRY

DRY.
WASH

STOR.

CL.

DRESSING

VANITY

RANGE

CL.

DN

VANITY

STEP

56'-0"

ENTRY

CURB

UP

CL.

MASTER BED RM.
13'⁰ x 15'²

TUB

BATH

SEAT

PORCH

GARAGE
21'⁴ x 21'⁸

Design V22701 First Floor: 1,909 square feet
Second Floor: 891 square feet; Total: 2,800 square feet

● A snack bar in the kitchen! Plus a breakfast nook and formal dining room. Whether it's an elegant dinner party or a quick lunch, this home provides the right spot. There's a wet bar in the gathering room. Built-in bookcases in the study. And between these two rooms, a gracious fireplace. Three large bedrooms. Including a luxury master suite. Plus a balcony lounge overlooking gathering room below.

OPEN TO GATHERING RM. BELOW

SLOPED CEILING

B.

BED RM.
10'⁴ x 14'⁰

LOUNGE
19'⁴ x 11'¹⁰

RAILING

CL.

DN.

BATH

WALK-IN CLOSET

BED RM.
18'⁰ x 13'⁶

CL.

Design V22782

First Floor: 2,060 square feet
Second Floor: 897 square feet
Total: 2,957 square feet

D

● What makes this such a distinctive four bedroom design? Let's list some of the features. This plan includes great formal and informal living for the family at home or when entertaining guests. The formal gathering room and informal family room share a dramatic raised-hearth fireplace. Other features of the sunken gathering room include: high, sloped ceilings, built-in planter and sliding glass doors to the front entrance court. The kitchen has a snack bar, many built-ins, a pass-thru to dining room and easy access to the large laundry/wash room. The master bedroom suite is located on the main level for added privacy and convenience. There's even a study with a built-in bar. The upper level has three more bedrooms, a bath and a lounge looking down into the gathering room.

Design V22906 First Floor: 2,121 square feet
Second Floor: 913 square feet; Total: 3,034 square feet

D

● This striking Contemporary with Spanish good looks offers outstanding living for lifestyles of today. A three-car garage opens to a mudroom, laundry, and washroom to keep the rest of the house clean. An efficient, spacious kitchen opens to a spacious dining room, with pass-thru also leading to a family room. The family room and adjoining master bedroom suite overlook a backyard terrace. Just off the master bedroom is a sizable study that opens to a foyer. Steps just off the foyer make upstairs access quick and easy. The center point of this modern Contemporary is a living room that faces a front courtyard and a lounge above the living room. Three second-story bedrooms and an upper foyer join the upstairs lounge.

Design V22834 First Floor: 1,775 square feet
Second Floor: 1,041 square feet; Lower Level: 1,128 square feet
Total: 3,944 square feet

● This passive solar design offers 3,900 square feet of livability situated on three levels. The primary passive element will be the lower level sun room which admits sunlight for direct-gain heating. The solar warmth collected in the sun room will radiate into the rest of the house after it passes the sliding glass doors. During the warm summer months, shades are put over the skylight to protect it from direct sunlight. This design has the option of incorporating active solar heating panels to the roof. The collectors would be installed on the south-facing portion of the roof. They would absorb the sun's warmth for both domestic water and supplementary space heating. An attic fan exhausts any hot air out of the house in the summer and circulates air in the winter. With or without the active solar panels, this is a marvelous two-story contemporary.

Design V22831 First Floor: 1,758 square feet
Second Floor: 1,247 square feet; Total: 3,005 square feet

D

Design V22944 Main Level: 1,545 square feet; Upper Level: 977 square feet; Lower Level: 933 square feet; Total: 3,455 square feet

● This eye-catching contemporary features three stacked levels of livability. And what livability it will truly be! The main level has a fine U-shaped kitchen which is flanked by the informal breakfast room and formal dining room. The living room will be dramatic, indeed. Its sloping ceiling extends through the upper level. It overlooks the lower level activities room and has wonderfully expansive window areas for full enjoyment of surrounding vistas. A two-way fireplace can be viewed from dining, living and media rooms. A sizable deck and two cozy balconies provide for flexible outdoor living. Don't miss the music alcove with its wall for stereo equipment. Upstairs, the balcony overlooks the living room. It serves as the connecting link for the three bedrooms. The lower level offers more cheerful livability with the huge activities room plus lounge area. Note bar, fireplace.

Design V22910 First Floor: 1,221 square feet
Second Floor: 767 square feet; Total: 1,988 square feet

● This two-story home offers excellent zoning by room functions and modern amenities for comfort. A two-story gathering room, with attached dining room, serves the needs of any get-together, both formal and informal.

Sliding glass doors on either side of this room lead to two separate terrace areas. A third terrace can be reached via sliding glass doors in the breakfast room. Be sure to note the special features of this home: dramatic ceiling

heights, built-in storage areas, and pass-throughs. Notice also the media room for stereos/VCRs, plush master bedroom with a whirlpool, modern kitchen, and balcony.

BALCONY	BALCONY
BED RM. 11⁸ x 13⁸	BUNK RM. 11⁸ x 19⁰

UPPER GATHERING RM.

BALCONY   RAILING

CL   CL

BATH   RAILING   DN.

UPPER FOYER   CL

TERRACE

ACTIVITIES RM. 15⁴ x 18⁴

BUNK RM. OPTIONAL 11⁴ x 15⁸   BASEMENT

RAISED HEARTH   AIR COND.

BATH   STORAGE CABINETS   CL   LT.   WASH.   DRY.   UP

Design V22511

Main Level: 1,043 square feet
Upper Level: 703 square feet
Lower Level: 794 square feet
Total: 2,540 square feet

L **D**

40'-4"

52'-0"

DECK

GATHERING RM. 15⁴ x 18⁴

BALCONY

STUDY-BED RM. 11⁸ x 13⁸

DINING RM. 11⁸ x 11⁸

SNACK BAR

LINEN   CL

BATH   FOYER   DN.   UP   KITCHEN 11⁸ x 9⁸

CL   PNTR.   REF.   RANGE

PORCH

ENTRANCE COURT   OPEN TRELLIS

STORAGE

CARPORT 11⁸ x 20⁰

● Study this outstanding multi-level with its dramatic outdoor deck and balconies. This home is ideal if you are looking for a home that is new and exciting. The livability that it offers will efficiently serve your family.

Design V22823

First Floor: 1,370 square feet
Second Floor: 927 square feet
Total: 2,297 square feet

L **D**

● The street view of this contemporary design features a small courtyard entrance as well as a private terrace off the study. Inside the livability will be outstanding. This design features spacious first floor activity areas that flow smoothly into each other. In the gathering room a raised hearth fireplace creates a dramatic focal point. An adjacent covered terrace, featuring a skylight, is ideal for outdoor dining and could be screened in later for an additional room.

Design V22892 First Floor: 1,623 square feet; Second Floor: 160 square feet; Total: 1,783 square feet

● What a striking contemporary! It houses an efficient floor plan with many outstanding features. The foyer has a sloped ceiling and an open staircase to the basement. To the right of the foyer is the work center. Note the snack bar, laundry and covered dining porch, along with the step-saving kitchen. Both the gathering and dining rooms overlook the back yard. Each of the three bedrooms has access to an outdoor area. Now, just think of the potential use of the second floor loft. It could be used as a den, sewing room, lounge, TV room or anything else you may need. It overlooks the gathering room and front foyer. Two large skylights will brighten the interior.

Design V22887
First Floor: 1,338 square feet; Second Floor: 661 square feet; Total: 1,999 square feet

● This attractive, contemporary one-and-a-half story will be the envy of many. First, examine the efficient kitchen. Not only does it offer a snack bar for those quick meals but also a large dining room. Notice the adjacent dining porch. The laundry and garage access are also adjacent to the kitchen.

An exciting feature is the gathering room with fireplace. The first floor also offers a study with a wet bar and sliding glass doors that open to a private porch. This will make those quiet times cherishable. Adjacent to the study is a full bath followed by a bedroom. Upstairs a large master bedroom suite oc-

cupies the entire floor. It features a bath with an oversized tub and shower, a large walk-in closet with built-ins and an open lounge with fireplace. Both the lounge and master bedroom, along with the gathering room, have sloped ceilings. Develop the lower level for additional space.

Design V22729 First Floor: 1,590 square feet
Second Floor: 756 square feet; Total: 2,346 square feet

L

● Entering this home will be a pleasure through the sheltered walk-way to the double front doors. And the pleasure and beauty does not stop there. The entry hall and sunken gathering room are open to the upstairs for added dimension. There are fine indoor-outdoor living relationships in this design. Note the private terrace, a living terrace plus the balcony.

Design V21783
First Floor: 2,412 square feet
Second Floor: 640 square feet
Total: 3,052 square feet

Design V23352

First Floor: 1,148 square feet
Second Floor: 1,010 square feet
Total: 2,158 square feet

L **D**

WIDTH 47'
DEPTH 54'-8"

● Rustic looking with a contemporary feel—that's the beauty of this design. Interior rooms include an open gathering room with through-fireplace to cozy study, formal dining room near the kitchen/breakfast room combination and three bedrooms on the upper level. Note the balcony lounge overlooking the gathering room and the well-appointed master bath.

Design V22920 First Floor: 3,067 square feet
Second Floor: 648 square feet; Total: 3,715 square feet

L **D**

● Utilizing the same floor plan as Design V22921, this contemporary design also has a great deal to offer. Study the living areas. A fireplace opens up to both the living room and country kitchen. Privacy is the key word when describing the sleeping areas. The first floor master bedroom is away from the traffic of the house and features a dressing/exercise room, whirlpool tub and shower and a spacious walk-in closet. Two more bedrooms and a full bath are on the second floor. The three-car garage is arranged so that the owners have use of a double-garage with an attached single on reserve for guests.

Design V23557

First Floor: 2,897 square feet
Second Floor: 835 square feet
Total: 3,732 square feet

● The owners of this home will be giving themselves a real treat. A large master bedroom is accompanied by a pampering master bath and dressing area with walk-in closet. The master suite also provides access to the media room with bay window and fireplace. A sunken gathering room suits formal or informal occasions. The kitchen contains a snack bar and is convenient to the breakfast and dining rooms. Two large bedrooms upstairs are accompanied by two full baths.

Design V22780

First Floor: 2,006 square feet
Second Floor: 718 square feet
Total: 2,724 square feet

● This 1½-story contemporary has more fine features than one can imagine. The livability is outstanding and can be appreciated by the whole family. Note the fine indoor-outdoor living relationships.

Design V22772 First Floor: 1,579 square feet

Second Floor: 1,240 square feet; Total: 2,819 square feet

● This four-bedroom two-story contemporary design is sure to suit your growing family needs. The rear U-shaped kitchen, flanked by the family and dining rooms, will be very efficient to the busy homemaker. Parents will enjoy all the convenience of the master bedroom suite.

Design V22771 First Floor: 2,087 square feet
Second Floor: 816 square feet; Total: 2,903 square feet

● This design will provide an abundance of livability for your family. The second floor is highlighted by an open lounge which overlooks both the entry and the gathering room below.

Design V22562

First Floor: 2,884 square feet
Second Floor: 864 square feet
Total: 3,748 square feet

D

● Here is an exciting contemporary design for the large, active family. It can be called upon to function as either a four or five bedroom home. As a four bedroom home the parents will enjoy a wonderful suite with study and exceptional bath facilities. Note stall shower, plus sunken tub. The upstairs features the children's bedrooms and a spacious balcony lounge which looks down to the floor below. The sunken gathering room will be just that with its sloped beamed ceiling, dramatic raised hearth fireplace and direct access to the rear terrace.

Design V23556

First Floor: 1,828 square feet
Second Floor: 1,344 square feet
Total: 3,172 square feet

● Contemporary styling on the exterior, an amenity-filled floor plan—what more could you ask for in a luxury home? First-floor livability includes a huge gathering room/dining room combination with fireplace and terrace access. Another area with fireplace is found just off the kitchen. A sunken media room with greenhouse area is located to the right of the entry foyer. The second floor holds four bedrooms and three full baths. The master bedroom contains a sloped ceiling, a convenient dressing area with double-bowl vanity, and His and Hers walk-in closets. A compartmented toilet and whirlpool tub grace the bath.

● Varying roof planes, wide overhangs, interestingly shaped blank wall areas and patterned, double front doors provide the distinguishing characteristics of this contemporary design. The extension of the front wall results in a private, outdoor patio area accessible from the living room. There is a fine feeling of spaciousness inside this plan. The living area features open planning. Upstairs, four good-sized bedrooms and two baths.

Design V22602 First Floor: 1,154 square feet
Second Floor: 1,120 square feet; Total: 2,274 square feet

● This is a refreshingly dramatic contemporary. The use of the vertical paned windows highlight the exterior. Upon entrance to this home, one will enjoy the openness. An indoor-outdoor living relationship is present throughout this design. Note the lounge on the second floor. It is open on two sides so you can look down into the gathering room and entry hall below.

Design V22749 First Floor: 1,716 square feet
Second Floor: 1,377 square feet; Total: 3,093 square feet

● This exciting contemporary has dramatic roof lines and appealing glass areas. The interior planning is, indeed, unique. The spaciousness of the dining/family room will make entertaining a memorable occasion. Note the privacy of the master bedroom. The second floor is devoted to the activities of the younger generation. The lounge looks down into the gathering room.

Design V22530 First Floor: 1,616 square feet
Second Floor: 997 square feet; Total: 2,613 square feet

Design V22390 First Floor: 1,368 square feet
Second Floor: 1,428 square feet; Total: 2,796 square feet

D

● If yours is a large family and you like the architecture of the Far West, don't look further. Particularly if you envision building on a modest sized lot. Projecting the garage to the front contributes to the drama of this two-story. Its stucco exterior is beautifully enhanced by the clay tiles of the varying roof surfaces. The focal point, of course, is the five bedroom, three bath second floor. Four bedrooms have access to the outdoor balcony.

Design V22377 First Floor: 1,170 square feet
Second Floor: 815 square feet; Total: 1,985 square feet

● What an impressive, up-to-date home. Its refreshing configuration will command a full measure of attention. Note that all of the back rooms on the first floor are a couple steps lower than the entry and living room area. Separating the living room and the slightly lower level is a thru-fireplace, which has a raised hearth in the family room. Four bedrooms, serviced by two full baths, comprise the second floor which looks down into the living room.

Design V21877 First Floor: 1,162 square feet
Second Floor: 883 square feet; Total: 2,045 square feet

D

● This simple, straightforward plan has much to offer in the way of livability and economical construction costs. Worthy of particular note are the excellent traffic patterns and the outstanding use of space. There is no wasted space here. Notice the cozy family room with its raised-hearth fireplace, wood box and sliding glass doors to the sweeping outdoor deck. The efficient kitchen is flanked by the informal snack bar and the formal dining area. Open planning between the living and dining areas promotes a fine feeling of spaciousness.

Design V22309 First Floor: 1,719 square feet
Second Floor: 456 square feet; Total: 2,175 square feet

● Study this floor plan carefully. The efficiency of the kitchen could hardly be improved upon. It is strategically located to serve the formal dining room, the family room and even the rear terrace. The sleeping facilities are arranged in a most interesting manner. The master bedroom with its attached bath and dressing room will enjoy a full measure of privacy on the first floor. A second bedroom is also on this floor and has a full bath nearby. Upstairs, there are two more bedrooms and a bath.

Design V22781

First Floor: 2,132 square feet
Second Floor: 1,156 square feet
Total: 3,288 square feet

L **D**

● This beautifully designed two-story could be considered a dream house of a
lifetime. The exterior is
sure to catch the eye of
anyone who takes sight of
its unique construction.
The front kitchen features
an island range, adjacent
breakfast nook and pass-
thru to formal dining room.
The master bedroom suite
with its privacy and con-
venience on the first floor
has a spacious walk-in
closet and dressing room.
The side terrace is accessible through sliding glass
doors from the master bedroom, gathering room and
study. The second floor has
three bedrooms and storage
space galore. Also notice
the lounge which has a
sloped ceiling and a sky-
light above. This delightful
area looks down into the
gathering room. The out-
door balconies overlook the
wrap-around terrace. Surely an outstanding trend
house for decades to come.

Design V22708

First Floor: 2,108 square feet
Second Floor: 824 square feet
Total: 2,932 square feet

D

● Here is a one-and-a-half story home whose exterior is distinctive. It has a contemporary feeling, yet it retains some of the fine design features and proportions of traditional exteriors. Inside the appealing double front doors there is livability galore. The sunken rear living-dining area is delightfully spacious and is looked down into from the second floor lounge. The open end fireplace, with its raised hearth and planter, is another focal point. The master bedroom features a fine compartmented bath with both shower and tub. The study is just a couple steps away. The U-shaped kitchen is outstanding. Notice the pantry and laundry. Upstairs provides children with their own sleeping, studying and TV quarters. Absolutely a great design! Study all the fine details closely with your family.

TERRACE

54'-8"

DECK

HOT TUB
SKYLITE

STUDY /
BED RM
11⁰ x 11⁰

GREAT RM
16⁰ x 14²

COVERED
PORCH

LOUNGE ABOVE

MASTER
BED RM
12⁰ x 14⁶

CL

LINEN

DINING
14⁰ x 9⁴

GL SHLVS

PANTRY

BATH

LINEN

UP
DN

FOYER

BRM

KITCHEN
13⁰ x 8⁰

OVEN

DW

WALK-IN
CLOSET

DRESSING RM.

VANITY

TUB

LAUND

W

D

RANGE

REF'G

CL

52'-0"

SEAT

PORCH
OPEN ABOVE

CURB

ROOF LINE

GARAGE
21⁴ x 21⁸

UPPER GREAT RM

RAILING

CL

LOUNGE / HOBBIES
16⁰ x 9²

SKYLITE

CL

DN

UPPER
FOYER

STOR /
BATH

RAILING

RAILING

Design V22822

First Floor: 1,363 square feet
Second Floor: 351 square feet
Total: 1,714 square feet

L

● Here is a truly unique house whose interior was designed with the current decade's economies, lifestyles and demographics in mind. While functioning as a one-story home, the second floor provides an extra measure of livability when required. In addition, this two-story section adds to the dramatic appeal of both the exterior and the interior. Within only 1,363 square feet, this contemporary delivers refreshing and outstanding living patterns for those who are buying their first home, those who have raised their family and are looking for a smaller home and those in search of a retirement home.

BALCONY

LOUNGE / GUEST RM. /
GRANDCHILDREN'S RM.
16⁰ x 19²

CL

CL

DN

RAILING

UPPER
FOYER

BATH

RAILING

ALTERNATE SECOND FLOOR

Design V23439

First Floor: 1,443 square feet
Second Floor: 937 square feet
Total: 2,380 square feet

● Featuring a facade of wood and window glass, this home presents a striking first impression. It's floor plan is equally as splendid. Formal living and dining areas flank the entry foyer—both are sunken a step down. Also sunken from the foyer is the family room with attached breakfast nook. A fireplace in this area sits adjacent to a built-in audiovisual center. A nearby study with adjacent full bath doubles as a guest room. Upstairs are three bedrooms including a master suite with whirlpool spa and walk-in closet. Plant shelves adorn the entire floor plan.

65'-2"

52'-10"

TERRACE

FAMILY RM
12² X 18⁶

VAULTED CEILING

STUDY
12⁰ X 12⁰

AUDIO/VISUAL CENTER

BOOKS

NOOK
14² X 8⁰

LINE OF FLOOR ABOVE

SLOPED ROOF WINDOWS ABOVE

DW

S

PLANT SHELVES ABOVE

KITCHEN
12⁶ X 12⁰

BUTLER'S PANTRY

COOK TOP

REF'S

PTRY

OPT'J CL

BATH

LINEN

DN

UP

W D

LAUNDRY

B.C.

RAILING

CL

LIVING RM
12² X 12²

DN FOYER DN

VAULTED CEILING

DINING RM
9⁸ X 11⁸

VAULTED CEILING

VAULTED CEILING

COVERED PORCH

2 CAR GARAGE
14¹⁰ X 16⁴

CUSTOMIZABLE
Custom Alterations? See page 413 for customizing this plan to your specifications.

BEDROOM
11⁶ X 10⁶

OPEN TO FAMILY RM BELOW

PLANT SHELF

LINEN

BATH

DN

RAILING

BALCONY

BEDROOM
10⁶ X 10⁴

RAILING

OPEN TO FOYER BELOW

OPEN TO DINING RM BELOW

RAILING

NICHE

CL

PLANT SHELF

PLANT SHELF

SEAT

S

MASTER BATH

WHIRLPOOL

MASTER BEDROOM
13⁰ X 14⁰

WALK-IN CLOSET

Design V22905

First Floor: 1,342 square feet
Second Floor: 619 square feet
Total: 1,961 square feet

L

● All of the livability in this plan is in the back! Each first floor room, except the kitchen, has access to the rear terrace via sliding glass doors. A great way to capture an excellent view. This plan is also ideal for a narrow lot seeing that its width is less than 50 feet. Two bedrooms and a lounge, overlooking the gathering room, are on the second floor.

Design V22928

First Floor: 1,917 square feet
Second Floor: 918 square feet
Total: 2,835 square feet

First Floor labels:
TERRACE
TERRACE
MUSIC ALCOVE 9⁴ x 9⁸
GATHERING RM. 14⁰ x 21²
GREENHOUSE 11⁴ x 6⁸
MASTER BEDROOM 12⁰ x 15⁴
SECOND FLOOR LINE
COUNTRY KITCHEN 27 x 15⁴ - 17⁰
W.R.
SNACK BAR
MUD RM.
DRSG
LIN.
DN. RAILING OPEN
CL
WALK IN CLOSET
BATH
FOYER
DINING RM. 12⁰ x 11⁴ + BAY
CURB
COVERED PORCH
GARAGE 23⁴ x 21⁴

54'-0"
68'-4"

Second Floor labels:
UPPER GATHERING ROOM
ROOF
ROOF
BEDROOM 12⁰ x 9⁰
LOUNGE 15⁸ x 12⁴
BATH
BEDROOM 12⁰ x 11⁸ + BAY
DN. RAILING
UPPER FOYER
BEDROOM 12⁰ x 13⁰ + BAY
ROOF
ROOF

Design V22582

First Floor: 1,195 square feet
Second Floor: 731 square feet
Total: 1,926 square feet

● This distinctive two-story will command attention wherever built. One of its significant features is that it doesn't require a huge piece of property. In slightly less than 2,000 square feet it offers tremendous livability. As a bonus, the basement can function as the family recreation and hobby areas. Of particular interest is the first floor laundry room. Don't miss the fine kitchen layout, the formal and informal dining facilities and the sloping ceiling of the living room. Notice the outstanding outdoor living facilities. Upstairs, three bedrooms and two baths will be found.

Design V22904

First Floor: 2,724 square feet
Second Floor: 1,019 square feet
Total: 3,743 square feet

● This four-bedroom Contemporary Trend Home is loaded with extras that include a spacious garden room with its own whirlpool, snack bar off the kitchen, and deluxe master bedroom suite. The master bedroom has access to an exercise room with its own bath and view of a backyard terrace. Adjacent to the master bedroom is a spacious living room with sloped ceiling. Three other bedrooms are isolated upstairs. Two upstairs rooms have their own balconies.

TWO COUPLES/SINGLES RESIDENCE

CONVERTIBLE ONE-FAMILY RESIDENCE

Design V22828 First Floor (Living Area): 817 square feet; Foyer & Laundry: 261 square feet
Second Floor (Living Area): 852 square feet; Foyer & Storage: 214 square feet; Total: 2,144 square feet

● This contemporary home has been designed as a two-couples/singles residence. A home of this type could be bought jointly by two couples or one couple could buy the entire home and rent out one of the units. Complete livability is offered on each floor of this two-story. Each floor has a living room, dining room, interior kitchen, bedroom and bath. At a later date this home could be converted into a one-family residence. The second floor unit would now be a bedroom area.

BASEMENT PLAN

Design V22884 First Floor: 1,855 square feet
Second Floor: 837 square feet; Total: 2,692 square feet

● The greenhouse in this design enhances its energy-efficiency and allows for spacious and interesting living patterns. Being a one-and-a-half story design, the second floor could be developed at a later date when the space is needed. The greenhouses add an additional 418 sq. ft. to the above quoted figures.

Design V22925 First Floor: 1,128 square feet; Second Floor: 844 square feet; Total: 1,972 square feet

● What a refreshing and exciting two-story contemporary. The expansive wide-overhanging roofs make a distinctive design statement. This is also true of the effective uses of varying exterior materials and surface textures. The front entry area is noteworthy for its panelled double doors below the large radial head window. This window and the two vertical strips of glass to its right permit an abundance of natural light to flood the foyer and open staircases. While enjoying privacy from the street, the various rooms enjoy wonderful views of the rear and side yards. The cathedral ceiling of the gathering room and its windowed wall will make this the family's favorite area. A thru-fireplace serves both the gathering and dining rooms at the same time. The corner kitchen serves both dining areas well. The media room will house all that hi-tech equipment. Upstairs, two bedrooms and baths.

Design V23347 First Floor: 1,915 square feet
Second Floor: 759 square feet; Total: 2,674 square feet

● Open living is the key to the abundant livability of this design. The gigantic gathering room/dining room area shares a through-fireplace with a unique sunken conversation area. An L-shaped kitchen has a pass-through snack bar to the breakfast room. On the second floor, two bedrooms are separated by a lounge with a balcony overlook.

Design V23404

First Floor: 3,358 square feet
Second Floor: 868 square feet
Total: 4,226 square feet

L **D**

● Farmhouse design does a double take in this unusual and elegant rendition. Notice that most of the living takes place on the first floor: formal living room and dining room, gigantic family room with enormous firepit and porch access, guest bedroom or den and master bedroom suite. Upstairs there are two smaller bedrooms and a dramatic balcony overlook to the family room below.

Design V23438

First Floor: 1,489 square feet
Second Floor: 741 square feet
Total: 2,230 square feet

● A unique farmhouse plan which provides a grand floor plan, this home is comfortable in country or suburban settings. Formal entertaining areas share first-floor space with family gathering rooms and work and service areas. The master suite is also on this floor for convenience and privacy. Upstairs is a guest bedroom, private bath and loft area that makes a perfect studio. Special features make this a great place to come home to.

Design V23409

First Floor: 1,481 square feet
Second Floor: 1,287 square feet
Total: 2,768 square feet

● Glass block walls and a foyer with barrel vaulted ceiling create an interesting exterior. Covered porches to the front and rear provide for excellent indoor/outdoor living relationships. Inside, a large planter and through-fireplace enhance the living room and family room. The dining room has a stepped ceiling. A desk, eating area and snack bar are special features in the kitchen. The master suite features a large walk-in closet, bath with double bowl vanity and separate tub and shower, and a private deck. Three additional bedrooms share a full bath.

Design V23403

First Floor: 2,240 square feet
Second Floor: 660 square feet
Total: 2,900 square feet

L **D**

● There is no end to the distinctive features in this Southwestern contemporary. Formal living areas are concentrated in the center of the plan, perfect for entertaining. To the right of the plan, the kitchen and family room function well together as a working and living area. Also note the separate laundry room. The optional guest bedroom or den and the master bedroom are located to the left of the plan. Upstairs, the remaining two bedrooms are reached by a balcony overlooking the living room and share a bath with twin vanities.

371

Design V22926 First Floor: 1,570 square feet
Second Floor: 598 square feet; Lower Level: 1,080 square feet
Total: 2,650 square feet

● This striking contemporary design offers plenty of leisure living on three levels including an activities room with bar, exercise room with sauna, a gathering room, circular glass windows, and skylights. Note the outstanding master bedroom suite with skylight over the bath, adjoining lounge, and adjacent upper gathering room.

SUN COUNTRY HOMES...

display the spirit and diversity of a relaxed lifestyle. From California Craftsman, Spanish Mission and Monterey to Santa Fe-style, these homes spread across the Southwest in the beginning of the 20th Century. Currently, these styles can be seen in scattered areas throughout the country. Unique features include red tile roofs, towers, exterior porches and balconies. Indoor/outdoor relationships are given special attention.

Design V23322
First Floor: 1,860 square feet
Second Floor: 935 square feet; Total: 2,795 square feet

● This cleverly designed Southwestern-style home takes its cue from the California Craftsman and Bungalow styles that have seen such an increase in popularity lately. Nonetheless, it is suited to just about any climate. Its convenient floor plan includes living and working areas on the first floor in addition to a master suite. The second floor holds two family bedrooms and a guest bedroom. Note the abundance of window area to the rear of the plan.

CUSTOMIZABLE

Custom Alterations? See page 413 for customizing this plan to your specifications.

Design V23449

First Floor: 1,336 square feet
Second Floor: 1,186 square feet
Total: 2,522 square feet

● A covered porch leads inside to a wide, tiled foyer. A curving staircase makes an elegant expression in the open space including the living and dining rooms with two-story ceilings. A through-fireplace warms the nook and family room with wet bar and glass shelves. The nook also includes planters on two sides. Just above, light spills into the whirlpool in the master bath with dual vanities and walk-in closet. The master bedroom includes a sitting area, two more closets, and access to a private covered deck. Two family bedrooms share a full bath with dual vanities.

CUSTOMIZABLE
Custom Alterations? See page 413 for customizing this plan to your specifications.

Design V23441

First Floor: 2,022 square feet
Second Floor: 845 square feet
Total: 2,867 square feet

● Special details make the difference between a house and a home. A snack bar, audio/visual center and a fireplace make the family room livable. A desk, island cook top, bay, and skylights enhance the kitchen area. The dining room features two columns and a plant ledge. The first-floor master suite includes His and Hers walk-in closets, a spacious bath, and a bay window. On the second floor, one bedroom features a walk-in closet and private bath, while two additional bedrooms share a full bath.

CUSTOMIZABLE

Custom Alterations? See page 413 for customizing this plan to your specifications.

Design V23417 First Floor: 875 square feet
Second Floor: 731 square feet; Total: 1,606 square feet

CUSTOMIZABLE
Custom Alterations? See page 413 for customizing this plan to your specifications.

● Perfect for a starter home, this design is compact yet features great livability. The plan provides both formal and informal living areas. There's a living room with bay window and adjacent dining area. Open to the kitchen, the spacious family room is large enough to accommodate an informal eating area. The second floor boasts a balcony lounge overlooking the family room, master bedroom with bay window and two smaller family bedrooms.

CUSTOMIZABLE
Custom Alterations? See page 413 for customizing this plan to your specifications.

Design V23418

First Floor: 1,283 square feet
Second Floor: 552 square feet
Total: 1,835 square feet

● This home is ideal for the economically minded who don't want to sacrifice livability. The entry foyer opens directly into the two-story living room with fireplace. To the right, the kitchen with peninsula cooktop and snack bar conveniently serves both the breakfast room and the formal dining room. Also on this level, the master bedroom boasts an enormous bath with a whirlpool and His and Hers walk-in closets. Three other bedrooms are located upstairs to ensure peace and quiet. Also notice the abundant storage space in the attic.

Design V23420 First Floor: 1,617 square feet
Second Floor: 658 square feet; Total: 2,275 square feet

● Here is a moderate-sized house with a wealth of amenities typical of much larger homes. Interesting window treatments include two bay windows, one in the living room and one in the breakfast room. In the kitchen there's a snack bar pass-through to the family room which boasts a corner raised-hearth fireplace. Also on this level, the master suite features a large bath with whirlpool and access to the rear covered porch. Upstairs are three more bedrooms and a shared bath. Notice the attic storage space.

CUSTOMIZABLE

Custom Alterations? See page 413 for customizing this plan to your specifications.

BEDROOM
10⁸ x 10⁸

BEDROOM
10² x 12⁶

BATH

LINEN

BEDROOM
12⁶ x 11²

DN

UPPER LIVING RM

CL

RAILING   RAILING

CL

UPPER FOYER

WHIRLPOOL

WALK-IN CLOSET

LEDGE

MASTER BATH

ROOF   ROOF

MASTER
BEDROOM
19⁰ x 13¹⁰

CUSTOMIZABLE

Custom Alterations? See page 413 for customizing this plan to your specifications.

Design V23427 First Floor: 1,574 square feet
Second Floor: 1,177 square feet; Total: 2,751 square feet

COVERED PORCH

BRKFST RM
8⁴ x 10⁶

FAMILY RM
19² x 16⁴

PORCH

DINING RM
12⁶ x 12²

KITCHEN
12⁸ x 12⁶

DW

REFG   PANTRY

STUDY
12⁶ x 11²

CABINET BOOKS

BATH

RAILING

FOYER

WH   FURN   LAUNDRY
MECH RM   W D

DN   UP   DN

LIVING RM
16² x 20⁴ • BAY

PORCH

COVERED PORCH

CURB

GARAGE
19⁰ x 20⁴

59'-10"

46'-0"

● Varying rooflines and unusual window treatments will make this home a standout anywhere. The transom-lit foyer opens onto a cozy study and a spacious living room with dramatic bay window. To the rear, the kitchen easily serves the dining room and the bay-windowed breakfast room. The family room features a large fireplace. Upstairs are four bedrooms including a master with whirlpool bath.

Design V23428 First Floor: 2,623 square feet
Second Floor: 551 square feet; Total: 3,174 square feet

● High sloping ceilings and plenty of windows lend a light, airy feel to this Southwestern design. Flanking the two-story foyer are the sleeping areas, the regal master suite to the left and three more bedrooms (or two plus study) to the right. Overlooking the back yard are the dining room and living room with raised-hearth fireplace. The U-shaped kitchen has a pass-through to the family room which also has a fireplace. Doors here and in the dining room open onto the covered porch. Notice the pot shelves scattered throughout the plan.

CUSTOMIZABLE
Custom Alterations? See page 413 for customizing this plan to your specifications.

Design V23425

First Floor: 1,776 square feet
Second Floor: 1,035 square feet
Total: 2,811 square feet

L **D**

CUSTOMIZABLE

Custom Alterations? See page 413 for customizing this plan to your specifications.

● Here's a two-story Spanish design with an appealing, angled exterior. Inside is an interesting floor plan containing rooms with a variety of shapes. Formal areas are to the right of the entry tower: a living room with fireplace and large dining room. The kitchen has loads of counter space and is complemented by a bumped-out breakfast room. Note the second fireplace in the family room and the first-floor bedroom. Three second-floor bedrooms include a master suite with balcony.

Design V22801
First Floor: 1,172 square feet
Second Floor: 884 square feet
Total: 2,056 square feet

L D

● The great room in this design will be just that. It is sunken two steps, has a beamed ceiling, the beauty of a fireplace and two sets of sliding glass doors to a front and rear courtyard. A built-in wet bar and fireplace are the features of the family room. The foyer of this Spanish design is very spacious and houses a powder room. Four bedrooms and two baths are on the second floor. Don't miss the two enclosed courtyards.

Design V23414
First Floor: 2,024 square feet
Second Floor: 1,144 square feet; Total: 3,168 square feet

● Though seemingly compact from the exterior, this home allows for "wide-open-spaces" living. The two-story entry connects directly to a formal living/dining area, a fitting complement to the more casual family room and cozy breakfast room. Split-bedroom planning puts the master suite on the first floor for utmost privacy. Up the curved staircase are three family bedrooms, a guest room with deck, and two full baths.

CUSTOMIZABLE
Custom Alterations? See page 413 for customizing this plan to your specifications.

381

CUSTOMIZABLE
Custom Alterations? See page 413 for customizing this plan to your specifications.

Design V23429

First Floor: 1,739 square feet
Second Floor: 1,376 square feet
Total: 3,115 square feet

● From the dramatic open entry to the full-width back porch, this home delivers a full measure of livability in Spanish design. Formal living areas (living room and dining room) have a counterpoint in the family room and glassed-in breakfast room. The kitchen is a hub for both areas. Notice that the first-floor study has an adjacent bath, making it a fine guest room when needed. On the second floor, the central loft serves two family bedrooms and a grand master suite.

CUSTOMIZABLE
Custom Alterations? See page 413 for customizing this plan to your specifications.

● You'll find plenty about this Spanish design that will convince you that this is *the* home for your family. Enjoy indoor/outdoor living in the gigantic family room with covered porch access and a sunken conversation area sharing a through fireplace with the study. An L-shaped kitchen has an attached, glass-surrounded breakfast room and is conveniently located next to the formal dining room/living room combination. Besides the opulent master suite on the second floor, there are two family bedrooms and a full bath.

Design V23426 First Floor: 1,859 square feet
Second Floor: 969 square feet; Total: 2,828 square feet

● This design is carefully zoned for utmost livability. The entry foyer routes traffic to all areas of the house. To the rear is the living room/dining room combination with built-in china cabinet. To the left, the kitchen is open to the breakfast room and family room with fireplace. The master bedroom is on the right and features a whirlpool and a private porch. Upstairs are three more bedrooms and an outdoor balcony.

Design V23424 First Floor: 1,625 square feet
Second Flooor: 982 square feet; Total: 2,607 square feet

CUSTOMIZABLE
Custom Alterations? See page 413 for customizing this plan to your specifications.

Design V23447

First Floor: 2,296 square feet
Second Floor: 1,027 square feet
Total: 3,323 square feet

CUSTOMIZABLE

Custom Alterations? See page 413
for customizing this plan to your
specifications.

● Family activities of all types have a distinct place in this home. The first floor contains a game room, along with a living room/dining room combination with sloped ceiling and a family room with fireplace. The spacious, angled kitchen includes a snack bar, walk-in pantry, and adjacent breakfast area with a bay. A covered patio in the back makes for pleasant outside dining in any weather. An elegant staircase is accented by a niche and art gallery. The master bedroom features a private deck, two closets and a lavish bath. Two additional bedrooms share a full bath.

Design V23448

First Floor: 2,504 square feet
Second Floor: 1,673 square feet
Total: 4,168 square feet

● Spacious rooms are the rule in this home. A sunken living room stretches for a full 25 feet. The family room with fireplace is impressive in size, and even the kitchen abounds in space with a separate eating area (with coffered ceiling), a snack bar, island cook top, and a walk-in pantry. The first-floor master suite contains His and Hers walk-in closets, a three-way fireplace, whirlpool, and double bowl vanity. Three bedrooms upstairs share a compartmented bath. Back on the first floor, a fifth bedroom with private bath is perfect for guest quarters.

CUSTOMIZABLE

Custom Alterations? See page 413 for customizing this plan to your specifications.

Design V23323

First Floor: 1,923 square feet
Second Floor: 838 square feet
Total: 2.751 square feet

● This two-story southwestern home was designed to make living patterns as pleasant as they can be. Take a step down from the foyer and go where your mood takes you: a gathering room with fireplace and an alcove for reading or quiet conversations, a media room for enjoying the latest technology, or to the dining room with sliding glass doors to the terrace. The kitchen has an island range and eating space. Also on the first floor is a large master suite including a sitting area with terrace access, walk-in closet and whirlpool. An elegant spiral staircase leads to two family bedrooms sharing a full bath and a guest bedroom with private bath.

CUSTOMIZABLE

Custom Alterations? See page 413 for customizing this plan to your specifications.

Design V23450

First Floor: 1,801 square feet
Second Floor: 1,086 square feet
Total: 2,887 square feet

● A striking facade includes a covered front porch with four columns. To the left of the foyer is a large gathering room with a fireplace and bay window. The adjoining dining room leads to a covered side porch. The kitchen includes a snack bar, pantry, desk, and eating area. The first-floor master suite provides a spacious bath with walk-in closet, whirlpool and shower. Also on the first floor: a study and a garage workshop. Two bedrooms and a lavish guest suite share the second floor.

CUSTOMIZABLE
Custom Alterations? See page 413
for customizing this plan to your
specifications.

Design V23435

First Floor: 1,946 square feet
Second Floor: 986 square feet
Total: 2,932 square feet

● Here's a grand Spanish Mission home designed for family living. Enter at the angled foyer which contains a curved staircase to the second floor. Family bedrooms are here along with a spacious guest suite. The master bedroom is found on the first floor and has a private patio and whirlpool overlooking an enclosed garden area. Besides a living room and dining room connected by a through-fireplace, there is a family room with casual eating space. There is also a library with large closet. You'll appreciate the abundant built-ins and interesting shapes throughout this home.

CUSTOMIZABLE

Custom Alterations? See page 413 for customizing this plan to your specifications.

Design V23432

First Floor: 1,966 square feet
Second Floor: 831 square feet
Total: 2,797 square feet

● Unique in nature, this two-story Santa Fe-style home is as practical as it is lovely. The facade is elegantly enhanced by a large entry court, over-looked by windows in the dining room and a covered patio from one of two family bedrooms. The entry foyer leads to living areas at the back of the plan: a living room with corner fire-place and a family room connected to the kitchen via a built-in eating nook. Upstairs, the master suite features a grand bath and large walk-in closet. The guest bedroom has a private bath. Every room in this home has its own outdoor area.

CUSTOMIZABLE
Custom Alterations? See page 413 for customizing this plan to your specifications.

69'-6"

56'-0"

PORCH

KITCHEN
9⁶ X 11²

DINING
11² X 11²

MASTER BEDROOM
13⁰ X 16⁶

S DW

SNACK BAR

COOK TOP

REF'S

NOOK
8⁸ X 9²

CABINETS BELOW

OVEN

CL

MECH

SLOPED CEILING

MASTER BATH

WHIRLPOOL

S

LINEN

BALCONY ABOVE

BOOKS

WALK-IN CLOSET

D

W

LAUNDRY

RAILING

SLOPED CEILING

SLOPED CEILING

ARCHED OPENING

UP

POWDER RM

FOYER

GATHERING
11¹⁰ X 14⁰

RAISED HEARTH

RAISED HEARTH

WB

OPEN THRU

MEDIA/ LIBRARY
10² X 12⁸

WORK SHOP

STORAGE

COVERED PORCH

2 CAR GARAGE
19⁶ X 23⁸

CUSTOMIZABLE

Custom Alterations? See page 413 for customizing this plan to your specifications.

Design V23437

First Floor: 1,522 square feet
Second Floor: 730 square feet
Total: 2,252 square feet

● This two-story Spanish Mission-style home has character inside and out. The first-floor master suite features a fire-place and gracious bath with walk-in closet, whirlpool, shower, dual vanities, and linen storage. A second fireplace serves both the gathering room and media room or library. The kitchen with island cook top includes a snack bar and an adjoining breakfast nook. Three bedrooms and two full baths occupy the second floor.

GUEST BEDROOM
10⁶ X 11⁰

BEDROOM
10⁶ X 11⁰

CL

LINEN

S

BATH

CL

DN

BALCONY

RAILING

BATH

MECH

CL

OPEN TO BELOW

OPEN TO GATHERING RM BELOW

BEDROOM
11² X 10⁴

MOST POPULAR ONE-STORY HOUSES . . .

a bonus feature we present for your inspection. From the one-story designs most requested by our customers, this grouping offers a diversity of floor plans and exteriors. Encompassing many of the most popular styles, from Contemporary to Western, they host a wealth of highlights: gathering rooms, luxury master suites, private studies, and great indoor-outdoor relationships.

Design V22220
Square Footage: 2,646

D

● The gracious formality of this home is reminiscent of a popularly accepted French styling. The hip-roof, the brick quoins, the cornice details, the arched window heads, the distinctive shutters, the recessed double front doors, the massive center chimney, and the delightful flower court are all features which set the dramatic appeal of this home. This floor plan is a favorite of many. The four bedroom, two bath sleeping wing is a zone by itself. Further, the formal living and dining rooms are ideally located. For entertaining they function well together and look out upon the pleasant flower court. Overlooking the raised living terrace at the rear are the family and breakfast rooms and work center. Don't miss the laundry, extra wash room and work shop in garage.

Clutter Room, Media Room To The Fore

● Something new? Something new, indeed!! Here is the introduction of two rooms which will make a wonderful contribution to family living. The clutter room is strategically placed between the kitchen and garage. It is the nerve center of the work area. It houses the laundry, provides space for sewing, has a large sorting table, and even plenty of space for the family's tool bench. A handy potting area is next to the laundry tray. Adjacent to

the clutter room, and a significant part of the planning of this whole zone, are the pantry and freezer with their nearby counter space. These facilities surely will expedite the unloading of groceries from the car and their convenient storing. Wardrobe and broom closets, plus washroom complete the outstanding utility of this area. The location of the clutter room with all its fine cabinet and counter space means that the often numerous family projects

can be on-going. This room is ideally isolated from the family's daily living patterns. The media room may be thought of as the family's entertainment center. While this is the room for the large or small TV, the home movies, the stereo and VCR equipment, it will serve as the library or study. It would be ideal as the family's home office with its computer equipment. Your family will decide just how it will utilize this outstanding area.

Design V22915 Square Footage: 2,758

L **D**

● The features of this appealing contemporary design go far beyond the clutter and media rooms. The country kitchen is spacious and caters to the family's informal living and dining activities. While it overlooks the rear yard it is just a step from the delightful greenhouse. Many happy hours will be spent here enjoying to the fullest the outdoors from within. The size of the greenhouse is 8'x18' and contains 149 sq. ft. not included in the square footage quoted above. The formal living and dining areas feature spacious open planning. Sloping ceiling in the living room, plus the sliding glass doors to the outdoor terrace enhance the cheerfulness of this area. The foyer is large and routes traffic efficiently to all areas. Guest coat closets and a powder room are handy. The sleeping zone is well-planned. Two children's bedrooms have fine wall space, good wardrobe facilities and a full bath. The master bedroom is exceptional. It is large enough to accommodate a sitting area and has access to the terrace. Two walk-in closets, a vanity area with lavatory and a compartmented bath are noteworthy features. Observe the stall shower in addition to the dramatic whirlpool installation. The floor plan below is identical with that on the opposite page and shows one of many possible ways to arrange furniture.

FURNITURE LAYOUT

Design V22534 Square Footage: 3,262

L

● The angular wings of this ranch home surely contribute to the unique character of the exterior. These wings effectively balance what is truly a dramatic and inviting front entrance. Massive masonry walls support the wide overhanging roof with its exposed wood beams. The patterned double front doors are surrounded by delight- ful expanses of glass. The raised planters and the masses of quarried stone (make it brick if you prefer) enhance the exterior appeal. Inside, a distinctive and practical floor plan stands ready to shape and serve the living patterns of the active family. The spacious entrance hall highlights sloped ceiling and an attractive open stairway to the lower level recreation area. An impressive fireplace and an abundance of glass are features of the big gathering room. Interestingly shaped dining room and study flank this main living area. The large kitchen offers many of the charming aspects of the family-kitchen of yesteryear. The bedroom wing has a sunken master suite.

Design V21829
Square Footage: 1,800

● All the charm of a traditional heritage is wrapped up in this U-shaped home with its narrow, horizontal siding, delightful window treatment and high-pitched roof. The massive center chimney, the bay window and the double front doors are plus features. Inside, the living potential is outstanding. The sleeping wing is self-contained and has four bedrooms and two baths. The large family and living rooms cater to the divergent age groups. Pay attention to the carefully thought-out room arrangement with living room and dining room to the fore, family room and kitchen to the rear. A service area with laundry and half bath is conveniently located. A rear terrace will surely be a favorite outdoor space.

Design V22565

Square Footage: 1,540

L D

● This modest sized floor plan has much to offer in the way of livability. It may function as either a two or three bedroom home. The living room is huge and features a fine, raised hearth fireplace. The open stairway to the basement is handy and will lead to what may be developed as the recreation area. In addition to the two full baths, there is an extra wash room. Adjacent is the laundry room and the service entrance from the garage. The blueprints you order for this design will show details for each of the three delightful elevations above. Which is your favorite? The Tudor, the Colonial or the Contemporary?

Design V22505
Square Footage: 1,366

L **D**

● This design offers you a choice of
three distinctively different exteriors.
Which is your favorite? Blueprints
show details for all three optional
elevations. A study of the floor plan
reveals a fine measure of livability. In
less than 1,400 square feet there are
features galore. An excellent return on
your construction dollar. In addition to
the two eating areas and the open
planning of the gathering room, the
indoor-outdoor relationships are of
great interest. The basement may be
developed for recreational activities.
Be sure to note the storage potential,
particularly the linen closet, the pantry,
the china cabinet and the broom closet.

When You're Ready To Order ...

Let Us Show You Our Home Blueprint Package.

Building a home? Planning a home? Our Blueprint Package contains nearly everything you need to get the job done right, whether you're working on your own or with help from an architect, designer, builder or subcontractors. Each Blueprint Package is the result of many hours of work by licensed architects or professional designers.

QUALITY

Hundreds of hours of painstaking effort have gone into the development of your blueprint set. Each home has been quality-checked by professionals to insure accuracy and buildability.

VALUE

Because we sell in volume, you can buy professional-quality blueprints at a fraction of their development cost. With our plans, your dream home design costs only a few hundred dollars, not the thousands of dollars that custom architects charge.

SERVICE

Once you've chosen your favorite home plan, you'll receive fast efficient service whether you choose to mail your order to us or call us toll free at 1-800-521-6797.

SATISFACTION

Our years of service to satisfied home plan buyers provide us the experience and knowledge that guarantee your satisfaction with our product and performance.

ORDER TOLL FREE 1-800-521-6797

After you've studied our Blueprint Package and Important Extras on the following pages, simply mail the accompanying order form on page 413 or call toll free on our Blueprint Hotline: 1-800-521-6797. We're ready and eager to serve you.

Each set of blueprints is an interrelated collection of floor plans, interior and exterior elevations, dimensions, cross-sections, diagrams and notations showing precisely how your house is to be constructed.

Here's what you get:

Frontal Sheet
This artist's sketch of the exterior of the house, done in two-point perspective, gives you an idea of how the house will look when built and landscaped. Large ink-line floor plans show all levels of the house and provide a quick overview of your new home's livability, as well as a handy reference for studying furniture placement.

Foundation Plan
Drawn to 1/4-inch scale, this sheet shows the complete foundation layout, including support

walls, excavated and unexcavated areas, if any and foundation notes. If slab construction rather than basement, the plan shows footings and details for a monolithic slab. This page, or another in the set, also includes a sample plot plan for locating your house on a building site.

Detailed Floor Plans

Complete in 1/4-inch scale, these plans show the layout of each floor of the house. All rooms and interior spaces are carefully dimensioned and keys are provided for cross-section details given later in the plans. The position of all electrical outlets and switches are clearly shown.

House Cross-Sections

Large-scale views, normally drawn at 3/8-inch equals 1 foot, show sections or cut-aways of the foundation, interior walls, exterior walls,

floors, stairways and roof details. Additional cross-sections are given to show important changes in floor, ceiling or roof heights or the relationship of one level to another. Extremely valuable for construction, these sections show exactly how the various parts of the house fit together.

Interior Elevations

These large-scale drawings show the design and placement of kitchen and bathroom cabinets, laundry areas, fireplaces, bookcases and other built-ins. Little "extras," such as mantelpiece and wainscoting drawings, plus moulding sections, provide details that give your home that custom touch.

Exterior Elevations

Drawings in 1/4-inch scale show the front, rear and sides of your house and give necessary notes on exterior materials and finishes. Particular attention is given to cornice detail, brick and stone accents or other finish items that make your home distinctive.

House Cross-Sections

Detailed Floor Plans

Exterior Elevations

Interior Elevations

Foundation Plans

Frontal Sheet

Important Extras To Do The Job Right!

Introducing seven important planning and construction aids developed by our professionals to help you succeed in your home-building project.

To Order, Call Toll Free 1-800-521-6797

To add these important extras to your Blueprint Package, simply indicate your choices on the order form on page 413 or call us Toll Free 1-800-521-6797 and we'll tell you more about these exciting products.

MATERIALS LIST

For many of the designs in our portfolio, we offer a customized materials take-off that is invaluable in planning and estimating the cost of your new home. This comprehensive list outlines the quantity, type and size of material needed to build your house (with the exception of mechanical system items). Included are:

- framing lumber
- roofing and sheet metal
- windows and doors
- exterior sheathing material and trim
- masonry, veneer and fireplace materials
- tile and flooring materials
- kitchen and bath cabinetry
- interior drywall and trim
- rough and finish hardware
- many more items

(Note: Because of differing local codes, building methods, and availability of materials, our Materials Lists do not include mechanical materials. To obtain necessary take-offs and recommendations, consult heating, plumbing and electrical contractors. Materials Lists are not sold separately from the Blueprint Package.)

This handy list helps you or your builder cost out materials and serves as a ready reference sheet when you're compiling bids. It also provides a cross-check against the materials specified by your builder and helps coordinate the substitution of items you may need to meet local codes.

SPECIFICATION OUTLINE

This valuable 16-page document is critical to building your house correctly. Designed to be filled in by you or your builder, this booklet lists 166 stages or items crucial to the building process.

For the layman, it provides a comprehensive review of the construction process and helps in making the specific choices of materials, models and processes. For the builder, it serves as a guide to preparing a building quotation and forms the basis for the construction program.

Designed primarily as a reference for the homeowner, this Specification Outline can become a legally binding document. Once it is filled out and agreed upon by owner and builder, it becomes a complete Project Specification.

When combined with the blueprints, a signed contract and schedule, the Specification Outline becomes a legal document and record for the building of your home. Many home builders find it useful to order two of these outlines—one as a worksheet in formulating the specifications and another to be carefully completed as a legal document.

Plan-A-Home®

PLUMBING

The Blueprint Package includes locations for all the plumbing fixtures in your new house, including sinks, lavatories, tubs, showers, toilets, laundry trays and water heaters. However, if you want to know more about the complete plumbing system, these 24x36-inch detail sheets will prove very useful. Prepared to meet requirements of the National Plumbing Code, these six fact-filled sheets give general information on pipe schedules, fittings, sump-pump details, water-softener hookups, septic system details and much more. Color-coded sheets include a glossary of terms.

ELECTRICAL

The locations for every electrical switch, plug and outlet are shown in your Blueprint Package. However, these Electrical Details go further to take the mystery out of household electrical systems. Prepared to meet requirements of the National Electrical Code, these comprehensive 24x36-inch drawings come packed with helpful information, including wire sizing, switch-installation schematics, cable-routing details, appliance wattage, door-bell hookups, typical service panel circuitry and much more. Six sheets are bound together and color-coded for easy reference. A glossary of terms is also included.

Plan-A-Home® is an easy-to-use tool that helps you design a new home, arrange furniture in a new or existing home, or plan a remodeling project. Each package contains:

- More than *700 peel-off planning symbols* on a self-stick vinyl sheet, including walls, windows, doors, all types of furniture, kitchen components, bath fixtures and many more. All are made of durable, peel-and-stick vinyl you can use over and over.

- A reusable, transparent, *1/4-inch scale planning grid* made of tough mylar that matches the scale of actual working drawings (1/4 -inch equals 1 foot). This grid provides the basis for house layouts of up to 140x92 feet.

- *Tracing paper* and a protective sheet for copying or transferring your completed plan.

- A *felt-tip pen*, with water-soluble ink that wipes away quickly.

With Plan-A-Home®, you can make basic planning decisions for a new house or make modifications to an existing house. Use with your Blueprint Package to test modifications to rooms or to plan furniture arrangements before you build. Plan-A-Home® lets you lay out areas as large as a 7,500 square foot, six-bedroom, seven-bath house.

CONSTRUCTION

The Blueprint Package contains everything an experienced builder needs to construct a particular house. However, it doesn't show all the ways that houses can be built, nor does it explain alternate construction methods. To help you understand how your house will be built—and offer additional techniques—this set of drawings depicts the materials and methods used to build foundations, fireplaces, walls, floors and roofs. Where appropriate, the drawings show acceptable alternatives. These six sheets will answer questions for the advanced do-it-yourselfer or home planner.

MECHANICAL

This package contains fundamental principles and useful data that will help you make informed decisions and communicate with subcontractors about heating and cooling systems. The 24 x 36-inch drawings contain instructions and samples that allow you to make simple load calculations and preliminary sizing and costing analysis. Covered are today's most commonly used systems from heat pumps to solar fuel systems. The package is packed full of illustrations and diagrams to help you visualize components and how they relate to one another.

D *The Deck Blueprint Package*

Many of the homes in this book can be enhanced with a professionally designed Home Planners' Deck Plan. Those home plans highlighted with a **D** have a matching or corresponding deck plan available which includes a Deck Plan Frontal Sheet, Deck Framing and Floor Plans, Deck Elevations and a Deck Materials List. A Standard Deck Details Package, also available, provides all the how-to information necessary for building *any* deck. Our Complete Deck Building Package contains 1 set of Custom Deck Plans of your choice, plus 1 set of Standard Deck Building Details all for one low price. Our plans and details are carefully prepared in an easy-to-understand format that will guide you through every stage of your deck-building project. See these pages for 25 different Deck layouts to match your favorite house.

SPLIT–LEVEL SUN DECK
Deck Plan D100

BI–LEVEL DECK WITH COVERED DINING
Deck Plan D101

FRESH–AIR CORNER DECK
Deck Plan D102

BACK–YARD EXTENDER DECK
Deck Plan D103

WRAP–AROUND FAMILY DECK
Deck Plan D104

DRAMATIC DECK WITH BARBECUE
Deck Plan D105

SPLIT–PLAN COUNTRY DECK
Deck Plan D106

DECK FOR DINING AND VIEWS
Deck Plan D107

BOLD, ANGLED CORNER DECK
Deck Plan D108

SPECTACULAR "RESORT–STYLE" DECK
Deck Plan D109

TREND–SETTER DECK
Deck Plan D110

TURN–OF–THE–CENTURY DECK
Deck Plan D111

WEEKEND ENTERTAINER DECK
Deck Plan D112

STRIKING "DELTA" DECK
Deck Plan D113

CENTER–VIEW DECK
Deck Plan D114

KITCHEN–EXTENDER DECK
Deck Plan D115

BI–LEVEL RETREAT DECK
Deck Plan D116

SPLIT–LEVEL ACTIVITY DECK
Deck Plan D117

OUTDOOR LIFESTYLE DECK
Deck Plan D118

TRI–LEVEL DECK WITH GRILL
Deck Plan D119

CONTEMPORARY LEISURE DECK
Deck Plan D120

ANGULAR WINGED DECK
Deck Plan D121

DECK FOR A SPLIT–LEVEL HOME
Deck Plan D122

GRACIOUS GARDEN DECK
Deck Plan D123

TERRACED DECK FOR ENTERTAINING
Deck Plan D124

For Deck Plan prices and ordering information, see page 408.

 Or call **Toll Free**, 1-800-521-6797.

L The Landscape Blueprint Package

For the homes marked with an L in this book, Home Planners has created a front-yard landscape plan that matches or is complementary in design to the house plan. These comprehensive blueprint packages include a Frontal Sheet, Plan View, Regionalized Plant & Materials List, a sheet on Planting and Maintaining Your Landscape, Zone Maps and Plant Size and Description Guide. These plans will help you achieve professional results, adding value and enjoyment to your property for years to come. Each set of blueprints is a full 18" x 24" in size with clear, complete instructions and easy-to-read type. See the following pages for 40-different front-yard Landscape Plans to match your favorite house.

Regional Order Map

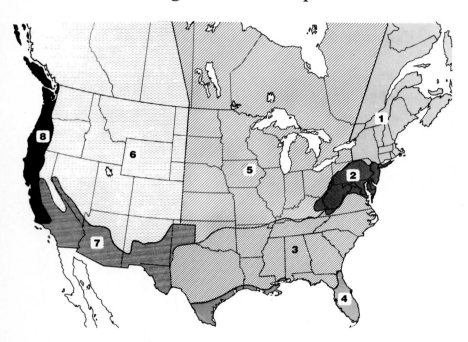

Most of the Landscape Plans shown on these pages are available with a Plant & Materials List adapted by horticultural experts to 8 different regions of the country. Please specify Geographic Region when ordering your plan. See page 408-411 for prices, ordering information and regional availability.

Region 1	Northeast
Region 2	Mid-Atlantic
Region 3	Deep South
Region 4	Florida & Gulf Coast
Region 5	Midwest
Region 6	Rocky Mountains
Region 7	Southern California & Desert Southwest
Region 8	Northern California & Pacific Northwest

CAPE COD TRADITIONAL
Landscape Plan L200

WILLIAMSBURG CAPE
Landscape Plan L201

CAPE COD COTTAGE
Landscape Plan L202

GAMBREL–ROOF COLONIAL
Landscape Plan L203

CENTER–HALL COLONIAL
Landscape Plan L204

CLASSIC NEW ENGLAND COLONIAL
Landscape Plan L205

SOUTHERN COLONIAL
Landscape Plan L206

COUNTRY–STYLE FARMHOUSE
Landscape Plan L207

PENNSYLVANIA STONE FARMHOUSE
Landscape Plan L208

RAISED–PORCH FARMHOUSE
Landscape Plan L209

NEW ENGLAND BARN–STYLE HOUSE
Landscape Plan L210

NEW ENGLAND COUNTRY HOUSE
Landscape Plan L211

TRADITIONAL COUNTRY ESTATE
Landscape Plan L212

FRENCH PROVINCIAL ESTATE
Landscape Plan L213

GEORGIAN MANOR
Landscape Plan L214

GRAND–PORTICO GEORGIAN
Landscape Plan L215

BRICK FEDERAL
Landscape Plan L216

COUNTRY FRENCH RAMBLER
Landscape Plan L217

FRENCH MANOR HOUSE
Landscape Plan L218

ELIZABETHAN TUDOR
Landscape Plan L219

TUDOR ONE–STORY
Landscape Plan L220

ENGLISH–STYLE COTTAGE
Landscape Plan L221

MEDIEVAL GARRISON
Landscape Plan L222

QUEEN ANNE VICTORIAN
Landscape Plan L223

GOTHIC VICTORIAN
Landscape Plan L224

BASIC RANCH
Landscape Plan L225

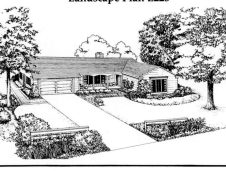

L–SHAPED RANCH
Landscape Plan L226

SPRAWLING RANCH
Landscape Plan L227

TRADITIONAL SPLIT–LEVEL
Landscape Plan L228

SHED–ROOF CONTEMPORARY
Landscape Plan L229

WOOD–SIDED CONTEMPORARY
Landscape Plan L230

HILLSIDE CONTEMPORARY
Landscape Plan L231

FLORIDA RAMBLER
Landscape Plan L232

CALIFORNIA STUCCO
Landscape Plan L233

LOW–GABLE CONTEMPORARY
Landscape Plan L234

NORTHERN BRICK CHATEAU
Landscape Plan L235

MISSION–TILE RANCH
Landscape Plan L236

ADOBE–BLOCK HACIENDA
Landscape Plan L237

COURTYARD PATIO HOME
Landscape Plan L238

CENTER–COURT CONTEMPORARY
Landscape Plan L239

For Landscape Plan prices and ordering
information, see page 408.

 Or call **Toll Free,**
1-800-521-6797.

Price Schedule & Plans Index

House Blueprint Price Schedule
(Prices guaranteed through December 31, 1994)

	1-set Study Package	4-set Building Package	8-set Building Package	1-set Reproducible Sepias
Schedule A	$210	$270	$330	$420
Schedule B	$240	$300	$360	$480
Schedule C	$270	$330	$390	$540
Schedule D	$300	$360	$420	$600
Schedule E	$390	$450	$510	$660

Additional Identical Blueprints in same order.................$50 per set
Reverse Blueprints (mirror image)....................$50 per set
Specification Outlines...........................$7 each
Materials Lists:
      Schedule A-D $40
      Schedule E $50

Deck Plans Price Schedule

CUSTOM DECK PLANS

Price Group	Q	R	S
1 Set Custom Plans	$25	$30	$35

   Additional identical sets ....$10 each
   Reverse sets (mirror image).................................$10 each

STANDARD DECK DETAILS
1 Set Generic Construction Details.....................$14.95 each

COMPLETE DECK BUILDING PACKAGE

Price Group	Q	R	S
1 Set Custom Plans, plus 1 Set Standard Deck Details	$35	$40	$45

Landscape Plans Price Schedule

Price Group	X	Y	Z
1 set	$35	$45	$55
3 sets	$50	$60	$70
6 sets	$65	$75	$85

Additional Identical Sets ....$10 each
Reverse Sets (mirror image)...............................$10 each

These pages contain all the information you need to price your blueprints. In general the larger and more complicated the house, the more it costs to design and thus the higher the price we must charge for the blueprints. Remember, however, that these prices are far less than you would normally pay for the services of a licensed architect or professional designer.

Custom home designs and related architectural services often cost thousands of dollars, ranging from 5% to 15% of the cost of construction. By ordering our blueprints you are potentially saving enough money to afford a larger house, or to add those "extra" amenities such as a patio, deck, swimming pool or even an upgraded kitchen or luxurious master suite.

Index

To use the Index below, refer to the design number listed in numerical order (a helpful page reference is also given). Note the price index letter and refer to the House Blueprint Price Schedule above for the cost of one, four or eight sets of blueprints or the cost of a reproducible sepia. Additional prices are shown for identical and reverse blueprint sets, as well as a very useful Materials List. Also note in the Index below those plans that have matching or complementary Deck

Plans or Landscape Plans. Refer to the schedules above for prices of these plans. Some of our plans can be customized through Home Planners' Home Customizer® Service. These plans are indicated below with this symbol: ♠. See page 413 for more information.

To Order: Fill in and send the order form on page 413—or call toll free 1-800-521-6797.

DESIGN	PRICE	PAGE	CUSTOMIZABLE	DECK	DECK PRICE	LANDSCAPE	LANDSCAPE PRICE	REGIONS
V21082	B	137						
V21104	A	88						
V21141	B	54						
V21142	B	41						
V21179	B	22						
V21196	A	92						
V21202	B	40						
V21208	A	195						
V21228	D	218		D124	S	L217	Y	1-8
V21239	C	122						
V21241	A	93		D117	S	L225	X	1-3,5,6,8
V21260	B	220						
V21266	B	40						
V21269	B	136						
V21278	B	50						
V21285	B	135		D117	S	L205	Y	1-3,5,6,8
V21304	B	127				L225	X	1-3,5,6,8
V21318	A	132						
V21339	B	127						
V21354	A	128		D105	R	L200	X	1-3,5,6,8
V21361	A	128		D117	S	L225	X	1-3,5,6,8

DESIGN	PRICE	PAGE	CUSTOMIZABLE	DECK	DECK PRICE	LANDSCAPE	LANDSCAPE PRICE	REGIONS
V21365	A	103		D113	R			
V21368	A	129						
V21372	A	82						
V21394	A	83		D105	R	L202	X	1-3,5,6,8
V21700	C	22						
V21701	B	101		D117	S			
V21711	D	209						
V21715	B	322		D100	Q	L204	Y	1-3,5,6,8
V21718	B	76		D114	R	L210	Y	1-3,5,6,8
V21719	A	29		D105	R	L203	Y	1-3,5,6,8
V21723	A	129						
V21728	C	122						
V21736	B	99						
V21745	B	67						
V21763	C	32						
V21766	B	100		D100	Q			
V21767	C	156						
V21773	B	195						
V21777	B	58						
V21783	C	344						
V21787	C	138		D117	S			

DESIGN	PRICE	PAGE	CUSTOMIZABLE	DECK	DECK PRICE	LANDSCAPE	LANDSCAPE PRICE	REGIONS
V21791	B	80		D114	R	L205	Y	1-3,5,6,8
V21793	C	101		D100	Q			
V21794	C	303						
V21814	B	33						
V21816	C	212						
V21827	B	60						
V21829	B	395		D113	R	L226	X	1-8
V21849	B	37						
V21852	C	158						
V21856	A	36		D117	S			
V21858	C	147		D101	R			
V21868	B	134						
V21870	B	80						
V21877	B	355		D114	R			
V21887	B	68						
V21900	C	24						
V21901	A	88						
V21902	B	77						
V21903	B	89						
V21905	C	130						
V21907	B	318						
V21914	B	66						
V21933	B	136		D117	S	L205	Y	1-3,5,6,8
V21955	B	122						
V21956	A	132	🏠	D117	S			
V21957	A	323		D100	Q	L228	Y	1-8
V21966	B	319						
V21967	B	97						
V21970	C	105		D100	Q			
V21972	B	321						
V21986	B	58				L203	Y	1-3,5,6,8
V21987	B	77		D101	R	L203	Y	1-3,5,6,8
V21991	B	277						
V21993	D	221				L213	Z	1-8
V21996	B	126		D114	R	L205	Y	1-3,5,6,8
V22102	C	35						
V22103	B	46		D124	S			
V22107	A	194						
V22124	B	100		D114	R	L203	Y	1-3,5,6,8
V22127	B	258						
V22128	B	250		D100	Q	L205	Y	1-3,5,6,8
V22131	B	61		D117	S	L203	Y	1-3,5,6,8
V22132	C	151				L201	Y	1-3,5,6,8
V22133	D	208		D106	S	L214	Z	1-3,5,6,8
V22138	B	51						
V22139	C	157						
V22140	C	201				L206	Z	1-6,8
V22141	C	251						
V22145	A	78				L209	Y	1-6,8
V22146	A	79		D114	R	L203	Y	1-3,5,6,8
V22148	C	267						
V22162	A	82		D103	R	L202	X	1-3,5,6,8
V22172	C	133						
V22175	B	277						
V22176	B	156		D112	R	L206	Z	1-6,8
V22184	C	186						
V22185	C	187						
V22188	C	49						
V22190	B	259						
V22192	D	154		D117	S	L218	Z	1-6,8
V22211	B	36		D117	S	L201	Y	1-3,5,6,8
V22220	C	391		D114	R	L217	Y	1-8
V22221	C	158						
V22222	B	216						
V22223	B	131		D112	R	L205	Y	1-3,5,6,8
V22224	B	67				L210	Y	1-3,5,6,8
V22225	D	139						
V22230	D	177						
V22239	C	255						
V22242	B	254		D112	R			
V22250	C	159						
V22253	C	22						
V22274	C	269						
V22276	B	269						
V22278	C	279						
V22281	C	216		D106	S			
V22283	C	175		D114	R	L206	Z	1-6,8
V22286	B	278						
V22295	C	52						
V22308	C	46						
V22309	B	355						
V22320	C	69						
V22322	B	52		D100	Q			
V22324	B	268						
V22325	B	321						
V22326	C	217						
V22336	C	211						
V22342	D	219						
V22346	B	53						
V22356	D	245		D119	S	L219	Z	1-3,5,6,8
V22364	B	60						
V22373	B	280						
V22377	A	354						
V22379	B	331		D120	R	L212	Z	1-8
V22390	C	353		D101	R			
V22391	C	276						
V22395	B	74						
V22396	B	80		D100	Q			
V22399	B	19						
V22488	A	325	🏠	D102	Q			
V22490	A	326	🏠					
V22491	A	261	🏠					
V22500	B	97		D100	Q	L204	Y	1-3,5,6,8
V22503	C	220						
V22505	A	397	🏠	D113	R	L226	X	1-8
V22507	C	220						
V22508	C	250						
V22510	A	83		D105	R	L200	X	1-3,5,6,8
V22511	B	340		D108	R	L229	Y	1-8
V22513	C	310						
V22520	B	169		D105	R	L201	Y	1-3,5,6,8
V22521	B	110						
V22524	A	212		D105	R			
V22530	B	353						
V22531	B	58						
V22534	D	394				L227	Z	1-8
V22538	B	55		D113	R	L201	Y	1-3,5,6,8
V22539	B	54						
V22540	B	319		D113	R	L205	Y	1-3,5,6,8
V22541	C	275						
V22543	D	215		D107	S	L218	Z	1-6,8
V22553	C	197						
V22556	C	164		D103	R			
V22559	B	102		D112	R			
V22562	D	350		D122	S			
V22563	B	74	🏠	D114	R	L201	Y	1-3,5,6,8
V22565	B	396		D101	R	L225	X	1-3,5,6,8
V22568	C	262						
V22569	A	102		D112	R	L200	X	1-3,5,6,8
V22571	A	86		D114	R	L202	X	1-3,5,6,8
V22582	A	362						
V22585	B	141		D113	R	L205	Y	1-3,5,6,8
V22586	A	259						
V22596	B	99		D114	R	L201	Y	1-3,5,6,8
V22598	A	45						
V22599	C	320		D100	Q			
V22600	C	165						
V22602	B	352						
V22610	C	48		D114	R	L204	Y	1-3,5,6,8
V22614	C	304		D114	R			
V22615	D	107		D106	S	L211	Y	1-8
V22618	B	263						
V22622	A	45	🏠	D103	R	L200	X	1-3,5,6,8
V22623	B	33		D100	Q	L205	Y	1-3,5,6,8
V22625	C	32						
V22627	A	213						
V22629	B	272						
V22630	B	272						
V22631	B	104		D112	R	L201	Y	1-3,5,6,8
V22633	C	146						

DESIGN	PRICE	PAGE	CUSTOMIZABLE	DECK	DECK PRICE	LANDSCAPE	LANDSCAPE PRICE	REGIONS
V22636	A	109						
V22637	B	263						
V22638	C	150						
V22639	C	162		D114	R	L215	Z	1-6,8
V22640	B	38		D114	R			
V22641	C	34						
V22644	B	94						
V22645	C	232				L224	Y	1-3,5,6,8
V22646	B	232		D114	R	L224	Y	1-3,5,6,8
V22647	D	233				L224	Y	1-3,5,6,8
V22649	C	39						
V22650	B	121		D117	S	L201	Y	1-3,5,6,8
V22653	C	30						
V22654	A	25						
V22655	A	84				L200	X	1-3,5,6,8
V22656	B	85		D105	R	L203	Y	1-3,5,6,8
V22657	B	98				L200	X	1-3,5,6,8
V22658	A	71						
V22659	B	27		D113	R	L205	Y	1-3,5,6,8
V22660	D	193						
V22661	A	95	🏠	D113	R	L202	X	1-3,5,6,8
V22662	C	153				L216	Y	1-3,5,6,8
V22663	B	214						
V22664	B	192		D113	R			
V22665	D	183						
V22666	B	13						
V22667	B	189				L216	Y	1-3,5,6,8
V22668	B	188				L214	Z	1-3,5,6,8
V22673	C	198						
V22674	C	278						
V22676	C	302						
V22680	C	70		D114	R			
V22681	B	31						
V22682	A	72	🏠	D115	Q	L200	X	1-3,5,6,8
V22683	D	148		D101	R	L214	Z	1-3,5,6,8
V22684	C	207		D114	R	L204	Y	1-3,5,6,8
V22686	C	204		D112	R	L209	Y	1-6,8
V22687	C	18		D117	S	L204	Y	1-3,5,6,8
V22688	B	206						
V22690	C	161						
V22691	B	20						
V22693	D	202						
V22694	C	112				L209	Y	1-6,8
V22695	C	168						
V22696	D	176						
V22697	C	205						
V22699	C	106				L211	Y	1-8
V22700	C	199						
V22701	C	333						
V22708	C	357		D112	R			
V22711	B	332	🏠	D105	R	L229	Y	1-8
V22718	C	310		D105	R			
V22722	C	299						
V22724	C	302						
V22729	B	344				L234	Y	1-8
V22731	B	51		D114	R	L205	Y	1-3,5,6,8
V22732	B	254						
V22733	B	44		D100	Q	L205	Y	1-3,5,6,8
V22748	A	332						
V22749	C	352						
V22752	B	140						
V22757	C	311						
V22762	C	196						
V22771	C	349						
V22772	C	348						
V22774	B	115	🏠	D100	Q	L207	Z	1-6,8
V22775	B	114				L207	Z	1-6,8
V22776	B	117	🏠	D113	R	L207	Z	1-6,8
V22780	C	348						
V22781	C	356		D121	S	L230	Z	1-8
V22782	C	334		D101	R			
V22794	C	246						
V22798	A	224		D100	Q	L200	X	1-3,5,6,8
V22799	A	28						
V22800	B	282		D113	R	L220	Y	1-3,5,6,8
V22801	B	381		D105	R	L232	Y	4,7
V22822	A	358				L229	Y	1-8
V22823	B	341		D112	R	L229	Y	1-8
V22826	B	301	🏠	D116	R			
V22828	B	364						
V22829	D	231		D113	R	L219	Z	1-3,5,6,8
V22831	C	337		D113	R			
V22834	D	336						
V22839	C	200						
V22852	A	86		D105	R	L202	X	1-3,5,6,8
V22853	C	325						
V22854	B	282	🏠	D112	R	L220	Y	1-3,5,6,8
V22855	B	249	🏠	D103	R	L219	Z	1-3,5,6,8
V22865	C	119		D114	R			
V22870	A	29						
V22883	C	297						
V22884	B	365						
V22887	A	343						
V22889	D	171		D107	S	L215	Z	1-6,8
V22890	C	116		D114	R			
V22891	B	64						
V22892	B	342						
V22897	C	65						
V22898	C	185		D118	R			
V22899	C	184						
V22904	C	363						
V22905	B	360		D121	S	L229	Y	1-8
V22906	C	335		D114	R			
V22907	B	124						
V22908	B	125	🏠	D117	S	L205	Y	1-3,5,6,8
V22909	B	300		D103	R			
V22910	B	339						
V22915	C	392		D114	R	L212	Z	1-8
V22920	D	346		D104	S	L212	Z	1-8
V22921	D	90		D104	S	L212	Z	1-8
V22923	B	312						
V22924	B	190						
V22925	B	366						
V22926	D	372						
V22927	B	299	🏠	D100	Q			
V22928	C	361						
V22939	B	266		D108	R			
V22940	E	288		D114	R			
V22944	C	338						
V22945	B	120	🏠					
V22946	C	118	🏠	D114	R	L207	Z	1-6,8
V22951	E	286						
V22952	E	290				L235	Z	1-3,5,6,8
V22953	E	285		D111	S	L223	Z	1-3,5,6,8
V22954	E	284				L223	Z	1-3,5,6,8
V22955	E	287						
V22956	E	291						
V22957	D	247		D107	S	L218	Z	1-6,8
V22959	B	264						
V22960	B	248						
V22963	D	111						
V22964	B	265						
V22965	D	253						
V22967	B	252						
V22968	E	289						
V22969	C	227		D110	R	L223	Z	1-3,5,6,8
V22970	D	235				L223	Z	1-3,5,6,8
V22971	C	225				L223	Z	1-3,5,6,8
V22972	B	226				L223	Z	1-3,5,6,8
V22973	B	226	🏠			L223	Z	1-3,5,6,8
V22974	A	239				L223	Z	1-3,5,6,8
V22975	D	152						
V22977	D	203				L214	Z	1-3,5,6,8
V22978	C	26						
V22979	C	170						
V22980	C	160						
V22981	D	113						
V22982	C	155						
V22983	A	56						
V22984	E	174						

DESIGN	PRICE	PAGE	CUSTOMIZABLE	DECK	DECK PRICE	LANDSCAPE	LANDSCAPE PRICE	REGIONS
V22987	D	172						
V22988	B	62		D120	R	L201	Y	1-3,5,6,8
V22989	D	17						
V22990	D	15						
V22991	D	210		D111	S	L215	Z	1-6,8
V22992	E	43		D103	R	L203	Y	1-3,5,6,8
V22993	D	173						
V22994	E	16						
V22995	E	63		D106	S	L217	Y	1-8
V22996	E	196						
V22998	D	14						
V22999	E	42						
V23126	A	75		D114	R	L203	Y	1-3,5,6,8
V23189	A	86		D113	R			
V23300	E	292						
V23301	E	294						
V23302	A	260	🏠					
V23303	D	181						
V23304	E	295						
V23305	E	293						
V23307	C	241		D111	S	L207	Z	1-6,8
V23308	E	228						
V23309	B	244						
V23313	B	328						
V23316	A	329						
V23318	B	324	🏠			L202	X	1-3,5,6,8
V23320	D	178						
V23321	C	327	🏠	D116	R	L209	Y	1-6,8
V23322	C	373	🏠	D118	R	L234	Y	1-8
V23323	C	386	🏠	D120	R	L223	Z	1-3,5,6,8
V23330	A	308						
V23331	A	281						
V23333	C	191						
V23334	C	309						
V23335	C	256						
V23337	D	180						
V23338	B	298						
V23339	B	179						
V23341	B	306						
V23342	B	257						
V23343	C	307						
V23347	D	367						
V23349	E	163		D107	S	L216	Y	1-3,5,6,8
V23351	C	108		D115	Q	L209	Y	1-6,8
V23352	B	345		D108	R	L229	Y	1-8
V23353	C	330		D113	R	L206	Z	1-6,8
V23354	E	273		D104	S	L212	Y	1-8
V23356	C	315		D103	R	L217	Y	1-8
V23363	C	305						
V23364	D	296						
V23365	C	167						
V23367	D	166						
V23369	E	270						
V23370	D	315		D119	S	L235	Z	1-3,5,6,8

DESIGN	PRICE	PAGE	CUSTOMIZABLE	DECK	DECK PRICE	LANDSCAPE	LANDSCAPE PRICE	REGIONS
V23371	E	274		D115	Q	L214	Z	1-3,5,6,8
V23372	C	92		D102	Q	L200	X	1-3,5,6,8
V23379	B	21						
V23380	E	223						
V23381	E	316						
V23382	C	238		D110	R	L202	X	1-3,5,6,8
V23383	C	236		D111	S	L205	Y	1-3,5,6,8
V23384	C	236		D115	Q	L207	Z	1-6,8
V23385	C	240		D100	Q	L207	Z	1-6,8
V23386	E	229		D111	S	L216	Y	1-3,5,6,8
V23387	E	243		D110	R	L224	Y	1-3,5,6,8
V23388	D	230		D111	S	L207	Z	1-6,8
V23389	C	234		D115	Q	L205	Y	1-3,5,6,8
V23390	C	240		D106	S	L207	Z	1-6,8
V23391	C	237		D116	R	L207	Z	1-6,8
V23392	D	242		D110	R	L223	Z	1-3,5,6,8
V23393	C	234		D115	Q	L207	Z	1-6,8
V23394	D	230		D111	S	L207	Z	1-6,8
V23395	E	283		D111	S	L223	Z	1-3,5,6,8
V23396	C	144		D111	S	L207	Z	1-6,8
V23397	D	142		D110	R	L209	Y	1-6,8
V23398	C	145		D111	S	L224	Y	1-3,5,6,8
V23399	C	143		D110	R	L224	Y	1-3,5,6,8
V23403	C	371		D115	Q	L237	Y	7
V23404	D	368		D106	S	L230	Z	1-8
V23409	C	370						
V23414	C	381	🏠					
V23417	A	376	🏠					
V23418	A	376	🏠					
V23420	B	377	🏠					
V23424	B	383	🏠					
V23425	C	380	🏠					
V23426	C	383	🏠					
V23427	C	378	🏠					
V23428	C	379	🏠					
V23429	C	382	🏠					
V23432	C	389	🏠			L233	Y	3,4,7
V23435	D	388	🏠	D104	S	L227	Z	1-8
V23437	C	390	🏠					
V23438	C	369				L209	Y	1-6,8
V23439	C	359	🏠					
V23441	C	375	🏠					
V23447	D	384	🏠	D120	R	L237	Y	7
V23448	E	385	🏠			L233	Y	3,4,7
V23449	C	374	🏠					
V23450	C	387	🏠	D106	S	L229	Y	1-8
V23550	D	313						
V23551	D	317						
V23552	C	47						
V23553	D	96						
V23554	E	271						
V23555	D	314						
V23556	D	351						
V23557	D	347						

Before You Order . . .

Before completing the coupon at right or calling us on our Toll-Free Blueprint Hotline, you may be interested to learn more about our service and products. Here's some information you will find helpful.

Quick Turnaround

We process and ship every blueprint order from our office within 48 hours. On most orders, we do even better. Normally, if we receive your order by 5 p.m. Eastern Time, we'll process it the same day and ship it the following day. Because of this quick turnaround, we won't send a formal notice acknowledging receipt of your order.

Our Exchange Policy

Since blueprints are printed in response to your order, we cannot honor requests for refunds. However, we will exchange your entire first order for an equal number of blueprints at a price of $40 for the first set and $10 for each additional set; $60 total exchange fee for 4 sets; $90 total exchange fee for 8 sets... *plus* the difference in cost if exchanging for a design in a higher price bracket or *less* the difference in cost if exchanging for a design in a lower price bracket. (Sepias are not exchangeable.) All sets from the first order must be returned before the exchange can take place. Please add $8 for postage and handling via ground service; $20 via 2nd Day Air.

About Reverse Blueprints

If you want to build in reverse of the plan as shown, we will include an extra set of reversed blueprints (mirror image) for an additional fee of $50. Although lettering and dimensions appear backward, reverses will be a useful visual aid if you decide to flop the plan. Right-reading reverses of Customizable Plans are available through our Customization Service. Call for more details.

Modifying or Customizing Our Plans

With such a great selection of homes, you are bound to find the one that suits you. However, if you need to make alterations to a design that is customizable, you need only order our Customizer® kit or call our Customization representative at 1-800-322-6797, ext. 800, to get you started (see additional information on next page). It is possible to customize many of our plans that are not part of our Home Customizer® Service. If this is the case for the home you have chosen, information about customizing the plans will be included in your blueprint package.

If you decide to revise plans significantly that are not customizable through our service, we strongly suggest that you order reproducible sepias and consult a licensed architect or professional designer to help you redraw the plans.

Architectural and Engineering Seals

Some cities and states are now requiring that a licensed architect or engineer review and "seal" your blueprints prior to construction. This is often due to local or regional concerns over energy consumption, safety codes, seismic ratings, etc. For this reason, you may find it necessary to consult with a local professional to have your plans reviewed. This can normally be accomplished with minimum delays, for a nominal fee. In some cases, Home Planners can seal your plans through our Customization Service. Call for more details.

Compliance with Local Codes and Regulations

At the time of creation, our plans are drawn to specifications published by Building Officials Code Administrators (BOCA), the Southern Standard Building Code, or the Uniform Building Code and are designed to meet or exceed national building standards. Some states, counties and municipalities have their own codes, zoning requirements and building regulations. Before starting construction, consult with local building authorities and make sure you comply with local ordinances and codes, including obtaining any necessary permits or inspections as building progresses. In some cases, minor modifications to your plans by your builder, local architect or designer may be required to meet local conditions and requirements. Home Planners may be able to make these changes to Customizable Plans providing you supply all pertinent information from your local building authorities.

Foundation and Exterior Wall Changes

Most of our plans are drawn with either a full or partial basement foundation. Depending upon your specific climate or regional building practices, you may wish to convert this basement to a slab or crawlspace. Most professional contractors and builders can easily adapt your plans to alternate foundation types. Likewise, most can easily convert 2x4 wall construction to 2x6, or vice versa. If you need more guidance on these conversions, our handy Construction Detail Sheets, shown on page 401, describe how such conversions can be made. For Customizable Plans, Home Planners can easily provide the necessary changes for you.

How Many Blueprints Do You Need?

A single set of blueprints is sufficient to study a home in greater detail. However, if you are planning to obtain cost estimates from a contractor or subcontractors—or if you are planning to build immediately—you will need more sets. Because additional sets are cheaper when ordered in quantity with the original order, make sure you order enough blueprints to satisfy all requirements. The following checklist will help you determine how many you need:

_____ Owner

_____ Builder (generally requires at least three sets; one as a legal document, one to use during inspections, and at least one to give to subcontractors)

_____ Local Building Department (often requires two sets)

_____ Mortgage Lender (usually one set for a conventional loan; three sets for FHA or VA loans)

_____ TOTAL NUMBER OF SETS

 Toll Free 1-800-521-6797

Normal Office Hours:
8:00 a.m. to 8:00 p.m. Eastern Time
Monday through Friday
Our staff will gladly answer any questions during normal office hours. Our answering service can place orders after hours or on weekends.

If we receive your order by 5:00 p.m. Eastern Time, Monday through Friday, we'll process it the same day and ship it the following business day. When ordering by phone, please have your charge card ready. We'll also ask you for the Order Form Key Number at the bottom of the coupon. Please use our Toll-Free number for blueprint and book orders only.
For Customization orders call 1-800-322-6797, ext. 800.

By FAX: Copy the Order Form on the next page and send it on our International FAX line: 1-800-224-6699.

Canadian Customers
Order Toll-Free 1-800-561-4169

For faster service and plans that are modified for building in Canada, customers may now call in orders directly to our Canadian supplier of plans and charge the purchase to a charge card. Or, you may complete the order form at right, adding 30% to all prices and mail in Canadian funds to:

The Plan Centre
20 Cedar Street North
Kitchener, Ontario N2H 2W8

By FAX: Copy the Order Form on the next page and send it via our Canadian FAX line: 1-519-743-1282.

The Home Customizer®

Many of the plans in this book are customizable through our Home Customizer® service. Look for this symbol 🏠 on the pages of home designs. It indicates that the plan on that page is part of The Home Customizer® service.

Some changes to customizable plans that can be made include:

- exterior elevation changes
- kitchen and bath modifications
- roof, wall and foundation changes
- room additions
- and much more!

If the plan you have chosen to build is one of our customizable homes, you can easily order the Home Customizer® kit to start on the path to making your alterations. The kit, priced at only $19.95, may be ordered at the same time you order your blueprint package by calling on our toll-free number or using the order blank at right. Or you can wait until you receive your blueprints, spend some time studying them and then order the kit by phone, FAX or mail. If you then decide to proceed with the customizing service, the $19.95 price of the kit will be refunded to you after your customization order is received. The Home Customizer® kit includes:

- instruction book with examples
- architectural scale
- clear acetate work film
- erasable red marker
- removable correction tape
- ¼" scale furniture cutouts
- 1 set of Customizable Drawings with floor plans and elevations

The service is easy, fast and *affordable*. Because we know and work with our plans and have them available on state-of-the-art computer systems, we can make the changes efficiently at prices much lower than those charged by normal architectural or drafting services. In addition, you'll be getting custom changes directly from Home Planners—the company whose dedication to excellence and long-standing professional experience are well recognized in the industry.

Call now to learn more about how simple it can be to have the *custom home* you've always wanted.

☎ Toll Free
1-800-322-6797, Ext. 800

Have You Seen Our Newest Designs?

Home Planners is one of the country's most active home design firms, creating nearly 100 new plans each year. And at least 50 of our latest creations are featured in each edition of our New Design Portfolio. You may have received a copy with your latest purchase by mail. If not, or if you purchased this book from a local retailer, just return the coupon below for your FREE copy. Make sure you consider the very latest of what Home Planners has to offer!

Yes!

Please send my FREE copy of your latest New Design Portfolio.

Name _____

Address _____

City _____ State _____ Zip _____

V2NDP

ORDER FORM

HOME PLANNERS, INC., 3275 WEST INA ROAD
SUITE 110, TUCSON, ARIZONA 85741

THE BASIC BLUEPRINT PACKAGE
Rush me the following (please refer to the Plans Index and Price Schedule in this section):
_____ Set(s) of blueprints for plan number(s) _____. $_____
_____ Set(s) of sepias for plan number(s) _____. $_____
_____ Additional identical blueprints in same order @ $50 per set. $_____
_____ Reverse blueprints @ $50 per set. $_____
_____ Home Customizer® Kit(s) for Plan(s)_____ @ $19.95 per kit. $_____

IMPORTANT EXTRAS
Rush me the following:
_____ Materials List: @ $40 Schedule A-D; $50 Schedule E $_____
_____ Specification Outlines @ $7 each. $_____
_____ Detail Sets @ $14.95 each; any two for $22.95; any three for $29.95; all four for $39.95 (save $19.85). $_____
❏ Plumbing ❏ Electrical ❏ Construction ❏ Mechanical
(These helpful details provide general construction advice and are not specific to any single plan.)

DECK BLUEPRINTS
_____ Set(s) of Deck Plan _____. $_____
_____ Additional identical blueprints in same order @ $10 per set. $_____
_____ Reverse blueprints @ $10 per set. $_____
_____ Set of Standard Deck Details @ $14.95 per set. $_____
_____ Set of Complete Building Package (Best Buy!)
Includes Custom Deck Plan _____.
(See Index and Price Schedule)
Plus Standard Deck Details $_____

LANDSCAPE BLUEPRINTS
_____ Set(s) of Landscape Plan _____. $_____
_____ Additional identical blueprints in same order @ $10 per set. $_____
_____ Reverse blueprints @ $10 per set. $_____
Please indicate the appropriate region of the country for Plant & Material List. (See Map on page 404): Region _____
SUB-TOTAL $_____
SALES TAX (Arizona residents add 5% sales tax; Michigan residents add 4% sales tax.) $_____

POSTAGE AND HANDLING	1-3 sets	4 or more sets	
DELIVERY (Requires street address - No P.O. Boxes)			
•Regular Service Allow 4-6 days delivery	❏ $6.00	❏ $8.00	$_____
•2nd Day Air Allow 2-3 days delivery	❏ $12.00	❏ $20.00	$_____
•Next Day Air Allow 1 day delivery	❏ $22.00	❏ $30.00	$_____
POST OFFICE DELIVERY If no street address available. Allow 4-6 days delivery	❏ $8.00	❏ $12.00	$_____
OVERSEAS AIR MAIL DELIVERY Note: All delivery times are from date Blueprint Package is shipped.	❏ $30.00	❏ $50.00	$_____
	❏ Send COD		

TOTAL (Sub-total, tax, and postage) $_____

YOUR ADDRESS (please print)

Name _____

Street _____

City _____ State _____ Zip _____

Daytime telephone number (_____) _____

FOR CREDIT CARD ORDERS ONLY
Please fill in the information below:
Credit card number _____
Exp. Date: Month/Year _____
Check one   ❏ Visa ❏ MasterCard ❏ Discover Card

Signature _____

Please check appropriate box: Order Form Key
❏ Licensed Builder-Contractor
❏ Home Owner   V2BP

☎ **ORDER TOLL FREE**
1-800-521-6797

413

Additional Plans Books

THE DESIGN CATEGORY SERIES

1.

ONE-STORY HOMES
A collection of 470 homes to suit a range of budgets in one-story living. All popular styles, including Cape Cod, Southwestern, Tudor and French. **384 pages. $8.95 ($11.95 Canada)**

2.

TWO-STORY HOMES
478 plans for all budgets in a wealth of styles: Tudors, Salt-boxes, Farmhouses, Victorians, Georgians, Contemporaries and more. **416 pages. $8.95 ($11.95 Canada)**

3.

MULTI-LEVEL AND HILL-SIDE HOMES 312 distinctive styles for both flat and sloping sites. Includes exposed lower levels, open staircases, balconies, decks and terraces. **320 pages. $6.95 ($9.95 Canada)**

4.

VACATION AND SECOND HOMES 258 ideal plans for a favorite vacation spot or perfect retirement or starter home. Includes cottages, chalets, and 1-, 1½-, 2-, and multi-levels. **256 pages. $5.95 ($7.95 Canada)**

THE EXTERIOR STYLE SERIES

9.

THE ESSENTIAL GUIDE TO TRADITIONAL HOMES
Over 400 traditional homes in one special volume. American and European styles from Farmhouses to Norman French. "Readers' Choice" highlights best sellers in four-color photographs and renderings. **304 pages. $9.95 ($12.95 Canada)**

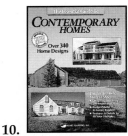

10.

THE ESSENTIAL GUIDE TO CONTEMPORARY HOMES More than 340 contemporary designs from Northwest Contemporary to Post-Modern Victorian. Four-color section of best sellers; two-color illustrations and line drawings throughout the remainder. **304 pages. $9.95 ($12.95 Canada)**

11.

VICTORIAN DREAM HOMES 160 Victorian and Farmhouse designs by three master designers. Victorian style from Second Empire homes through the Queen Anne and Folk Victorian era. Beautifully drawn renderings accompany the modern floor plans. **192 pages. $12.95 ($16.95 Canada)**

12.

WESTERN HOME PLANS
Over 215 home plans from Spanish Mission and Monterey to Northwest Chateau and San Francisco Victorian. Historical notes trace the background and geographical incidence of each style. **208 pages. $8.95 ($11.95 Canada)**

OUR BEST PLAN PORTFOLIOS

NEW ENCYCLOPEDIA OF HOME DESIGNS
Our best collection of plans is now bigger and better than ever! Over 500 plans organized by architectural category including all types and styles and 269 brand-new plans. The most comprehensive plan book ever.

15. **352 pages. $9.95 ($12.95 Canada)**

AFFORDABLE HOME PLANS For the prospective home builder with a modest or medium budget. Features 430 one-, 1½-, two-story and multi-level homes in a wealth of styles. Included are cost saving ideas for the budget-conscious.

16. **320 pages. $8.95 ($11.95 Canada)**

LUXURY DREAM HOMES At last, the home you've waited for A collection of 150 of the best luxury home plans from seven of the most highly regarded designers and architects in the United States. A dream come true for anyone interested in designing, building or remodeling luxury home.

17. **192 pages. $14.95 ($17.95 Canada)**

HOME IMPROVEMENT AND LANDSCAPE BOOKS

5.

THE HOME REMODELER
A revolutionary book of 31 remodeling plans backed by complete construction-ready blueprints and materials lists. Sections on kitchens, baths, master bedrooms and much more. Ideas galore; helpful advice and valuable suggestions. **112 pages. $7.95 ($10.95 Canada)**

6.

DECK PLANNER 25 practical plans and details for decks the do-it-yourselfer can actually build. How-to data and project starters for a variety of decks. Construction details available separately. **112 pages. $7.95 ($10.95 Canada)**

7.

THE HOME LANDSCAPER
55 fabulous front and back-yard plans that even the do-it-youselfer can master. Complete construction blueprints and regionalized plant lists available for each design. **208 pages. $12.95 ($16.95 Canada)**

8.

BACKYARD LANDSCAPER
Sequel to the popular *Home Landscaper*, contains 40 professionally designed plans for backyards to do yourself or contract out. Complete construction blueprints and regionalized plant lists available. **160 pages. $12.95 ($16.95 Canada)**

INTRODUCING THE NEW BLUE RIBBON DESIGNER SERIES

13.

200 FARMHOUSES & COUNTRY HOME PLANS Styles and sizes to match every taste and budget. Grouped by type, the homes represent a variety from Classic Farm-houses to Country Capes & Cottages. Introductions and expert-ly drawn floor plans and render-ings enhance the sections. **224 pages. $6.95 ($9.95 Canada)**

14.

200 BUDGET-SMART HOME PLANS The definitive source for the home builder with a limited budget, this volume shows that you can have your home and enjoy it, too! Amenity-laden homes, in many sizes and styles, can all be built from our plans. **224 pages. $6.95 ($9.95 Canada)**

Please fill out the coupon below. We will process your order and ship it from our office within 48 hours. Send coupon and check for the total to:

HOME PLANNERS, INC.
3275 West Ina Road, Suite 110, Dept. BK
Tucson, Arizona 85741

THE DESIGN CATEGORY SERIES—A great series of books edited by design type. Complete collection features 1376 pages and 1273 home plans.

1. _____One-Story Homes @ $8.95 ($11.95 Canada) .... $ _____
2. _____Two-Story Homes @ $8.95 ($11.95 Canada) .... $ _____
3. _____Multi-Level & Hillside Homes @ $6.95 ($9.95 Canada) .... $ _____
4. _____Vacation & Second Homes @ $5.95 ($7.95 Canada) .... $ _____

HOME IMPROVEMENT AND LANDSCAPE BOOKS

5. _____The Home Remodeler @ $7.95 ($10.95 Canada) .... $ _____
6. _____Deck Planner @ $7.95 ($10.95 Canada) .... $ _____
7. _____The Home Landscaper @ $12.95 ($16.95 Canada) .... $ _____
8. _____The Backyard Landscaper @ $12.95 ($16.95 Canada) .... $ _____

THE EXTERIOR STYLE SERIES

9. _____Traditional Homes Plans @ $9.95 ($12.95 Canada) .... $ _____
10. _____Contemporary Homes Plans @ $9.95 ($12.95 Canada) .... $ _____
11. _____Victorian Dream Homes @ $12.95 ($16.95 Canada) .... $ _____
12. _____Western Home Plans @ $8.95 ($11.95 Canada) .... $ _____

THE BLUE RIBBON DESIGNER SERIES

13. _____200 Farmhouse & Country Home Plans @ $6.95 ($9.95 Canada) $ _____
14. _____200 Budget-Smart Home Plans @ $6.95 ($9.95 Canada) .... $ _____

OUR BEST PLAN PORTFOLIOS

15. _____New Encyclopedia of Home Designs @ $9.95 ($12.95 Canada) $ _____
16. _____Affordable Home Plans @ $8.95 ($11.95 Canada) .... $ _____
17. _____Luxury Dream Homes @ $14.95 ($17.95 Canada) .... $ _____

Sub-Total .... $ _____
Arizona residents add 5% sales tax; Michigan residents add 4% sales tax $ _____
ADD Postage and Handling .... $ __3.00__
TOTAL (Please enclose check) .... $ _____

Name (please print) _____
Address _____
City _____ State _____ Zip _____

CANADIAN CUSTOMERS: Order books Toll-Free 1-800-561-4169. Or, complete the order form above, using Canadian prices and adding postage, and mail with your check in Canadian funds to: The Plan Centre, 20 Cedar Street North, Kitchener Ontario N2H 2W8. FAX: 1-519-743-1282.

 TO ORDER BOOKS BY PHONE CALL TOLL FREE 1-800-322-6797

V2BK

OVER 3 MILLION BLUEPRINTS SOLD

"We instructed our builder to follow the plans including all of the many details which make this house so elegant... Our home is a fine example of the results one can achieve by purchasing and following the plans which you offer... Everyone who has seen it has assured us that it belongs in 'a picture book.' I truly mean it when I say that my home 'is a DREAM HOUSE.'"

S.P.
Anderson, SC

"We have had a steady stream of visitors, many of whom tell us this is the most beautiful home they've seen. Everyone is amazed at the layout and remark on how unique it is. Our real estate attorney, who is a Chicago dweller and who deals with highly valued properties, told me this is the only suburban home he has seen that he would want to live in."

W. & P.S.
Flossmoor, IL

"Home Planners' blueprints saved us a great deal of money. I acted as the general contractor and we did a lot of the work ourselves. We probably built it for half the cost! We are thinking about more plans for another home. I purchased a competitor's book but my husband only wants your plans!"

K.M.
Grovetown, GA

*"We are **very** happy with the product of our efforts. The neighbors and passersby appreciate what we have created. We have had many people stop by to discuss our house and kindly praise it as being the nicest house in our area of new construction. We have even had one person stop and make us an unsolicited offer to buy the house for much more than we have invested in it."*

K. & L.S.
Bolingbrook, IL

"The traffic going past our house is unbelievable. On several occasions, we have heard that it is the 'prettiest house in Batavia.' Also, when meeting someone new and mentioning what street we live on, quite often we're told, 'Oh, you're the one in the yellow house with the wrap-around porch! I love it!'"

A.W.
Batavia, NY

"I have been involved in the building trades my entire life... Since building our home we have built two other homes for other families. Their plans from local professional architects were not nearly as good as yours. For that reason we are ordering additional plan books from you."

T.F.
Kingston, WA

"The blueprints we received from Home Planners were of excellent quality and provided us with exactly what we needed to get our successful home-building project underway. We appreciate Home Planners' invaluable role in our home-building effort."

T.A.
Concord, TN